Recent Developments in Curriculum Studies

Edited by Philip H. Taylor

NFER–NELSON

Published by the NFER–NELSON Publishing Company Ltd.,
Darville House, 2 Oxford Road East,
Windsor, Berkshire SL4 1DF

and in the United States of America by

NFER–NELSON, 242 Cherry Street, Philadelphia,
PA 19106 – 1906
Tel: (215) 238 0939. Telex: 244489.

First Published 1986

**LIBRARY OF CONGRESS CATALOGING IN
PUBLICATION DATA**

Photoset by David John Services Ltd., Maidenhead.

Printed in Great Britain by A. Wheaton & Co. Ltd., Exeter

ISBN 0–7005–1041–9
Code 8239 02 1

Contents

7142167

Contributors

Suzanne de Castell is an assistant professor and **Allan Luke** is a doctoral student with the Faculty of Education, Simon Fraser University, Burnaby, British Columbia, Canada. They are engaged in research on literacy, educational history and educational media. Related work has appeared in *Curriculum Inquiry, Journal of Educational Thought, Educational Philosophy and Theory* and the *Canadian Journal of Education*.

David Hamilton is Lecturer in Education at the University of Glasgow. His general interest is the analysis of pedagogy. He is currently working on a research programme entitled 'Studies in the development of schooling – with special reference to the pedagogy of the classroom system'.

David Harris is Lecturer in Education at the Centre for Science and Mathematics Education, Chelsea College, University of London. His research interests include the history and philosophy of pragmatism.

Magdalene Lampert has taught in several school systems in the New England area and is currently Curriculum Co–ordinator and teacher of mathematics in grades four through six at Buckingham Browne and Nichols School in Cambridge, Massachusetts. Her research interest is in the nature of teachers' work.

Sverker Lindblad is Assistant Professor at the Department of Education, University of Uppsala. He is at present dealing with research on teachers' experiments to change teaching.

Neil McEwen is Senior Lecturer in Geographical Education in the Faculty of Education, Birmingham Polytechnic. He has taught geography in secondary schools and participated in Schools Council curriculum development projects. He has a particular interest in the problems of teaching mixed–ability classes.

William F Pinar teaches in the Graduate School of Education and Human Development of the University of Rochester. He has written on theory and practice, autobiography, sexuality and gender. At present he is working on a gender critique of Marxist educational theory.

Thomas S Popkewitz is Professor of Curriculum and Instruction at the University of Wisconsin–Madison. He is co–author of *The Study of Schooling: Field Methodology in Educational Research and Evaluation* and *Recent Trends in Soviet and American Research on Teaching and Learning* (both published by Praeger). His research interests are in problems of institutional change and stability and the ideologies of professional occupations.

Christopher Portal is Lecturer in Education at the University of Manchester and local evaluator for the Schools Council project 'Instrumental Enrichment'. He is interested in the development of heuristic methods for various forms of learning.

William A Reid is Reader in Curriculum Theory at the University of Birmingham. He has co-authored several books in the curriculum field and wrote *Thinking About the Curriculum*. For several years he was European Editor of the *Journal of Curriculum Studies*.

Thomas W Roby is Professor of Humanities and Philosophy in the City College of Chicago and also teaches at St Xavier Colleges in Chicago. He holds the PhD degree in the Philosophy of Education and Curriculum from the University of Chicago. He is the author of papers on classroom questioning, curriculum deliberation and Socratic inquiry.

Michael Taylor teaches physics at Northfields Upper School, Dunstable, Bedfordshire and is currently researching into teachers' perceptions of science and how these relate to the views of philosophers of science.

J J Wellington is Lecturer in Education at Sheffield University. After graduating from the University of Bristol in 1971 he taught in two London comprehensive schools and studied philosophy of education at the London Institute of Education. His interests include epistemology and the philosophy and teaching of science.

Acknowledgements
Grateful thanks are due to Taylor & Francis Ltd., publishers of the *Journal of Curriculum Studies*, for permission to reproduce the papers that appear in this volume, all of which were published in the Journal.

Introduction

The purpose of a field of study or discipline once established is to grow and develop. It is scholars who *'till'* the field of study or *'work'* within a discipline that make growth and change possible. Essentially growth is an addition to the *'stock'* of knowledge available to a field of study or a discipline. It is also the acquisition of improved methods of research, reflection and inquiry.

New knowledge and improved methods of research may arise from the employment of new paradigms or from the restructured essential exemplifications of the field or from addressing a new set of questions. In the first instances old assumptions are replaced by new as was the case with 'new wave evaluators', especially Eisner and exemplified in his *'The Educational Imagination'* (1979) with its reliance on an aesthetic perspective. It was also the case with the Reconceptualists as the most cursory glance at the *Journal of Curriculum Theorizing* will show. The Reconceptualists do not concentrate on the personal consciousness of teacher and taught merely as a reaction to the positivist rationality of much educational and psychological theory of the past quarter of a century, but because they cannot see how one can account for curricular reality without considering the impact of decisions about what to teach on the self-awareness of teachers and the self-consciousness of pupils.

In an altogether different direction a paradigm based partly in Marxism and partly in phenomenological sociology has developed. Its flavour permeates a recent and successful text in educational sociology, Meighan's *A Sociology of Educating* (1981). It is the burden of this 'radical' paradigm that the reform of schooling is not possible without the reform of society at large. Michael Apple (1982) is perhaps the most vigorous exponent of this perspective.

Each new paradigm has spawned new forms of inquiry and research. Education and gender, knowledge and control, the 'hidden curriculum', the sociology of assessment and of educational research all are topics arising from the efforts of scholars working within the radical paradigm.

Equally radical though in a different direction is a developing interest in education and modernity. A good example of this is to be found in Musgrove's *Education and Anthropology*, subtitled 'Other Cultures and the Teacher' (1982). Its radicalism lies in such arguments as:

> One of the jobs of the school is to open windows onto wider worlds. The culture concept [of curriculum] closes them. There has often been a spirited and surprisingly successful opposition to the application of the culture concept of the school curriculum in many of the 'other cultures' of this book. They have refused to be confirmed by schooling in their traditional entities. Their culture has relevance in the curriculum only at its points of maximum tension with modernity. It is from this dialectical relationship of cultures in contact and conflict that a new synthesis, a third cultural reality is built up.

New paradigms clearly cast shadows before them for the study of the curriculum. But so do new questions.

Currently the most vigorous areas of new questioning concern curriculum history, an area of inquiry almost deliberately neglected by historians of education: new views of school subjects and new appreciations of the transactional curriculum. Equally, old questions persist about curriculum theory, curriculum change, innovation and evaluation. Both the new questions and the old preoccupations are reflected in this collection of papers.

Just as new questions emerge, so are new forms of curriculum research called for especially in response to changed approaches to curriculum development and evaluation. As school-based curriculum development supersedes the centre–periphery model, so a different form of research into its effectiveness is developing.

More importantly, however, the relationship between forms of curriculum knowledge and relevant styles of research are being forged. That this should be the case, and not before time, is developed elsewhere (Taylor P.H. and Richards, C.M., 1985). What matters here is that there is an increasing awareness that this should be so. After all, curriculum history is as much history as is the history of the medieval monarchy and empirical studies of the social context of the curriculum are every bit as empirical and social as the social context of actions of members of Parliament or of the U.S. Senate.

It is the aim of this collection of papers to illustrate the correlation between forms of curriculum knowledge and styles of research. Another aim is to illuminate the preoccupations of the field of curriculum studies which are in fact as they have always been, mainly with what should be and what is taught in schools and other educational institutions. And it is a bonus that this collection of papers also shows the developing sophistication and growing maturity of the scholarship of the field.

Not all that presently concerns those who study the curriculum can be illuminated in twelve papers. What can be shown (and it has been the intention to approach the task conservatively), are the efforts of some of those caught up in the on-going attempt to understand better the curriculum in its many aspects. To suggest that this selection of papers is exemplary, if by this is meant 'illustrative', would be more than fair. But of more importance is to see each paper as belonging to a movement in curriculum scholarship toward a sharper focus on the issues that confront those who deal with curriculum problems in the real world. It is just this that is a prime justification for the existence of a field of study.

References

TAYLOR, P.H. and RICHARDS, C.M. (1985) *An Introduction to Curriculum Studies: Second Edition.* Windsor, NFER-NELSON.

EISNER, E. (1979). *The Educational Imagination.* New York: Macmillan.

MEIGHAN, R. (1981). *A Sociology of Educating.* London: Holt, Rinehart & Winston.

MUSGROVE, F. (1982). *Education and Anthropology.* London: John Wiley.

APPLE, M. (1982). *Education and Power.* London: Routledge & Kegan Paul.

Part One

Curriculum Theory and Theorizing

'Theories' says Popper, the distinguished philosopher of science:

are nets to catch what we call 'the world': to rationalise, to explain, and to master it. We endeavour to make the mesh ever finer and finer.

He is of course referring to the world of atoms and molecules, plants and animals and to rocks and minerals, not the man–made world of curriculum decision, choice and action. Even so, something of what Popper[1] has to say needs to be held in mind when we come to reflect on the nature of curriculum theory and theorizing if only to moderate the view that curriculum theory is merely the result of either academic speculation or philosophical special pleading. On the contrary, it can be, and increasingly is, as Reid[2] has shown, directly related to the real world of teachers and teaching, and hence of practical thinking about the curriculum.

All the contributions to this section address the real world of the curriculum though not necessarily in all of its aspects. Wellington's sights are on the nature of knowledge, thought and understanding and how using a categorical framework one may argue that the curriculum should consist of broad categories of experience rather than the customary assembly of subjects, though one cannot, he avers, prove (in a philosophical sense) that this ought to be the case.

Pinar's paper moves in an altogether different direction toward accounting for the particular and personal that is the reality of the lived curriculum. Drawing on phenomenology, neo–Marxist sociology and existentialism, Pinar is concerned to show how we can slow down the reality of the lived curriculum long enough to understand it and grasp its qualities. It is not that he wishes to freeze it for all time. On the contrary he seeks a method whereby all the vibrancy of self and situation in the lived educational experience can be captured. It is through the autobiographical method that this can be achieved.

Pinar's theorizing has opened a new dimension in the curriculum field and been a considerable stimulus to others. Such is also true of Schwab's work but in an altogether different and possibly unintended direction, that of laying the foundations of what is coming to be called deliberative *curriculum theory. It was Schwab's contention that deliberation is at the heart of all dealings with the practical realities of the curriculum. Of it he says: '(Deliberation) treats both ends and means and must treat them as mutually determining one another.' It is this contention that is at the heart of deliberative curriculum theory in its search not for the* right *curricular alternative but the best. The practical problems which the process of deliberation sets is taken up in Roby's article. As a middle–ground, theory of practices, a–prescriptive and undoctrinal, Roby argues there is a need to operationalize the process of deliberation in concrete examples. This is what his paper attempts using negative as well as positive examples. His hope is that:*

> *When more deliberations are undertaken and recorded the process itself as a non–procedural practical enterprise will doubtless take more varied forms.*

References

1.   POPPER, K. (1959). *The Logic of Scientific Discovery.* London: Hutchinson.
2.   REID, W.A. (1978). *Thinking about the Curriculum.* London: Routledge and Kegan Paul.

Further Reading

BANKS, P. (1980). 'Herbert Spencer: Victorian curriculum theorist,' *Journal of Curriculum Studies,* 12, 2, 123–35.
LUNGREN, U.P. (1983). 'Social production and reproduction as a context for curriculum theorizing,' *Journal of Curriculum Studies,* 15, 2, 143–54.
PEREIRA, P. (1984). 'Deliberation and the arts of perception'. *Journal of Curriculum Studies,* 16, 4, 347–66.
POSNER, G.J. (1982). 'A cognitive science conception of curriculum and instruction,' *Journal of Curriculum Studies,* 14, 4, 343–51.
REID, L.A. (1981). 'Knowledge knowing and becoming education,' *Journal of Curriculum Studies,* 12, 2, 79–92.
SMITH, M.J.E. (1984). 'Mental skills: some critical reflections,' *Journal of Curriculum Studies,* 16, 3, 225–32.
THELEN, H.A. (1982). 'Authenticity, legitimacy and productivity: a study of the tensions among values underlying an educational activity,' *Journal of Curriculum Studies,* 14, 1, 29–41.

Determining a Core Curriculum: the Limitations of Transcendental Deductions

J.J. Wellington

Foundations for the curriculum

The search for a 'core curriculum', or a group of subjects indispensable to schools or education itself, is well under way in England and Wales after the prompting of Lady Young and the Department of Education and Science. Those participating in this quest and demanding a common core need to be made aware of a philosophical problem which has its roots in the 19th–century writings of Immanuel Kant.

Kant's main contribution to philosophy was the 'transcendental deduction' which he used in both epistemology and ethics by attempting to prove that 12 definite 'categories' are both unique and necessary for a complete understanding of the natural and moral worlds. Similar transcendental arguments have been employed by more recent philosophers such as Strawson,[1] and by some philosophers of education in showing that certain subjects or activities are indispensable to education.[2]

A clear example of Kant's influence on these philosophers of education can be seen by comparing his 12 categories with Hirst's seven forms of knowledge (see Figure 1). The empirical form of knowledge, especially in science, relies heavily on the notions of substance, causality (cause and effect), and dependence, i.e. Kant's categories of relation. The mathematical form is concerned with the categories of quantity (unity, plurality and totality) as well as those of negation and limitation. Philosophical knowledge, if there is such a thing, hinges on questions of existence and non–existence, necessity and contingency, possibility and impossibility. Religious and moral knowledge are clearly concerned with similar 'categories'. Kant tried to show that his 12 categories, and only these, were essential in acquiring objective knowledge. Hirst, in a similar way, argued that the seven forms of knowledge were indispensable to a balanced curriculum.

In an article entitled 'The impossibility of transcendental deductions,[3] Körner shows that no Kantian–style argument purporting to prove that certain 'categories' are necessary for the acquisition of knowledge can ever be logically valid. In the light of Körner's article I hope to show that any attempt to use arguments of a 'Kantian–transcendental' type in defining or justifying education, or in determining the subjects on a school curriculum is logically invalid. A particular set of disciplines or subjects comprising a school curriculum cannot be shown to be either necessary or sufficient 'tools' for the acquisition of knowledge.

(1)	Empirical form	(a)	Of relation Substance
(2)	Historical/sociological form		Causality Dependence
(3)	Mathematical form:	(b)	Of quantity Unity Plurality Totality
(4)	Philosophical form:	(c)	Of quality Reality Negation Limitation
(5)	Religious form:	(d)	Of modality Possibility-impossibility
(6)	Moral form:		Existence-non-existence Necessity-contingency
(7)	Aesthetic form		

Figure 1.   Hirst's seven forms of knowledge/Kant's 12 categories

No satisfactory *philosophical* proof exists to show that physics rather than pinball should be taught in school. Decisions affecting school curricula may have good sociological, psychological, political or economic grounds but as yet lack any firm, absolute philosophical foundation. Any criteria for establishing a 'core curriculum' must recognize the non–uniqueness or dispensability of our disciplines and forms of inquiry, and admit the possibility of categorical change.

The nature of transcendental deductions

Before any modern writer is accused of using a transcendental argument, the nature of Kant's attempts must be briefly sketched. These occur in his major work: *The Critique of Pure Reason.*[4] In the *Critique*, Kant is determined to prove that what he calls objective knowledge is only possible through the application of certain definite 'categories' to our experience. In other words, our knowledge can only be obtained by perceiving the outside world (the world of 'phenomena'[5]) by means of certain conceptual schemes.

Only by our imposing our 'categories' onto the jumbled experiences we receive can we make any sense of them. The categories are the 'active' element of perception, whose application leads to our knowledge of the world.

Who would disagree that Kant's claim that, unless we categorize or conceptualize in some way the varied and constant bombardment of our senses, knowledge is impossible? Our categories or conceptual schemes impose the form or structure necessary to make sense of our experience.

Knowledge is only possible when we have both a perception and a concept working together: 'Thoughts without content are empty. Perceptions without concepts are blind.'[6] However Kant set out to prove a lot more than this. He 'explained' his 12 categories and then attempted to prove that knowledge is only possible when gained through this structure.

These categories make sense of our experience, they create order from chaos. His attempt to show that only these categories could provide us with objective knowledge is known as a *transcendental deduction*.

Unfortunately the merits and insights of Kant's deduction cannot be examined here. What is important for this article, however, is the nature and form of this deduction since it was the first (though not the last) of its kind.

Firstly, a transcendental deduction always seeks to investigate the possibility, legitimacy or 'right to exist' of a certain set of concepts (or conceptual schemes), metaphysical beliefs (such as views of 'Space' and 'Time') or moral presuppositions. Thus the general format of a transcendental deduction can be expressed as follows: 'X is *only* possible through Y' or, 'Y is both a necessary and sufficient condition for X'. For example, Kant's transcendental deductions fit into this format as follows:

(a) 'Euclidean geometry is only possible on Kant's view of Space.'
(b) 'Newtonian mechanics is only possible on Kant's view of Time.'
(c) 'Objective knowledge is only possible through the 12 categories.'

In seeking to prove that the 12 categories are necessary conditions for objective knowledge, Kant is justifying their 'right to exist'. For this reason, I will often use the words 'justification' and 'deduction' as synonyms.

Another feature of transcendental justifications worth noting is their apparent circularity. This point is more difficult to express, but I think it arises because of their refusal to refer to extrinsic factors. A transcendental justification is, for this reason, in contrast with a utilitarian one. For example, two possible justifications of democracy as the best form of government might run as follows:

(i) Democracy is best because it *alone* produces the greatest happiness of the greatest number.
(ii) The basic principles of Justice and Respect for Persons are *only* possible in a democracy.[7]

The first refers to an extrinsic factor (a result or consequence), while the second refers only to certain absolute principles intrinsic to, presupposed by, or embodied in democracy.

Some modern transcendental tendencies

The limitations of transcendental arguments will be considered shortly, but first we must briefly review some more recent attempts to show the uniqueness of certain forms of thought or categories. In his article entitled 'Liberal education and the nature of knowledge'[8] Hirst sets out to analyse and then justify the notion of 'liberal education'. In doing so he develops the thesis that there are clearly distinguishable 'forms of knowledge' which are both necessary and sufficient in making experience intelligible to man. For example, he states that: 'The forms of knowledge are the basic articulations whereby the whole of experience has become intelligible to man, they are the fundamental achievement of mind.'[9] Hirst begins his article by criticizing attempts to define education in terms of mental powers or abilities and concludes that a satisfactory concept of education can only be worked out in terms of the forms of knowledge (which he claims, are logically *prior* to mental abilities). He defines forms of knowledge as 'complex ways of understanding experience which are publicly verifiable and gained through learning' (i.e. very similar to Kant's categories). By acquiring the forms of knowledge, Hirst continues, our experience is structured under some form of conceptual scheme – we acquire a conceptual apparatus for articulating various regions of experience. This account is clearly modelled on Kant's thesis that the categories are the means by which we understand and think about objective experience. The task Hirst now sets himself is that of justifying a liberal education by justifying the pursuit of rational knowledge. He does this by a transcendental argument which tries to make explicit the relations between the concepts of rational justification and the pursuit of knowledge: i.e. a justification of the pursuit of knowledge is only possible by the use of knowledge. Most people would accept that the pursuit of knowledge can only be justified by, in some way, using knowledge. Hirst's claim is stronger than this however. He argues that asking for a justification of the pursuit of knowledge or education logically implies a commitment to the seven forms of knowledge. This seemingly circular argument is the essential element in Hirst's attempt at a transcendental justification of the forms of knowledge. In a Kantian form it can be caricatured as: 'Knowledge is only possible through the seven forms.'

A more recent attempt to wield the transcendental argument was made by Allen Brent. Brent attempts his own transcendental argument to show that 'the empirical / mathematical / moral / religious / historico–sociological / aesthetic / philosophical distinction, however primitive or developed, is the indispensable means of preserving any human language or any human thinking from subjective chaos'.[10].

The impossibility of such a transcendental deduction will be discussed shortly, but firstly, a brief sketch is required of R.S. Peters's attempts to justify education as a pursuit, and also the presuppositions of morality.[11] To what basic principles is a person committed when he seriously asks the question 'what ought I to do?' or 'why do this rather than that?'. Peters answers: by the very act of asking these questions a person is committed to certain 'worthwhile activities'. His main concern is to justify the pursuit of educational (or curriculum) activities without referring to their instrumental, vocational or utilitarian value (indeed this must be the aim of any philosophical justification of the curriculum). Peter's justification must therefore refer to the intrinsic value of curriculum activities such as science, mathematics, the arts etc., and their difference from activities like golf, fishing, bridge and football. Peters finds four basic distinctive features of curriculum activities: their unending or infinite nature (since truth is their object), the width of their cognitive concern, their wide–ranging content, and their ability to 'change a man's view of the world'.[12] Having separated worthwhile activities from other kinds Peters now asks why, when a person asks seriously the question 'why do this rather than that?', he should be more committed to such activities than others. His answer is that these activities are all 'relevant to answering the sort of questions he is asking'. That is, curriculum activities, or *forms of inquiry*, like science, history, literature and philosophy are all relevant to answering the question 'why do this rather than that?'

Peters argues that these forms of inquiry are somehow built into the question itself, that they are the presuppositions of asking the question. To ask the question is to be committed to these special theoretical activities or forms of inquiry. Peters admits in this section of *Ethics and Education* that he is using a transcendental argument.[13] He uses a similar argument in justifying the presuppositions of moral discourse: justice, respect for persons, freedom and consideration of interests. Without commitment to these basic principles, or presuppositions, it would be impossible for a person to be moral. Moral discourse, and morality itself are only possible through the basic principles of justice, freedom, respect for and consideration of persons.[14]

The three transcendental arguments which are particularly relevant to the philosophy of education can be summarized as follows:

(a) Knowledge is only possible through seven particular forms (Hirst, Brent).

(b) Morality, or moral discourse, is only possible through rationality, freedom, and respect for persons (Peters).

(c) The question 'why do this rather than that?' can only be answered through certain forms of inquiry, or 'worthwhile activities' (Peters).

In each of these Kantian formulations of the three theses the word 'through' is used metaphorically.

The impossibility of transcendental deductions

The inherent limitations of this type of argument have been clearly demonstrated by a leading British philosopher, Stephen Körner.[15] He defines a transcendental deduction as 'A demonstration of the reasons why a particular categorical schema is not only in fact, but necessarily employed in differentiating a region of experience'. A 'categorical schema' is the means by which we understand the external world, or structure reality in different 'regions of experience', for example sensory, moral or aesthetic. In attempting a transcendental deduction a person must prove that any, and every, possible method of differentiating (or making sense of) a certain region of experience necessarily belongs to the chosen categorical schema. He must, as Körner puts it, 'demonstrate the schema's uniqueness'.

Now this might be attempted in three possible ways:

(a) By comparing the schema with experience which is not differentiated in any way. But this is impossible, Körner claims, since the statements used in the comparison could not be formulated without employing *some* kind of prior differentiation of experience.

(b) It might seem possible to demonstrate the schema's uniqueness by comparing it with other schemata as 'possible competitors'; but, clearly, this is self-defeating.

(c)   Finally, by examining the schema and its application entirely from within one might hope to demonstrate its uniqueness; but such an examination could only exhibit the schema and show how it works for a certain region of experience. It could not prove that every differentiation of that region belongs to the schema.

Körner concludes that a transcendental deduction, seeking to show that certain categories or schemes for making sense of experience are unique, cannot succeed. In fairness to Kant, Körner points out that his attempts to show their uniqueness have a largely historical explanation. In his day, Kant and his contemporaries strongly believed that the mathematics and physics of that time, and even the moral code, were true beyond all doubt. Kant thus assumed that the schemata employed in mathematical, physical and moral thinking were unique and could not be otherwise. In 1981 we have non–Euclidean geometry, Einstein's relativistic view of the space–time continuum, Heisenberg's 'uncertainty principle' and the knowledge that Newtonian physics only applies to slow–moving objects. Kant's category of cause and effect has been replaced by the statistical probability that one event will follow another, while modern physicists assure us that 'matter' (Kant's category of substance) is mostly empty space, and particles often behave like waves.

In the light of these alternative 'categorical schemata' or ways of understanding the world, who would be bold enough to even attempt such a transcendental deduction today? An argument to show that certain *formal* conditions, for example certain laws of logic, are necessary presuppositions of objective understanding or knowledge may well be possible. Kant actually succeeds in showing that *some* group of categories, or conceptual framework, is necessary for an understanding of the objective world. However, he cannot prove that *certain definite* categories are indispensable: he cannot justify the 'non–formal conditions of objective thought'.[16] Similar constraints apply to any attempt at deducing the content of a school curriculum. Körner's criticisms of Kant can be easily and directly applied to Hirst's transcendental claims for the forms of knowledge and Peters's arguments for the uniqueness of certain forms of inquiry and moral presuppositions. One cannot prove that certain forms of inquiry or theoretical activities are *unique* in our understanding of the 'human predicament' or situation, or are indispensable to a liberal education. To do so would involve a proof that certain categorical schemata, which constitute these forms of inquiry, are unique in our understanding of experience. This proof has been shown to be impossible.

Alternative criteria for the curriculum

The clear message so far is: beware of any transcendental tendencies in defining and justifying curriculum decisions. Any useful definition of education must admit the possibility of 'categorical change'. Moreover, because the forms of knowledge are necessarily non–unique, the barriers between them must be subject to change. Thus there can be no logical or conceptual criteria which are fully adequate in dividing our knowledge of the world into separate distinguishable compartments, like the forms of knowledge. How then can a liberal education possibly be defined and its pursuit justified? A notion which recognizes the non–uniqueness of conceptual schemes, the existence of categorical change, and the lack of conceptual barriers between disciplines is that of a *categorical framework*, developed by Körner.[17] His ideas suggest an alternative account of the nature of education and even give some guidelines for deciding on a school curriculum.

Our categorical frameworks depend, he says, on the way we classify or group objects together, on the distinctions we make, on the logic underlying our thinking and even more on what objects we recognize as existing. (For example, gods, fairies, giants, substances, atoms, minds etc.) Of course, education has a great influence on the way we classify objects, and thereby structure our experience. We learn to separate subjects from predicates, vertebrates for invertebrates, metals from non–metals, speed from velocity and so on. Briefly, a categorical framework is the structure within which all our thinking proceeds.

Our categorical frameworks are determined by our backgrounds, our attitudes, our interests, our innate abilities, by the society we live in and even by the 'social class' we belong to within that society. Since our thought and understanding are determined by our categorical frameworks both will be enriched as we acquire more and more ways of conceptualizing experience. Three distinct regions of experience which can be recognized are: the empirical region, both scientific and non–scientific; the non–empirical covering mathematics and philosophy for example; and the realm of value judgements, such as moral and aesthetic. New categorical frameworks or conceptual schemes can enrich our experience in each of these regions by applying a novel, or more sophisticated structure to it. Herein lies the aim of, and justification for, education as a pursuit. The more we 'put in' to an experience, the more we get from it: just as a long, boring car journey can be improved by learning to distinguish motor cars by their make, model, age, origin, etc., any experience is enriched when we learn new distinctions and differences (such as vertebrate/invertebrate, mammal/reptile) or apply new concepts (say friction, social class, supply and demand, etc.) to it. To the uninitiated, some might say uneducated, football can be seen as 22 men kicking a bag of wind between two wooden posts. A dedicated (or educated) football follower sees it through rather different eyes. The way we 'see' things is obviously determined by our education. By acquiring new categorical frameworks and new concepts we can structure, or enmesh experience in an increasingly 'educated' way.

Conclusion

I have tried to show that any transcendental argument for justifying the inclusion of certain subjects in the school curriculum is logically unsound. Unfortunately, at present, there seem to be no clear philosophical reasons for teaching certain subjects rather than other, apparently less fundamental ones.

By describing education in terms of the acquisition of categorical frameworks the possibility of flexibility, tolerance and change are built in. (A Marxist learns to interpret events in society as part of the struggle between classes, but this is only one way of perceiving them.)

This view of education obviously rests heavily on Körner's notion of a categorical framework and needs a lot more refining and clarifying. However, I am sure that one thing is clear: the key to a philosophical (as opposed to empirical, sociological or psychological) definition of education lies in a logical inquiry into the nature of thought and understanding – the kind of inquiry first attempted by Kant himself in the *Critique of Pure Reason.*

References

1. STRAWSON, P.F. (1964). *Individuals.* London: Methuen.
2. Cf. PETERS, R.S. (1966). *Ethics and Education.* London: George Allen & Unwin; and HIRST, P.H. (1965). 'Liberal Education and the nature of Knowledge'. In: ARCHAMBAULT, R.D. (1965). *Philosophical Analysis and Education.* London: Routledge & Kegan Paul.
3. KÖRNER, S. (1967). 'The impossibility of Transcendental Deductions'. *Monist,* 51, 3 (July 1967).
4. KANT, I. *Critique of Pure Reason.* Translated by Norman Kemp Smith (1968). London: Macmillan.
5. *Op. cit.,* p. 257.
6. *Op. cit.,* p. 93.
7. PETERS, R.S. (1966). *Ethics and Education.* pp. 304–6.
8. HIRST, *op. cit.,* pp. 113–38.
9. HIRST, *op. cit.,* pp. 122.
10. BRENT, A. (1978). *Philosophical Foundations for the Curriculum.* London: Allen & Unwin. pp. 168–211.
11. PETERS, *op. cit.,* Chapter 5.
12. *Op. cit.,* p. 159.
13. *Op. cit.,* p. 163.
14. *Op. cit.,* Chapters 6, 7 and 8.
15. KÖRNER, S. *op. cit.,* and 'Transcendental tendencies in recent philosphy', *Journal of Philosophy,* LXII, 19 (1966).
16. LACEY, A.R. (1976). *A Dictionary of Philosophy.* London: Routledge & Kegan Paul. p. 218.
17. KÖRNER, S. (1974). *Categorial Frameworks.* Oxford: Blackwell.

'Whole, Bright, Deep with Understanding': Issues in Qualitative Research and Autobiographical Method

William F. Pinar

Qualitative work 'aims at particular understanding', in contrast to quantitative research, which 'aims at *general* understanding'.[1] Willis's statement echoes one nearly 100 years earlier: 'Understanding has always the particular as its object.'[2] In this essay I will sketch the relation of particularity and understanding, noting its problematic issues. I will conclude with a summary of autobiographical method, thus situating the preceding discussion of issues in qualitative research in a specific form of curriculum research.

General and particular understanding

The rise of mainstream social science in the 20th century accompanies increasing control of human life. Lasch[3] has documented the invasion of the family by the 'helping professions' (an extension of the corporate state), Habermas[4] the rationalizing function of social science in the control of professional life, Marcuse[5] the influence of media and cultural life in maintaining the individual's alienation from himself and his community. The collapse of epistemology into philosophy of science parallels the hegemony of quantification and measurement in the social sciences. One issue is control, knowledge that what holds true in any specific situation will hold true in others. The movement toward increasing political control has its epistemological correlate: Zygmunt Bauman describes the interest in general understanding and the desire for control:

Only if I can be sure that what I have grasped is from now on immutable and immune to contingencies of fate, can my knowledge give me the feeling of genuine mastery over the object. The real trouble, therefore (the real reason of our anxiety) is not the endemic structure of theoretical understanding, but *the practical lack of control over the life situation* which a most perfect interpretation will still be helpless to redress. *Objective understanding appears, so to speak, as a substitute for practical control over the situation;* as an 'intellectual socialization' of the conditions of action which in reality are privately owned. *This is why attempts to gain objective understanding will always be repeated: and this is why they will never be successful.* That is, unless an entirely different situation of action deprives them of their goal. Paradoxically, *a truly objective understanding would be accessible only in conditions which do not require it: which do not posit such an understanding as a problem.*[6]

Understood in this way, the interest which guides an epistemological and methodological search for objective understanding has a psycho-political, finally historical origin. Perhaps the interest in control is rooted in the effort to stabilize economic systems, and, in the effort to ensure economic stability, other important realms of human life are also regularized. The dangers – political and psychological – have been understood for several generations.[7] I will focus briefly on the latter kind.

General understanding is useful as it permits some measure of control over situations which are, as Nietzsche noted, in fact in flux. Some control is necessary to carry about our business. It permits goal-directed behaviour which is efficient, and thereby more likely effective. One danger is that, relying upon rules of conduct and generalization concerning types of situations, one dulls new situations. They become like past ones. That is, of course, the meaning of generalization: looking for in the new what has been seen in the old. One focuses on what is general or common to the situations, not on what is unique to each. In teaching and classroom discourse, this means, as Huebner has pointed out,[8] we have ignored such significant, but difficult to conceptualize and quantify, dimensions of educational activity as the ethical, the aesthetic and the political. The more exclusively one relies upon *rules* of conduct – such as objectives for one's class to achieve – the more frozen becomes the situation. One is reminded of the 'smooth' conversation of some educational researchers, whose projects and achievements slide from their mouths in carefully modulated tones, the conversational equivalent of 'muzak'. Such individuals may manage new situations and new people predictably and efficiently. However, this routinized behaviour comes at the cost of spontaneity and individuality. He becomes a social type which we recognize. His specific self, now to some extent buried behind the mask, is probably as forgotten to him as it is hidden to us. Being with him elicits the social type in us, inhibiting the particular. Developmentally, to the extent one is a type, having regularized one's behaviour, and perhaps forgotten one's self-abandonment, one is arrested. One has self-control, often some control of situations, but at the cost of psychological fluidity and movement. This reduction of the individual to the social type numbs him to ethical, aesthetic and political considerations as these are subservient to and forgotten in this consuming effort to achieve his objectives. In a discipline's effort to achieve objective knowledge it absolutizes the relative, atemporalizes the historical, and rationalizes the political *status quo*. In its extreme formulation, fascism is the political correlate to psychological arrest.

To return to our colleague, he has his shadow. This is the person – whom we rarely see at formal meetings – who seems excessively, perhaps compulsively committed to his individuality, his particularity. Ignoring in situations what is expected or common, he causes awkwardness. When it is appropriate – or so others think – to behave efficiently, he may not. I think we would acknowledge the dangers in each of these caricatures, each of these types. I think we would tend to agree that balance between control and abandon, the common and the idiosyncratic, the particular and the general is desirable. Such balance is of course neither consensually determinable nor timeless. When one observes oneself to be a bit eccentric for one's tastes, then one blends in more with others, forever making appropriate adjustments.

The curriculum field is, in my view, imbalanced toward the general (so is mainstream social science). 'Traditionalists' have espoused principles of curriculum and instruction, general guides to development, implementation and evaluation which ignore the specificity of each situation. It was precisely this flight from particularity which Schwab attacked in his *The Practical: A Language for Curriculum*.[9] The traditionalists began to give way to 'conceptual-empiricists', social scientists who substituted categorization and quantification for stipulation. Among those whose work functions to reconceptualize the field, the politically- and economically-orientated curricularists have perpetuated this interest in generalization by utilizing concepts such as 'hegemony' and 'correspondence theory' to explain the politico-economic functions of curriculum. Autobiographic curriculum theory attempts to redress this imbalance by focusing upon concrete individuals in specific situations. Finally, however, work which acknowledges the relation between the general, the abstract, and the specific and concrete, and sketches this relation dialectically, so that each element contributes to the transformation of the other to achieve a higher-order synthesis, must be the objective of us all. But, as Bauman points out, such an ideal requires historical conditions which would make that work unnecessary. It is precisely the exploitation of the working classes by the bourgeoisie, more subtly the oppression of individuals by themselves, the mystification of concrete reality by abstract formulation, and the denial of the importance of the intellect by the philistine who accepts the concrete and everyday as natural and transparent which makes the theoretical agenda enunciated earlier necessary. Because our historical conditions make clear these inhuman practices we struggle to change them, and it is in the context of this historical struggle that autobiographical work must be situated.

Empathy and educational criticism

How is understanding of the particular attempted? One view suggests that one begins by reconstructing the intentions of those whose actions are under scrutiny. For instance, the attempt to achieve historical understanding might view the products of past peoples as evidence of the intentions which present-day historians aspire to reconstruct. The object, or end-product of intention, is necessarily a modified, mediated, ambiguous expression of that intention. 'The intention is always richer than its tangible traces, as these are invariably residues of its defeats.'[10] Labour is in this view a fundamentally artistic expression of spirit; labour is the mediation between the ideal vision of the spirit in us and the vicious materiality of this world.[11] To focus solely upon the object and its relation to other objects (as in exclusively economic interpretation) truncates the labour process by omitting its psycho-spiritual elements. Thus the effort to understand involves

> the capture of spirit, which expresses itself in, and lives through, monuments of intellectual and artistic creation, as well as ordinary forms of public life. The visible, tangible legacy of the past – tests, paintings, legal codes, recorded customs – had been thereby posited as *Ausserungen* – externalization of the Spirit, sentient leftovers of Spirit's self-estrangement, documents of its expressive powers; and the true object of understanding was perceived as standing behind them, never exhausted by them, always fuller and richer than any of its expression.[12]

At first it seems we have travelled far from this romantic view of objects and actions as deposits, as weaker, thinner, sedimentations of richer intention, of spirit. The focus of mainstream social scientists upon the observable does seem to abandon issues of origin and meaning. But the psychoanalytic and Marxian traditions, in ways different from each other and from the romantic view, preserve a sense of manifest and latent, refuse to accept the visible as the final and irreducible. In educational research aspects of the qualitative tradition suggest an interest in *interpretation*. For instance, Eisner's work on problems in evaluation, while utilizing neither a psychoanalytic nor a Marxian view or method, nonetheless *interprets* classroom practice. The examples of this work in his *The Educational Imagination*[13] and the essays by Robert Donmoyer,[14] Gail McCutcheon,[15] Elizabeth Vallance,[16] and Thomas Barone, Jr.[17] escape mere mirroring of what occurs. Such work, while not explicit about its criteria of criticism, contextualizes taken-for-granted educational activity more broadly, in the perspective of the critic. In this way Eisner's work understands what it studies more penetratingly than does another form of qualitative research, the ethnography, at least as this form is practised by Harry Wolcott in his study of *The Man in the Principal's Office,*[18] or by Louis Smith in his study of an urban classroom.[19]

What is praiseworthy in the Smith and Wolcott ethnographies is the effort to describe, and through description understand, the everyday life of those in an urban classroom and of him in a principal's office, respectively. But these examples of qualitative understanding are flawed as they fail to describe *lived* experience. Rather, events, behaviour, what is spoken, is recorded. How Ed Bell experienced his schedule, his colleague's intentions, the spirit behind the role, is veiled although not entirely absent. It is a newspaper account of his day, as is Smith's description of the urban classroom. The events of the day are described as 'news', from a perspectiveless perspective. In the attempt to be comprehensive and impartial the qualitativeness of these situations was omitted. What is felt, fantasized and thought – the reality beneath the words, events and schedules – is not made explicit. Neither do we sense who the authors are beyond their professional personae, what their immediate experience is, how they were affected by their work. The difficulty with these ethnographies is they collapse onto the surface of what they study, and in so doing, risk triviality.

The model-building in Smith's and Wolcott's books is finally only conceptual scaffolding, a building which does not elevate our position in order to see further; it only obscures what lies underneath. It is conceptualization born in scientistic obsession to categorize and schematize categories and schema which fail to penetrate the surface, the obvious. Nothing unexpected is discovered in these studies. The principal's day is pretty much as one anticipated; the urban classroom is as mundane and lifeless as we knew. Perhaps all ethnographic research suffers this identification with the surface of social life, but at least in anthropological depictions of so-called primitive cultures we are presented with the unfamiliar, and are so instructive and entertaining. The principal's job may be primitive, but it is hardly unfamiliar, and surely neither instructive nor entertaining.

What could be interesting is a study of (Wolcott's) Bell's 'underlife'. What fuels his competence? How is this job situated in his life; how does it provide a medium for his continued development; how does it block that development? An autobiographical account might provide such understanding, although only if the autobiographer worked persistently not to report his day as a newspaper journalist would, only if he free-associatively crept underneath his habitual explanations of his actions, outside his regularized statements of his objectives. To become more truly qualitative in their focus and method, ethnographies must relinquish their obsession with the obvious and the mundane, and become exegetical, must excavate layers of intention and experience which antedate and live below the text which is daily life, of which language and event are deposits.

In their insensitivity to ethical, aesthetic, political and poetic aspects of lived experience, ethnographies such as these contribute to the self–alienation and social amnesia which typify the historical present.[20] They have lost a sense of their own motives, adding information which no one has requested because everyone knows it. They originate and end in the mundane, and are here distinguishable from educational criticism formulated by Eisner and practised by his students. Their accounts also begin in the mundane but do not end there. By permitting the critic to make judgement, such accounts bring to form aspects of the lived experience of the situation. Implicitly these writers seem to understand that the individual's life-history provides the existential conditions for understanding. (I will return to this point later.) This view is indicated in the imagery Eisner employs to describe the work of an educational critic.

Eisner describes this work as 'rendering the essentially ineffable qualities constituting works of art into a language that will help others to perceive the work more deeply. In this sense, the critic's task is to function as a midwife to perception.'[21] The image of midwife does imply the presence of someone (the unborn child in the image, understanding in the analogy) present yet not visible, encapsulated in the mother's body (or situation not discerned, not yet brought to form). This sense of understanding a present yet not visible is also indicated in the preceding sentence by the use if 'ineffable'. Strictly speaking, 'ineffable' is hyperbole, meaning generally, 'indescribable', 'incapable of being expressed in words'. If this were true, the critic would face a hopeless task. Perhaps Eisner is thinking of a second, less common meaning of the word: 'not to be uttered, as in taboo'. If so, this use of 'ineffable' suggests a particularly important task of the critic, i.e. to break the silence maintained by authority, by tradition, the breaking of which represents the piercing of taboo. Such work becomes explicitly political as well as aesthetic, and raises problematic issues concerning the authority of the critic. Are his judgements matters of taste only, of political inclination? How does he legitimate them? As with a midwife, one senses one must have confidence in the critic's work. There would appear to be no criteria outside the critic's past record and reputation. I do not see this reliance upon the word of others as damaging, however. The quantitative critic is no different position finally. His numbers may disguise his political and aesthetic commitments, but they cannot transcend them.

One next step critical work (in Eisner's sense) might take is the specification of procedure, not in a vulgar, technical way, but in a way which makes explicit how the critic proceeds. It is some, but not sufficient help to say that the 'connoisseur'[22] is 'to attend to happenings of educational life in a focused, sensitive and conscious way'.[23] How does one achieve such focus, sensitivity and consciousness? In answering that question I believe autobiographical method can be of use, and I will suggest how in the final section.

Empathy and educational understanding

Being 'focused, sensitive and conscious' means, in part, being empathetic. We can observe this, for instance, in Robert Donmoyer's criticism of Miss Hill's fourth-grade classroom.[24] His view of her as reminiscent of Mary Hartmann is quickly clouded by coming to know her. He sees how her routinized teaching represents her effort to survive a situation organizationally-created and maintained. Further, he sees her outside the classroom where she is spontaneous and humane. He describes her, consequently, as a Jekyll-and-Hyde character.[25]

Empathy, however, conceals as it reveals. Empathy, a prerequisite for understanding the intentions of others, invites he who empathizes to participate in those intentions, intentions which can function as self-rationalizing, self-forgiving and obscuring ideas. At least she meant well. She has the highest ideals; it is her situation which prevents their realization. One easily risks complicity with another's delusions and legitimations. In serious autobiographical work one adopts a critical posture towards one's self-report, scrutinizing one's free-associative account looking for the *functions* of one's explanations of oneself. Similarly the critic must not abandon his critical task in his empathic effort to understand. He must not only mirror the self-report of the other, as in the ethnographies previously mentioned, as this results in a unidimensional and usually trivial account. Further, in the presence of another – especially when the other characterizes himself as 'critic' – one tends to give less free-associative and more defended accounts. The critic, as Eisner suggests with the image of midwife, brings to form what operates underneath the teacher's announced intentions, claimed limitations. The critic's empathy must not make him a political eunuch. As it is for the mother-to-be, bringing to awareness that which is denied, repressed, or simply not known is not a painless procedure. The midwife, for her part, must work to make the process as painless as possible. She must be a trusted colleague who wishes her client well, but in so wishing does not relinquish her independence or critical judgement.

Understanding in this sense is a socially negotiated undertaking. The critic reflects upon the report of the other, contextualizing it in his experience and commitments. What Eisner does not (yet) do and what may be part of a next step is the enunciation of a schema which represents a codification of experience and commitment, criteria by which the critic judges, or perhaps a method of judgement and understanding. The schema acts as a kind of sieve through which self-report and observation is poured. Schutz observes:

> Meaning is not a quality of certain lived experiences emerging distinctively in the stream of consciousness...It is rather the result of my explication of past lived experiences which are grasped reflectively from an actual now and from an actual valid reference scheme...Lived experiences first become meaningful, then, when they are explicated *post hoc* and become comprehensible to me as well-circumscribed experiences. Thus only those lived experiences are subjectively meaningful which are...examined as regards their constitution, and which are explicated in respect to their position in a reference schema that is at hand.[26]

The concept of 'valid reference scheme' implies a scientifically-derived scheme which obscures problematic political and aesthetic issues. However, Schutz's notion acknowledges the role of the researcher in the determination of meaning. The research does not merely mirror what he observes, as if meaning inhered 'out there', in the situation, and the dutiful researcher works to absent himself, and merely reflect back what occurred. This is the error of ethnography, an error which results from the interest in being scientific, from accepting the false dualism of subject and object. It is the researcher's 'eye', his capacity to penetrate the surface of situations – the language of the participants, their public intentions and their observable behaviour – to qualities discernible but not yet present, which makes possible understanding. The researcher is a midwife who assists in bringing to birth knowledge not yet born. Dewey, using different imagery, describes well this process of qualitative knowing.

When it is said that I have a feeling, or impression, of 'hunch', that things are thus and so, what is actually designated is primarily the presence of a dominating quality in a situation as a whole, not just the existence of a feeling as a psychical or psychological fact. To say I have a feeling or impression that so and so is the case is to note that the quality in question is not yet resolved into determinate terms and relations; it marks a conclusion without a statement of the reasons for it, the grounds upon which it rests. It is the first stage in the development of explicit distinctions. All thought in every subject begins with just an unanalyzed whole. When the subject-matter is reasonably familiar, relevant distinctions speedily offer themselves, and sheer qualitativeness may not remain long enough to be readily recalled. But it often persists and forms a haunting and engrossing problem. It is a common-place that a problem *stated* is well on its way to solution, for statement of the nature of a problem signifies that the underlying quality is being transformed into determinate distinctions of terms and relations or has become an object of articulate thought. But something presents itself as problematic before there is recognition of *what* the problem is. The problem is had or experienced before it can be stated or set forth; but it is had as an immediate quality of the whole situation. The sense of something problematic, of something perplexing and to be resolved, marks the presence of something pervading all elements and considerations. Thought is the operation by which it is converted into pertinent and coherent terms.[27]

In this passage Dewey nicely unites self and situation. Before turning to what else he does, let us note that the passage is somewhat overly enthusiastic. There are times when one's feeling is in fact psychological, private, not properly understood as part of the situation. The notion of projection denotes the capacity of the individual to distort the situation which he understands – rather, misunderstands – according to unconscious material which – being unconscious – he denies as he projects it onto others. Other orders of bias exist which, if they elude the researcher, function to misread qualitativeness. Gouldner's notion of 'domain assumptions' refers to the predispositions of the social theorists and investigators to shape their studies in ways which bias what they discover.

Domain assumptions about man and society might include, for example, dispositions to believe that men are rational or irrational; that society is precarious or fundamentally stable; that social problems will correct themselves with planned intervention; that human behavior is unpredictable; that man's true humanity resides in his feelings and sentiments.[28]

Erikson discusses the 'motivational dimensions' of the idea.[29] Robert Travers observes: 'Knowledge is preconditioned by the forms of our sensibility.'[30] With such words we move from pre–conscious or unconscious views of the constitution of human life to the psychological life of intellectual interests, to the fully empirical view that true knowledge lies outside the individual and one's sensibility conditions it.

When one is psychologically 'present' one can attune oneself to a situation, and one's experience of that situation does indeed depict that situation. We can become conscious of how life–history, commitments and assumptions operate in our experience of that situation. We become free of them as we become conscious of them. We then attune ourselves to the situation, allowing the problematic – the unknown, the tension – to state itself through us. The situation comes to form through us, and thus our sensibilities do not merely precondition knowledge; they make it possible. By focussing upon the 'underlife' of the situation we avoid restatement of the obvious and mundane. Such a focus brings the situation to form; in Dewey's words it becomes an object of articulate thought.

The observer meditates while in situation, keeping explicit his own material. He can later, when he goes over his account, explicate its presence, and delete it as appropriate if the statement is to become public. While in the room, he attempts to include as much as possible. He attunes himself, allowing himself to move through the room visually, emotionally, above all moving as a spirit throughout the room empathically, representing what is experienced though as yet not articulated. He works to sense the unstated problematic, what Dewey also terms 'an immediate quality of the whole situation'. Through thought and language we convert the unspoken, not–yet–understood 'into pertinent and coherent terms'. To achieve such understanding a second reading – a reading of the reading – may be necessary in which one applies, in Schutz's terms a 'valid reference scheme'.[31]

I want to return to the process of knowing, of being attuned to the situation, and expressing the indeterminate and problematic so that the 'underneath' as well as the surface of the situation is portrayed. Again, Dewey is helpful.

> The word 'intuition' has many meanings. But in its popular, as distinct from refined philosophical usage, it is closely connected with the single qualitativeness underlying all the details of explicit reasoning. It may be relatively dumb and inarticulate and yet penetrating; unexpressed in definite ideas which form reasons and justifications and yet profoundly right. To my mind, Bergson's contention that intuition precedes conception and goes deeper is correct. Reflection and rational elaboration spring from and make explicit a prior intuition. But there is nothing mystical about this fact, and it does not signify that there are two modes of knowledge, one of which is appropriate to one kind of subject matter, and the other mode to the other kind. Thinking and theorizing about physical matters set out from an intuition, and reflection about affairs of life and mind

consists in an ideational and conceptual transformation of what begins as an intuition. Intuition, in short, signifies the realization of a pervasive quality such that it regulates the determination of relevant distinction or of whatever, whether in the way of terms or relations, becomes the accepted object of thought.[32]

As he unites subject and object, Dewey unites the subjective and the objective, the humanities, art and the sciences. All knowing begins in intuition. It is the medium through which the qualities of situation become discerned, conceptualized and articulated. Intuition is the representation and meditation of situation and self. Thus, it behooves us to be interested in knowing how to cultivate the intuitive capacity, and to begin to utilize language to render our intuitions sensitively, hence more accurately. I am thinking of the ways in which gifted novelists and poets use language, painters use painting, dancers use movement. Linearity, or logical relations among words, is less important than a snug fit between word and the quality it signifies, less important than words' power to recreate the situation they portray. So used, language enables the reader or listener to empathically take part in the situation which he only hears about, or sees pictures of. Words need to be stretched to fit situations, not always compacted to compose a logical sentence. Attention needs to be paid to their rhythm as well as their sequence. 'How a poem means' helps comprise what it means.[33] The description of a classroom needs to be more experimental in a literary way, and mimic less the dry formalism of much theoretical language in psychology and sociology if we are to progress in our field.

Situations exhibit movement[34] to the extent one intuits them accurately, and articulates the intuitive reading so that it is accessible, indeed recognizable to one's students (or colleagues). Through this naming, the situation is brought to form, and becomes mature. Its articulation is its maturity. And as it matures, it disappears as a new situation arises in its place: immature, unnamed, perhaps not yet felt. As time passes the midwife works, the hidden becomes discernible, and through careful, cautious attunement to qualities these qualities present themselves as impressions or hunches. One gives this 'inner speech'[35] linguistic form, and through conversation, achieves understanding. True, it is possible that one understands more completely before conversation. *But for understanding to have social use, it must be negotiated socially.*

In order to achieve movement one must be willing to offer up one's 'reading'. Social negotiation can only occur when the participants are willing to give up aspects of their understanding for the sake of consensual articulation of the disciplinary situation. Further, when one is 'caught' in one's own views, one is less likely to accurately read the qualities of the situation, and one is less willing, less able to negotiate a consensual understanding. This is one meaning of 'ideological', that one projects, in this case not explicitly psychological material (although political views have their psychological functions and meaning), but unchallengeable, non-negotiable views of human life. Such views are akin to Gouldner's domain assumptions except they are quite conscious. Mannheim discusses this distortion of understanding and another, more temporally–based, distortion

knowledge is distorted and ideological when it fails to take account of the new realities applying to a situation, and when it attempts to conceal them by thinking of them in categories which are inappropriate...

In the same historical epoch and in the same society there may be several distorted types of inner mental structure, some because they have not yet grown up to the present, and others because they are already beyond the present.[36]

In the first paragraph of this passage we note the ideologue's deforming of the situation by adherence to categories generated and espoused before the situation has presented itself. Such individuals do not attune themselves to the situation, but vice versa. In the second paragraph two related distortions are noted. The mass of people of a given society are more–or–less sharing the same – the present – historical moment. Because they are the masses they constitute the present moment. Broadly speaking, they share ideas of what is possible, what is valuable and so on. But there are always groups and individuals who have yet to reach this historical stage, and the masses view them as 'backward'. As well, there is always an *avant–garde*, who have lived through already what the masses live through at the present time. Often the *avant–garde* forgets that the masses must live through their issues, cannot resolve them by passively accepting the knowledge of the *avant–garde*. Often the *avant–garde* forgets what Sartre does not: 'Ideas do not change men. Knowing the cause of a passion is not enough to overcome it; one must live it...in short one must "work oneself through".'[37]

Forgetting that historical stages must be lived through, not merely thought through, the *avant–garde* tends to succumb to smugness and self–superiority. It may offer its understanding of the historical present, but it is obliged to offer up this understanding, to allow the masses to dialectically oppose it in its movement to work through it. Thus each generation discovers anew what was understood before, if in now historically antiquated terms, in terms which do now bring to form the present historical situation. Collingwood understood this point well. 'Every new generation must rewrite history in its own way....The historian himself, together with the here–and–now which forms the total body of evidence available to him, is part of the process he is studying.'[38]

Not only specific truths change with each generation, but each generation's interests in those truths changes. Our interests are intimately linked to our interpretation of what is necessary to bring our situation to form, to discern its latent qualities. In this interpretive work, the effort to achieve nomological truth is little help. For interpretation and understanding of human affairs – educational and otherwise – cannot be achieved apart from time, history and human intention. This fundamental fact some of our quantitative colleagues have evidently forgotten. Part of our task is to remind them. Bauman notes:

> Suppose that somehow an empirical–statistical demonstration of the strictest sense is produced, showing that all men everywhere who have ever been placed in a certain situation have invariably reacted in the same way and to the same extent. Suppose that whenever this situation is reproduced, the same reaction invariably follows. Which is to say: suppose that this reaction is, in the most literal sense of the word, 'calculable'. Such a demonstration would not bring us a single step closer to the 'interpretation' of this reaction. By itself such a demonstration would contribute nothing to the project of

'understanding why' this reaction ever occurred and, moreover, 'why' it invariably occurs in the same way. As long as the 'inner', imaginative *reproduction* of the motivation responsible for the reaction remains impossible, we will be unable to acquire that understanding.[39]

Reproduction of motivation is impossible, given its situatedness in time, place and life–history. What quantitative research aspires for is in principle impossible. And, as Winch has argued, it is undesirable as well.[40]

Attunement

To focus more closely upon attunement, and its relation to understanding, I will summarize aspects of Heidegger's work, from which the term 'attunement' derives. For Heidegger, understanding is not a methodological problem: it is an ontological one. That is, understanding is a mode of being, not a technical problem for epistemologists or, more narrowly, philosophers of science. Understanding occurs only in the context of being–in–the–world,[41] It cannot occur for philosophers who abstract and reduce being–in–the–world to a set of technical problems. Rather, in Bauman's words, understanding only occurs in 'our pristine, straightforward, "prereflexive" being–in–the–world'.[42] In this state, if we are attuned, knowledge presents itself. Heidegger writes:

The essence of being is *physis*. Appearing is the power that emerges. Appearing makes manifest. Already we know then that being, appearings, causes emerge from concealment. Since the essent as such *is,* it places itself in and stands in *unconcealment, aletheia.* We translate, and at the same time thoughtlessly misinterpret, this word as 'truth'...The essent is true insofar as it is. The true as such is essent. This means: The power that manifests itself stands in unconcealment. In showing itself, the unconcealed as such comes to stand. Truth as unconcealment is not an appendage of being.[43]

Truth is what presents itself to us in situation. History is continually unconcealing. In specific situations, in a classroom for instance, we attune ourselves in order to see that which our everyday eyes do not see. We must close these eyes, listen and discover what lies concealed. This discovery is not final truth; it is not a logical or methodological exercise. It is not a matter of matching thoughts in me to actions out there. It is a matter of allowing reality, of which I am a spokesman, to speak itself. The original Greek for reality, for the essent, was *physis*. Bauman tells us that it was translated into Latin, through which it was passed on to the present time, as *natura*.[44] Heidegger notes the original meaning.

> What does the word *physis* denote? It denotes self–blossoming emergence (e.g. the blossoming of a rose), opening up, unfolding, that which manifests itself in such unfolding and perseveres and endures in it; in short, the realm of things that emerge and linger on...*Physis* means the power that emerges and the enduring real under its sway...*Physis* is the process of arising, of emerging from the hidden, whereby the hidden is first made to stand.[45]

Physis as understood by the Greeks derived from lived experience, not from the abstracted generalization associated with natural studies like physics. That *physis* is associated only with natural science, and not at all with the study of experience, underscrores the narrowness of the contemporary scientific age.[46]

Knowledge occurs in the experience of situation, in the context of daily life. Knowing is not properly a specialized activity practised by technicians isolated from the mainstream of life. Heidegger:

> We know from Heraclitus and Parmenides that the unconcealment of being is not simply given. Unconcealment occurs only when it is achieved by work: the work of the word in poetry, the work of stone in temple and statue, the work of the word in thought, the work of the *polis* as the historical place in which all this is grounded and preserved.[47]

Knowledge is not to be created simply for the sake of its creation, simply to add to 'the body of knowledge'. This is knowledge divorced from the intentions, needs and desires of concretely–existing individuals. Efforts to understand properly arise in the midst of a *felt* problematic.

Autobiographical method

We are not mere smudges on the mirror. Our life–histories are not liabilities to be exorcised but are the very precondition for knowing. It is our individual and collective stories in which present projects are situated, and it is awareness of these stories which is the lamp illuminating the dark spots, the rough edges. Dewey's 'intuition' and Heidegger's 'attunement' both refer to the reflexive grasp of problematic qualities of situations.

This image of grasp captures the unity of self and situation. Moulded together, the situation speaks through the self and the self through the situation. Qualitative understanding requires subtle and quiet attention to both. Autobiographical method can be employed to cultivate such attention: to situation as element of the self, to self as situation, and to transformation and reconstitution of both. [48] In such movement we glimpse dialectical development, the basic structural elements of intellectual and psycho–social development. We glimpse the role of texts and teachers and friends – the role of the curriculum – in our movement from the egocentric to the decentred, from provincial to broadminded, from ignorant to knowing human beings. It is a glimpse of this phenomenon previously portrayed in psychological and social theories now situated in the life of a particular individual – oneself.

Autobiographical method offers opportunities to return to our own situations, our 'rough edges', to reconstruct our intellectual agendas. The focus in such work is the felt problematic; its method is intuitive. One falls back on oneself – rather than upon the words of others – and must articulate what is yet unspoken, act as midwife to the unborn. One uncovers one's 'domain assumptions', one's projections – not in order to clean the slate but in order to understand the slate of which one is the existential basis, the basis which makes knowing possible. William Earle describes what we seek when we work autobiographically:

And while science and certain theoretical forms of philosophy look for *explanations* of phenomena, 'Know thyself' does not enjoin me to find explanations of myself in what lies outside myself, in what is *not* me. 'Knowing' is not necessarily explanatory, but it might be regarded as elucidation: that is, raising to explicit, reflexive consciousness that which is already implicitly grasped. It might be an effort to excavate the implicit buried sense of existence of a singular being by that singular being – in a word the 'autobiography' of the singular being. 'Know thyself' invites me to become explicit as to who I am, what it is for me to exist; what my singular existence has been, where it has been, where it is now, and what lies before me. 'Ontological autobiography', we shall call it, with not particular emphasis upon its 'graphical' or recorded character; it is a question of a form of consciousness rather than of literature.[49]

What we aspire to when we work autobiographically is not adherence to conventions of a literary form. Nor do we think of audience, of portraying our life to others. We write autobiography for ourselves, in order to cultivate our capacity to see through the outer forms, the habitual explanations of things, the stories we tell in order to keep others at a distance. It is against the taken-for-granted, against routine and ritual we work, for it is the regularized and the habitual which arrest movement – intellectual and otherwise. Arrested, we cannot see movement in others nor contribute to it. In this sense we seek a dialectical self-self relation, which then permits a dialectical relationship between self and work, self and others. Earle describes it as 'divestment':

> divestment may be taken as a 'purification' of the soul too much engrossed with what it is not, too much caught up in that deceptively tempting and deceptively rewarding domain of the impurities of existence, where the poor soul futilely sought itself...[Divestment]is a regressive shift of attention from objects or affairs back to the ego that was engrossed with them.[50]

Divestment does not represent retreat from the affairs of the world, from classrooms, politics and conflicts. It represents reflexive awareness of one's participation in the affairs of the world, a reflexivity which captures the mutual determinancy and mutual creation of both self and situation. Autobiographical method permits such awareness as it reconstructs the past, as it lays bare the relation between self and work, self and others which has prevailed in the past. It portrays, for instance, the ways in which intellectual interests functioned psychologically for us. Such portraits give us an order of information regarding the function of curriculum that we simply have not had before. Dewey recalls his interest in Hegel:

> There were, however, also 'subjective' reasons for the appeal that Hegel's thought made to me; it supplied a demand for unification that was doubtless an intense emotional craving, and yet was a hunger that only an intellectualized subject matter could satisfy...But the sense of divisions and separations that were, I suppose, born upon me as a consequence of a heritage of New England culture, divisions by way of isolation of self from the world, of soul from the body, of nature from God, brought a painful oppression – or rather, they were an inward laceration...Hegel's synthesis of subject and object, matter and spirit, the divine and the human was, however, no mere intellectual formula; it operated as an immense release, a liberation.[51]

We see how Hegel's work 'operated' for Dewey: it mended by its synthetical structure, his 'lacerations' and 'divisions'. In opposition to the felt fragmentation of childhood in New England is Hegel's series of unities, and the synthesis of dialectical interaction is specifically Deweyan, and American. It is pragmatism. Aspects of the synthetical character of Hegel are retained in this hybrid child. The 'isolation of self from the world' is ended as self is situation; situation is self, as we noted in the passage quoted from *Philosophy and Civilization*. This dialectical opposition to the atomization Dewey underwent as a child and boy constitutes, for Norman Holland, [52] biographic themes; but as David Bleich has pointed out, such themes do not statically reproduce themselves.[53] A biographic theme opposed by an antithetical theme blends creating a third, higher-order theme which, while containing elements of the previous two, is distinctly a hybrid. We see this evidenced in Dewey's work: atomization and dualism during childhood, Hegelian synthesis of consciousness and matter (situation in consciousness), then in adulthood Dewey's synthesis of consciousness and matter situated in matter, in situation. Viewed another way, these oppositions or antitheses can be understood as balances. Dewey describes his interest in this way:

> Probably there is in the consciously articulated ideas of every thinker an overweighting of just those things that are contrary to his intrinsic bent, and which, therefore, he has to struggle to bring to expression, while the native bent, on the other hand, can take care of itself. Anyway, a case might be made for the proposition that the emphasis upon the concrete, empirical, and 'practical' in my later writings is partly due to considerations of this nature. It was a reaction against what was more natural, and it served as a protest and protection against something in myself, which, in the pressure of the weight of actual experiences, I knew to be a weakness.[54]

To the extent one becomes conscious of the dialectics of one's intellectual development one can participate in them. Further, through one's self-understanding one comprehends – from a participant's rather than observer's point of view – the functions of ideas – and texts – in one's intellectual life, and the function of one's intellect in one's life. 'To understand is to rediscover you in me; the spirit retrieves itself on even higher levels of the configuration; identity of Spirit in me, in you, in every subject of our community, in every system of culture, finally in the totality of spirits and in universal history'.[55] Understanding of self is not narcissism; it is a precondition and a concomitant condition to the understanding of others. The process of education is not situated – and cannot be understood – in the observer, but in we who undergo it. In its extreme formulation, truth itself lies in the relation of self to situation, knower to known, in the mode of consciousness which allows the situation to articulate itself, allows the qualitative to surface, the problematic to be resolved. Kierkegaard observes:

> When the question of truth is raised subjectively, reflection is directed subjectively to the nature of the individual's

relationship; if only the mode of this relationship is in the truth, the individual is in the truth, even if he should happen to be thus related to what is not true.[56]

As scientific understandings of the natural and physical world change, so do understandings of the human world. The quantitative effort to capture, and make static our world derives from an interest to control and predict. Such an effort will continue to fail as long as human beings resist control. Qualitative research is politically progressive, as it is epistemologically sophisticated, because it understands that a basic meaning of human life is movement, conflict, resolution, conflict, resolution, each thesis and anti-thesis opposing each other in ways which give birth to a new orders of understanding and life. The task is not to control this movement, nor is it merely to portray it. It is to contribute to it, acting as midwives in the labour which is human history coming to form. This contribution can be made in work with ourselves, as well as work with others. It is work which cultivates the specificity of ourselves, the particularity of self and situation. Autobiographical method is one strategy by which this work can be conducted.

In another sense autobiographical work, because it focuses upon the self and its history, slows down movement, makes it stay, so it becomes more visible, its detail discernible. It is like a blow-up in a photographic sense. A character in Virginia Woolf's *The Years* seeks to see the same:

> There must be another life, here and now, she repeated. This is too short, too broken. We know nothing, even about ourselves. We're only just beginning, she thought, to understand, here and there. She held her hand hallowed; she felt that she wanted to enclose the present moment; to make it stay; to fill it fuller and fuller, with the past, the present and future, until it shone, whole, bright, deep with understanding.[57]

Acknowledgement

An earlier version of this paper was presented at the meeting of the American Educational Research Association in Boston (April 1980).

References and notes

1. WILLIS, G. (1978). 'Qualitative evaluation as the aesthetic, personal and political dimensions of curriculum criticism'. In: WILLIS, G. (ed) *Qualitative Evaluation: Concepts and Cases in Curriculum Criticism.* Berkeley, California: McCutcheon. pp. 7 and 8.
2. DILTHEY, W. quoted in BAUMAN, Z. (1978). *Hermeneutics and Social Science.* New York: Columbia University Press. p. 38.
3. LASCH, C. (1977). *Haven in a Heartless World.* New York: Basic Books.
4. HABERMAS, J. (1973). *Theory and Practice.* Boston: Beacon Press.
5. MARCUSE, H. (1978). *The Aesthetic Dimension.* Boston: Beacon Press.
6. BAUMAN, Z., *op. cit.,* p. 231 (see Note 2). Emphases in original.
7. The members of the Frankfurt School are among the most compelling analysts of these dangers. See JAY, M. (1973). *The Dialectical Imagination.* Berkeley, California: McCutcheon, for a summary of this work.
8. HUEBNER, D. (1975). 'Curricular language and classroom meanings'. In: PINAR, W.F. (Ed) *Curriculum Theorizing: The Reconceptualists.* Berkeley, California: McCutcheon. pp. 217–36.
9. SCHWAB, J.J. (1970). *The Practical: A Language for Curriculum.* Washington, D.C.: National Education Association.
10. BAUMAN, Z. *op cit.,* p. 25 (see Note 2).
11. See SARTRE, J.P. (1964). *Nausea* (New York: New Directions) for a novelistic portrait of vicosity.
12. BAUMAN, Z. *op. cit.,* p. 26 (see Note 2).
13. EISNER, E.W. (1979). *The Educational Imagination.* New York: Macmillan.
14. DONMOYER, R. (1980). 'The evaluator as artist', *Journal of Curriculum Theorizing,* 2, 2 (Summer).
15. McCUTCHEON, G. (1979). 'Educational criticism: methods and application', *Journal of Curriculum Theorizing,* 1, 2, (Summer).
16. VALLANCE, E. (1978). 'Scanning horizons and looking at weeds'. In: WILLIS, G. (ed) *op. cit.* (see Note 1).
17. BARONE, T. jr. (1979). 'Of Scott and Lisa and other friends'. In: EISNER, *op. cit.* pp. 240–5.
18. WOLCOTT, H.F. (1973). *The Man in the Principal's Office: An Ethnography.* New York: Holt, Rinehart and Winston.
19. SMITH, L.M. and GEOFFREY, W. (1968). *The Complexities of an Urban Classroom.* New York: Holt, Rinehart and Winston.
20. For a discussion of this phenomenon see JACOBY, R. (1975). *Social Amnesia.* Boston: Beacon Press.
21. EISNER, *op. cit.,* p. 191 (see Note 13).
22. 'Connoisseur' is, perhaps, an unfortunate choice of term: it implies

the bourgeois collector of art whose tastes are usually derived from others rather than from his experience as an artist.

23. EISNER, *op. cit.*,p. 195 (see Note 13).
24. DONMOYER, R. (1979). 'School and society revisited: an educational criticism of Miss Hill's fourth-grade classroom'. In: Eisner, *op. cit.*, pp. 229–40 (see Note 13).
25. *Ibid.*, p. 232.
26. SCHUTZ, A. quoted in BAUMAN, A., *op. cit.*, p. 180 (see Note 2).
27. DEWEY, J. (1970). *Philosophy and Civilization*. New York: G.P. Putnam's Sons, p. 100.
28. GOULDNER, A.W. s(1970). *The Coming Crisis of Western Sociology*. New York: Basic Books, p. 31.
29. ERIKSON, E. (1975). *Life History and Historical Moment*. New York: Norton.
30. TRAVERS, R.M.W. s(1978). 'Some comments on qualitative approaches to the development of scientific knowledge and the use of constructs derived from phenomenol experience'. In: WILLIS, (ed), *op. cit.* (see Note 1).
31. See Note 26.
32. DEWEY, *op. cit.*, pp. 100–1 (see Note 27).
33. CIARDI, J. (1959). *How Does a Poem Mean?* Cambridge, Mass.: Riverside Press.
34. For a full treatment of this notion see PINAR, W.F. (1980). 'Life history and educational experience', *Journal of Curriculum Theorizing*, 2, 2 (Summer).
35. VYGOTSKY, L.S. (1962). *Thought and Language*. Cambridge, Mass.: M.I.T. Press.
36. MANNHEIM, K. (1960). *Ideology and Utopia*. London: Routledge & Kegan Paul.
37. SARTRE, J.-P. (1963). *Search for a Method*. New York: Knopf, p.248.
38. COLLINGWOOD, R.G. (1973). *The Idea of History*. Oxford: Oxford University Press.
39. BAUMAN, *op. cit.*, p. 70. (see Note 2).
40. WINCH, P. (1971). *Ethics and Action*. London: Routledge & Kegan Paul.
41. BAUMAN, *op. cit.*, p. 148 (see Note 2).
42. *Ibid.*, p. 149.
43. *Ibid.*, p. 150.
44. *Ibid.*, p. 149–50.
45. *Ibid.*, p. 150.
46. *Ibid.*, p. 150
47. *Ibid.*, p. 151.
48. PINAR, W.F. (1979). 'The voyage out', *Journal of Curriculum Theorizing*, 2, 1 (Winter).
49. EARLE, W. (1977). *Autobiographical Consciousness: A Philosophical Inquiry into Existence*. Chicago, Illinois: Quadrangle

Books. p. 10.
50. *Ibid.,* pp. 58–9.
51. DEWEY, J. (1960). *On Experience, Nature and Freedom* (Bernstein, R.J. Ed.). Indianapolis, Indiana: Bobbs–Merrell. p. 10.
52. HOLLAND, N. (1973). *Poems in Persons: An Introduction to the Psychoanalysis of Literature.* New York: Norton.
53. BLEICH, D. (1978). *Subjective Criticism.* Baltimore, Maryland: Johns Hopkins University Press.
54. DEWEY, *op. cit.,* p. 8 (see Note 2).
55. BAUMAN, *op. cit.,* p. 35 (see Note 2).
56. KIERKEGAARD, S. In: BRETALL, R. (Ed) (1951). *A Kierkegaard Anthology.* Princeton, New Jersey: Princeton University Press. pp. 210–11.
57. WOOLF, V. (1937). *The Years.* New York: Harcourt, Brace. pp. 427–8.

Habits Impeding Deliberation

Thomas W. Roby

Introduction

For over a decade the literature on curriculum has been peppered
with articles, critiques and reviews concerning curriculum
deliberation. The advocates of this approach to constructing,
operationalizing and evaluating curricula have produced various
labels: from Schwab's first 'Practical' article through Reid's recent
'Deliberative Curriculum Theory' manifesto. A further sampling
would include, among others, Westbury on the art of curriculum,
Orpwood on deliberative curriculum inquiry, and Pereira on
perception and the practical arts. Related curriculum inquiry has
included action research, the teacher-as-researcher, reflection-in-
action, and decision theory, as well as various restatements of
Dewey.[1]

Yet, the various threads of discussion about curriculum
deliberation have a curious stop-start characteristic – a seeming
inability to sustain the discussion or coordinate the meanings of
the various terminologies. Partly the problem seems to lie in the
nature of curriculum deliberation itself, since it is an approach to
practice rather than a doctrine about it. Additional difficulties
arise from the doctrinal character of educational research itself,
where advocates tend to stake out and defend research areas with
novel terminologies. If curriculum can be 'reconceptualized' in this
way, then so can the novel terms of the reconceptualists. As this
process of stakeouts continues, each stakeholder flies her/his
favourite flag while often attacking those whose position is closest.

*This essay is a revision of a paper presented to the symposium 'What to
do about curriculum deliberation' at the annual meeting of the American
Educational Research Association in Montreal, April 1983.

What dialogue remains tends to be about 'curriculum' rather than actual practice. The amelioration of this state of affairs requires the advocates of curriculum deliberation to do something about operationalization of its ideas by way of a variety of teaching materials and approaches. Such activity can ground deliberative discourse in the concrete problems of schooling, provide a plurality of models to stimulate further activity, and focus the terms of the discourse on meaningful examples.

The ingredients of this essay are straightforward: a short description of the deliberative format, a description of some habits which impede deliberation – especially in its curricular form, and some suggestions for their amelioration. Since the process of deliberation is complicated, convoluted, and difficult to represent apart from concrete circumstances, I have tried to clarify it by reference to diverse examples and promising studies involving, though not limited to, curriculum. In the educational examples I refer primarily to three categories of curriculum students: prospective teachers engaged in undergraduate or graduate preparation for teaching; employed teachers hoping to improve their skills by a course in curriculum; and administrators with responsibility for curriculum supervision who are returning for a higher degree.

A variety of examples, however, or even extended illustrations in the curriculum literature, should *not* be taken as substitutes for practice. Beginning deliberators generally will do it less well than experienced ones, with results that may lead them to abandon the process. This raises a classic educational dilemma – if we acquire good habits and character by exercise, how can we exercise them when we don't yet have them? I present a partial answer – for curriculum students to engage in the process of practical reasoning on some simulated or actual problematic situation with an experienced mentor. Experience of success in deliberation provides one of the most successful arguments for changing existing habits.

Habits

Let us look at habits in the context of deliberation. Habits are identifiable patterns of behaviour which individuals or groups consciously or unconsciously employ to respond to the needs of a situation. Since situations are often typical, behaviour can repeat itself successfully. Problems arise when situations become atypical and behaviour anomolous. Our established patterns then lead to misperceptions of situation and remedy. For example, we have a habit of taking the 8:03 to work every morning. A rail strike disrupts the schedule, and we are forced to develop a new response. Often this is a not always successful modification of the old pattern. We all jump into our cars at 8:03 and arrive two hours late because of the ensuing traffic jam.

Habits are not only customary patterns of behaviour, but also dispositions to act in certain ways, based on our impulses to achieve certain ends, e.g., to get to work on time, to see the films we enjoy the most (and not the others), or to develop students' abilities for appreciating good stories. Habits manifest our pursuits and avoidances. They are also flexible responses. By judging ends and deciding upon means we can alter our habits to provide better ways of organizing the impulses. And we can consciously change habits on either a mechanical or a reflective basis. Mechanical habits, those we associate with operant conditioning and behaviour modification, are created by patterns of reinforcement.[2] Reflective habits, or arts, are closer to those advocated by Dewey in his various descriptions of the suspension and mediation of impulse by reason.[3] While both types have their uses, the latter seem most desirable for the present task: Ultimately our goal in education is autonomy, in this case to free students from impeding constraints. Self-criticism will be one of our chief means to this end.

In what follows I hope to show how certain habits impeding deliberation are played out when they are subject to the deliberative process. I envision two outcomes from this interaction. The first is modification of the impeding habits into the arts, or reflective habits, that facilitate deliberation. The second result is modification and complication of the serial format for deliberation, to be described in a moment, by its intersection with the habits. I propose that such use of the deliberative format in practical contexts reveals the spiral character of the deliberative process. Let us review this format.

The deliberative format

Schwab has described the practical arts, which are the basic format for deliberation, curricular or otherwise, in sequential fashion:

> These are arts by which we assign various possible meanings to perceived detail of the situation and group them in different ways in order to perceive and shape different formulations of 'the' problem posed by the displeasing situation. There are arts for weighing the alternative formulations of a problem thus achieved and for choosing one to follow further. There are arts for generating alternative possible solutions to the problem, arts for tracing each alternative solution to its probable consequences, arts for weighing and choosing among them. There are also reflexive arts for determining when the deliberation should be terminated and action undertaken.[4]

Below is an outline of this compressed passage:

1. Assignment of meaning to details in the problematic situation;
2. Formulation of meaningful details into discrete problems;
3. Weighing and choosing among problem formulations;
4. Formulation of solutions to chosen problem;
5. Rehearsal of consequences of solutions;
6. Weighing and choosing solution;
7. Termination and action.

The skeleton makes clear the serial character of this description, in which movement forward to the next stage or step depends upon completion of the task at the preceding one. Three of the steps concern the problem end of the sequence (1–3), while four concern the solution end (4–7). The term, 'rehearsal of consequences', at the solution end is borrowed from Schwab's earlier formulation of this task.[5]

To turn the above tasks into a specifically *curricular* deliberation, we must factor in four common components of education at each of the seven stages. These components, called 'commonplaces' by Schwab, are students, teachers, subject-matters, and milieux (i.e., economic, social and cultural contexts). So stated, they are abstract coordinates which require concrete specification. As coordinates, each can be given equal weight in a particular curriculum, or the four can be organized into various hierarchies in which one or more have greater importance than the others.*

Proper representation of the commonplaces requires competence in diverse disciplines and corresponding bodies of experience which are rarely found in a single person. Schwab recommends that curriculum deliberation be done by a group in which one or several individuals serve as advocates for each commonplace under the leadership of a chairperson who balances their various concerns against the curriculum-making process as a whole.[6] Concrete specification by such a curriculum group using the practical arts turns '*common*places' into '*particular*places.' When rightly used the arts involve the users, whatever their starting place, in a consideration of all four components and the complexities of their interrelations. When practical arts are not employed to specify the components, their usage is dictated either by avowedly theoretical considerations or by implicit generalizations which function in a quasi-theoretical manner.

These concerns complicate our earlier outline if we are to engage in the activity implicit in Schwab's writings:

1.	Assignment of meaning to details in the problematic situation	
2.	Formulation of meaningful details into discrete problems	by a group using the commonplaces of education
3.	Weighing and choosing among problem formulations	
4.	Formulation of solutions to chosen problem	
5.	Rehearsal of consequences of solutions	
6.	Weighing and choosing solution	
7.	Termination and action	

---

*In some of the recent discussion of curriculum, one or more of the components have been omitted, as in discussion whose appeal for new curricula is based exclusively on a traditional core of texts or a new view of subject matter, without any consideration of the needs, interests or past experiences of students, teachers and society.

Representations of deliberation

Among the few available accounts of curricular deliberation three
tend to follow the pattern just described. I summarized an
individual deliberation concerning the development of a remedial
programme for black students in an inner city community college
in the later 1960s.[7] The summary followed a diagnosis-prescription
model (in a quasi-medical mode) developed by Schwab, in which
diagnosis concerned stages 1–3, while prescription concerned
stages 4–7.[8] Schwab's deliberation was pitched at a more general
level, addressing as it did the liberal arts component in colleges
during the time of student unrest. To borrow a term which he
employs elsewhere, *College Curriculum and Student Protest*
constitutes an exercise in the arts of the 'quasi-practical'. This is
because its diagnoses and prescriptions, in order to be effective,
would need modification by considerations of the needs and
interests of a specific group of college students, as well as of the
teachers and subject matters available in their particular milieux.[9]
It is interesting that Schwab's recommendation in *College
Curriculum and Student Protest* for *simulated deliberation* has been
carried out by Townsend, but with a much different group –
educational administrators – from the college students originally
envisioned as its clientele.[10] Siegel in an imagined undertaking to
teach *Hamlet* to upwardly mobile, upper middle class suburban,
predominantly Jewish high school seniors, tended to exemplify
solutions provided by an eclectic treatment of the arts of literary
criticism.[11] Nonetheless, by moving back and forth between the
problems and solutions presented by each of the four
commonplaces of education she managed to convey something of
the spiral, as differentiated from the linear movement in
deliberation just outlined. We shall have more to say about this
distinction later.

Townsend aside, there are two difficulties with these
representations. First, they all are 'lone ranger' deliberations
which fail to do justice to its group character. Siegel especially
illustrates the difficulties for a single person adequately to
represent every commonplace adequately. Second, they are all
non-classroom deliberations. They concern the so-called preactive
and postactive, but not the interactive phases of teaching. Part of
the force of this omission is seen in the common notion that

curricula, once developed whether by deliberation or other means, are merely 'implemented in the classroom' without significant modification. To date, however, the only representation we have of *classroom* deliberation is my distillation of the experience of teaching both the curricular innovation just mentioned and the failed courses it replaced into parallel paradigmatic dialogues between students and teacher.[12]

Deliberation and its impeding habits

Curricular deliberation is complex and convoluted, though paradoxically, the terms of a completed deliberation, set forth in the earlier formats, appear serial and unforbidding. The retrospective neatening of the process into discrete, linear stages, when mistaken for the process itself, can circumscribe its dynamics. Still, the sequence of a completed deliberation does describe many, if not all, of its necessary terms: It can serve as a kind of a checklist to see if anything was left out. I use it as a convenient rhetorical structure on which to hang the impeding habits at each stage.

Habits fall into three main categories depending upon whether they impede a specific deliberative stage, its stages in a more general way, or its process. Three habits cluster at the solution end of the deliberative format. These are the 'rush to *the* solution' reinforced by 'crisis consciousness' and 'utopian anticipation'. Two habits interfere at the problematic beginnings, i.e., 'externalizing the elements of the problematic situation' and 'excluding or shortchanging commonplaces of education'. More general habits which appear in both problem–posing and solution-settings are 'global mentality,' 'pet formulation,' 'either...or thinking,' and 'lone ranger approach'. Finally there are two habits which can abort the process – 'the expectation of linear progress' and 'the intolerance of uncertainty'.[13]

Such habits alter the character of deliberation by leading to the omission of some terms of the process and by reversing the order of their serially conceived stages. Moreover, both deliberation and description are systematic: problems and solutions interact with each other; and habits likewise reinforce one another. As we concentrate on one we are constrained to refer to others. We shall begin with the habits that cluster at the solution end of deliberation, then show how curriculum students can be moved to reconsider and alter their dispositions by shifting to the problem area. As we proceed a comparative structure will emerge in which a teacher of curriculum students can get deliberation back on the track at various stages by utilizing the arts of each stage as well as those of the process.

When faced with a problematic situation, the first impeding habit is a 'rush to *the* solution'. Everyone prefers a solution, but nobody loves a problem. The impulsive deliberator prefers to begin with termination and action. This impulse can take several forms.

One is the move to a 'pet solution'.[14] Consider the example of the faculty in a small liberal arts college debating a core programme of general education.[15] The faculty fruitlessly wrangle over how many hours of each discipline must be put into the core, ignoring the possibility of formulating the situation in an interdisciplinary way. The result is a grimly divided faculty since there are never enough core hours to satisfy all the pets. Pet solutions often indicate subject matter biases, traditionalizing tunnel vision. When we are urged to go back to basics, there is a tendency to translate the basic into a pet subject matter. Such incomplete conception of the commonplaces means, for instance, that problems concerning students' needs, interests and talents are absorbed into mastery of the favoured basic.

The second habitual form that an impulse to *the* solution takes is 'global mentality'. Here are found such universal methods as Mastery Learning, Competency-Based Objectives, etc., whose predetermined solution fits all problems. The propaganda for such methods is often so enthusiastic that one scarcely hears of the specific problems which they originally addressed, much less of problems with their application. Since they purport to work with any subject matter, they become the Shakespearean answer to every question.[16]

Administrators and legislators, with their demands for universal panaceas from educational theorists, seem to prefer global solutions. Teachers, with their working repertory of working techniques, are less subject to educational fads and tend towards pet solutions. This distinction is by no means absolute, however, and both share the inclination to final, utopian solutions. The impulse to a final solution entails avoidance of the rehearsal of consequences. Whenever such solutions do get implemented there is surprise and chagrin at the modifications requisite upon the appearance of unanticipated problems. For instance, Mastery Learning assumes the student's ability to master nearly any given instructional task.[17] Yet the Chicago Mastery Learning Reading Program has had to change the subject matter content of the originally-given instructional tasks in order to reflect a better balance of positive and negative role models.[18] The solutions conceived at the global level of the generalized learner become the problems that must be dealt with in the milieux of the specific students. Another instance is from the college core curriculum mentioned above. One historian's pet solution for the core is thrown into doubt by the problems of persuading colleagues in his department to give up their specialty electives for the dubious rewards of retooling for a general course.

Reid points out 'if we look to academics or administrators for guidance on the design of curricula, we typically find that they try to turn something intrinsically complex and ambiguous into something clear cut and logical, and this is done in one of two ways: either by declaring a principle that *should* guide curriculum design or by proposing a set of procedural rules that designers *should* follow'. Tracing the course of a curricular development in Britain, he shows how the pattern of debate moved from vague feelings of unease about a situation to proposal for a solution, (a 'core curriculum') with no investigation of the sources of the unease. Reid's analysis shows how early deployment of a global principle such as 'core curriculum' skips over the problem appreciation phase of deliberation and short-circuits the process of practical reasoning. In the US, as he points out, procedural rules based on fixed objectives serve a similar purpose. Both principles and rules absorb problem-posing to solution-setting, e.g., 'Our problem is we need a core curriculum'. This leaves schools in the position of having solutions in search of problems rather than problems in search of solutions. Reid's example in a way combines the vices at the solution end of deliberation; as debate proceeded, the global solutions of the administrators in the Department of Education became assimilated to the pets of the teachers in the Schools Council.[19]

Two other habits often reinforce the rush of solution-orientated deliberators. One could be called 'crisis consciousness'. It is the reverse of Schwab's 'anticipatory generation of alternative'.[20] Anxiety at depressed reading scores sparks the felt need to go back to basics. This sort of orientation short-circuits the deliberate character of practical reasoning. Some administrators don't feel comfortable in a deliberation unless there is a real or imagined crisis. The spirit of the age has become premature consensus!

The other habit, which tends to prevail among teachers, is the 'lone ranger approach'. This was alluded to earlier in the deliberations of Roby, Schwab and Siegel. The global solutions of testers, theorists and bandwagon researchers wind up inside classrooms where they supply constraints upon individual teachers working with particular students. For teachers such solutions provide problems to be coped with, e.g. procedures to be instituted, forms to be filled out, etc.. The meetings they are called to most often are intended to facilitate the ready-made solutions of administrators. Consequently they are unused to deliberating in groups of peers. This gives their tendency to pet solutions an individualistic and even idiosyncratic cast.

Beginning remedies – promoting alternatives through arts of self-criticism

Let me begin my turn to the educational consequences of the analyses of curricular deliberation and its impeding habits. Those who rush to predetermined global or pet solutions need to face two sets of problems. First there are the problems generated by the solution, which pinpoint the finalistic, and often idealistic character of the preferred solution. Second there are the problems which the solution alleges it has solved. Introduction of both sets of problems brings into focus alternative competing solutions to their first impulses.

Consider idealism. Often curriculum students are unaware of the utopian nature of a preferred solution. They see it as realistic and feasible – albeit sometimes novel. A kind of magical thinking takes over. Failure does not lead to cynicism. Instead the idealism becomes dormant until able to fasten on the next universal innovation or opportunity to put forth the pet. Curriculum students need to face the idealistic character of the solution by distinguishing its feasible aspects from those which are unlikely to succeed within the circumstances of its introduction. Examination of the reasons for past failure (problems generated but ignored) in parallel innovations can be salutary.[21]

Curriculum students with field experience will often confess in non-threatening discussions their experience of failure in application of preferred solutions, the consequent scapegoating of the problematic situation that it failed to fix, and the resulting withdrawal into the ivory tower. The trick is to get the students to see a solution as utopian, then help them to develop more realistic alternatives which appropriate its usable elements for solving a specific problem. One way to separate the student's idealism overlaying the curricular reality is paradoxically by encouraging them to face and develop the utopian mode. Models such as Plato's *Republic* or Skinner's *Walden II* are useful for such elaboration.[22] This can result in an enriched ideal with more possibilities for application than the usually impoverished and one-dimensional concept initially put forth. Another way to promote realism is by development of devil's advocacy in the student, who must take a position opposing his or her own ideal. The separation of two alternatives, a competing ideal or even better a realistic one, is an important start. Such approaches mark the beginning of self-criticism – the art of scrutinizing one's formulations for hidden biases and limitations.[23]

Unfortunately at this point a promising beginning can be aborted by the 'either....or thinking' which pervades American culture at least. This mental set looks at two possibilities as exhaustive and exclusive: nuclear energy or coal, Republicans or Democrats, winners or losers. We need devices which will modify this habit.

Remedies through the deliberative process – backtracking to the problematic situation

Remedy for the cluster of habits which tend to group around the solution end of practical reasoning require assertion of the deliberative process. This means backtracking to its problematic origins, utilizing the commonplaces of education, and asserting its social character. Let us take these up in order.

From the viewpoint of practical reasoning, skipping ahead to a solution is not *per se* an undesirable movement. Often we hit on possible solutions early in the deliberative process. What short-circuits the process is the love of the solution which unreflectively forces premature closure. The initial movement is incomplete. Overquick deliberators must be persuaded to modify their habits by backtracking to the problematic situation and problem-posing stages. Having impulsively skipped ahead, they must artfully skip back. This backwards movement is not alien to the process, even in deliberations which initially work more diligently on the situation. Thus the terms of the process can utilize the incompleteness of the impeding habit.

Reid's analysis, referred to earlier, points out how often solutions in education have no clearly formulated problems, though they may prefigure problems, posed as it were in the solution. Thus we have a route for the return to the implicit problem formulation and, through it, to the details of the situation. Backtracking here concerns the movement from solution-mindedness to problem appreciation. Yet if curriculum students do not love problems (until married off to some convenient solution), they can quickly develop an active dislike for the complexity and indeterminacy of problematic circumstances. Frustration with lack of neatness and clarity fuels another rush to the solution. A quick look at the situation yields *the* problem, generally one which fits the pre–posed solution. Global mentality reinforces this tendency, since any solution more or less fits a problem posed in large enough terms. Moreover, as students backtrack to find *the* problem posed in their solution, another version of 'either/or thinking' appears, *viz.,* 'either you're part of the problem or part of the solution'.

Remedies using the social character of deliberation

The return to the situation should mean the possibility of generating more problems. Additional solutions should suggest themselves in terms of the later posings. We need a situation, either real or simulated, which will engage the students' interest sufficiently to overcome the simplifying tendencies of 'either/or thinking' while remaining sufficiently complex to resist the vagueness of global mentality. Here we also need to counter lone ranger approaches by introducing group processes. There are three possible procedures. One is through experience of the deliberative process itself as students confront its complexities. The second is by means of concrete examples of actual deliberations, both failed and successful. The third procedure involves critical reflection upon the sources of failure and success in the first two.

The three ways are coordinate. The first, as we have already pointed out, is crucial. Curriculum students need to face the dilemmas of the problematic situation in as concrete and engaging a manner as possible. Each of the three classes of students mentioned earlier stand in a different relation to this need. There are teachers (and/or administrators) with present, ongoing experience of curriculum problems, administrators (and/or teachers) that are between such experiences, and undergraduates (or graduates) whose teaching experience is prospective. Deliberative curricula for the first two classes have been developed and point to a way of treating the last group.

Pereira examined the role of discussion in teaching curricular deliberation to experienced teachers (in classes of 10 – 20) at the graduate level. Such students tend to enter a programme in curriculum without the expectation of gaining a useful approach to their own curricular problems. They expect simplistic recipes – objectives and algorithms. They exhibit reluctance or inability to articulate what is troubling them in their own situations. They are inexperienced in conceiving alternative formulations of problems and solutions. Finally, they become fearful when the initial consideration of alternatives only seems to complicate their viewpoints. Pereira meets these difficulties with a two-part discussion model.[24]

First there is an unstructured phase in which the teacher invites each student to explain what bothers her or him in the individual's problematic situation, probes for the various aspects of it, and encourages the other members of the class to act as resource persons. The teacher's role is not limited to that of a mere sounding board. Instead, s/he attempts to make the bothersome, but improvable, aspects of each situation visible and familiar to everyone – teacher, class and especially the student. This stage requires the ability to take time with each student, to tolerate a fair amount of confused striving, and to listen creatively – which is not merely to remain silent.

The second phase is more structured. Using an available model of deliberation[25] the teacher systematically helps the students to locate problems and solutions for formulation among the commonplaces of curriculum deliberation: students, teachers, subject matters and milieux. For this stage the students can discuss several models of systematic deliberation from those accounts cited earlier. *Pereira maintains that the earlier, freewheeling, 'inefficient,' stage of discussion is essential for the success of the later systematic stage.* Together they enable the students to focus their curricular discontents, tolerate and grasp the complexity of factors in deliberation, and shape these factors into alternative formulations.

For the second group, Townsend showed how administrators who are candidates for doctoral degrees can engage in simulated deliberation upon policy issues which engage their interests and abilities. This pattern of simulated deliberation involves division of a class into three to five 'task forces' (each with three to four students) which attempt to set policy for an educational context about which they have been given only basic unstructured facts. A simulated 'policy cycle' requires written or oral analyses by each task force of the problems, likely solutions, and implementation strategies seen by each. It includes both those problems, actions and strategies recommended by each group, those rejected, and the criteria for recommendation or rejection. The teacher functions as a 'data bank' to print out additional raw facts requested by the workgroups and to contrast each task force's work with the actual problem situation from which the given facts were originally drawn.[26]

A crucial aspect of the pattern is a reflective inquiry by each task force of the critical moments, periods and circumstances involved in their own problem-finding, solution-forming and implementation. The variety of possibilities which emerge vividly illustrate the reasons for different analyses and various solutions based on a diversity of talents and habits. The contrasting models for small group deliberation then become part of each task force's resources for succeeding policy cycle discussions. Thus the administrators experience the frustrations and satisfactions, benefits and dangers of constituting a school situation as a community of deliberators.

For curriculum students at the graduate or undergraduate level whose teaching experience is prospective, the recommendation would be for some kind of simulated deliberation along the lines set forth by Townsend and Schwab.[27]

Remedies using the commonplaces of education

We have seen how a group provides the variety of viewpoints, unavailable in individual deliberations, for coping with the complexity of problematic situations. In addition, we need organizers to help the students to shape and clarify the situation through assignment of meaning to its details. Here the commonplaces of education provide the resources. The commonplaces provide multiple foci for organizing the indeterminancy of the situation. Let us see how they develop meaning at the problematic stage, together with consideration of the impeding habits.

The educational commonplaces – students, teachers, subject matters and milieux – function as four coordinate foci in curriculum deliberations.[28] Multiple foci on a problematic situation enables deliberators to grasp a wide range of details with different slants on each. Curriculum students do not easily embrace this pluralistic comprehension. One way of avoidance is by concentrating on one or two commonplaces at the expense of the others. A favourite, already exhibited at the solution end, is pursuit of a pet subject matter. At other times, as Reid pointed out, the interest, skills and opinions of the teacher come to the fore.

The other way curriculum students avoid pluralism is through global mentality. They tend to generalize instead of perceiving and ordering details. The generalizations take the cast of sociological or educational stereotypes. For 'milieux' they put forth the univocal abstract socioeconomic container of schooling, e.g. the Ghetto, the Suburbs. For 'teachers' they refer to Classroom Managers. For 'students' they speak of the Adult Learner, the Disadvantaged Student, the Gifted Student, etc.

All this leaves curriculum students unable to convert the commonplaces into particularplaces, the key to weaving the commonplaces into a deliberation.[29] When faced with the need to coordinate all four commonplaces, they most easily adopt Schwab's metaphor of Chinese boxes fitted inside one another, e.g., the interaction of classroom, school, family, and neighbourhood communities.[30] They have much more difficulty comprehending the concrete ways that the milieux, in addition to providing educational contexts, function *inside* the students and teachers. The recent global solutions mentioned earlier, e.g., Mastery Learning, which concentrate on the 'learner', are not much help, since they treat students at a high level of generality and ignore the teacher, while leaving the subject matter emphasis intact.

In another essay, I have provided an illustration of these habitual difficulties involving subject matter bias and the inability to internalize student milieu.[31] Teachers and administrators (themselves nearly all former teachers) at an urban community college in a developing black ghetto created a special programme to cope with the increasing inability of their students to perform at grade level. Assuming that teachers are merely subject matter experts and communicators while students are its passive receptors, they constructed a special, non-college-credit programme of watered-down studies based on the regular coursework. This attempt to 'mainstream' disadvantaged students failed, since precious little attention was given to the racial and lower-class experience of the students. Dissonance between students' values and those of the middle class teachers – both black and whites – vitiated the well-intentioned efforts. Students continued to fail at about the same rate as before in the regular courses. The programme was terminated in confusion and misunderstanding.

Such failures arise from the habitual impulses to bring Greek drama or Newtonian physics to every student without examining either the differences between milieux of subject matter and student, which can block comprehension, or the similarities, which might promote understanding. Given that the graduate training of so many teachers in subject matter disciplines, it is small wonder that such impulses almost become conditioned reflexes.

This example also typifies curriculum students' difficulties in grasping the internal character of milieux in teachers and students by pointing out the general tendency to externalize the elements of the problematic situation. They can see themselves inside such *circumstances,* but are much less able to focus on the parts of the situation that are inside *themselves,* i.e. that they are part of the problem. Thus their discontents generally run to apparently remedial aspects of a situation outside themselves. They seldom indicate dissatisfaction with their own values or perceptions, and are disinclined to question their biases.

Using a classic historical illustration, Schwarz points out that:

> ...there is an almost built–in reflex to pose problems in terms of the observed external phenomena. This tendency is adaptive in conserving time and energy; for it is almost always more difficult to implement a solution which requires a change in what an individual thinks, believes, feels, or wants – even when the change will be more adaptive once accomplished. Solutions which include some alteration of internal structures almost always result in a temporary increase in potentially disruptive and painful effects. [32]

Schwartz's study of high school students' perceptions of their problems demonstrates how higher-level problem-posing requires the poser to include, as part of the problem situation, constructions internal to the poser him/herself. Looking back to my own example of the failed remedial programme, the white middle-class terms in which the teachers viewed their students led to the unrealistic expectation that the students should abandon their minority experience for the mainstream – but foreign – milieu. When instead the students dug in and demanded that the teachers modify the terms of instruction, the anxiety for some was comparable to that of Galileo's contemporaries contemplating the loss of the theological beliefs holding up the geocentric theory. This reluctance of deliberators to come to grips with the teacher commonplace involves tragic irony when the deliberators themselves are practising, or even prospective, teachers. Equally ironical is the expectation that students can abandon or modify the terms of their experience without parallel anxiety and a corresponding need for bridges between the old and the new.

Combining group processes with commonplaces

For curriculum students the group processes described by Pereira and Townsend can interact with the commonplaces, enabling members of a class to shape the details of the problematic situation in different ways. The voicing of discontents in Pereira's approach provides material to further the self-criticism begun earlier on the rush to pet or global solutions. The teacher is careful not to criticize directly any given formulation, but to encourage each student to take various roles, enacting the ways in which the various agents (students and teachers; parents and administrators) of the diverse milieux will react to proposed formulations. Thus the teacher asks questions involving personal parallels. For teachers infatuated with changing literary instruction from a traditional Aristotlean structure (plot, character, theme, etc.) to a more mythic construction (the 'journey of self discovery,' the 'dying and rising hero') the question might be 'How would you justify this change to parents or administrators concerned with the discipline of literature?' For administrators enamoured of behavioural objectives the teacher can ask, 'How would you teach the biology syllabus based on these goals?' Development of such role-taking not only helps the students to become more detached from their pet formulations but also to grasp their consequences in human terms rather than through mere generalities. Faced with a more vivid reality, curriculum students are forced to reconsider, modify or even abandon positions which under more threatening debate could harden into defensiveness.

In the second, more structured phase of Pereira's scheme a Devil's Advocacy can develop.[33] The teacher constitutes the class as a curriculum group in which various members take the role of expert on each commonplace. The assignments are made by reference to the biases revealed in the first phase, i.e. those with subject matter biases must marshall the case for student needs and interests; those overly concerned with students are forced to take a hard look at the resources of subject matter discipline. Such manoeuvres further the deliberation by making each deliberator more conscious of his/her limitations and thus more willing to accept differing positions as legitimate. The desired shift is from seeing alternatives as difficulties to be shunned to seeing them as resources to be cultivated and refined. Not just Devil's Advocacy of one's favourite solution should occur here, but a recognition and even experience of the feelings and motivations of the human deliberators and subjects of deliberation. Likewise in Townsend's simulated policy deliberations, the small groups can be structured in terms of the commonplaces while the teacher as Data Bank can function to provide further information on each.

Now we have reached a position to expand 'either/or thinking' significantly, if not unconditionally. Let us assume that consideration of each commonplace generates at least one particular problem formulation. The distinction between formulations internal or external to the deliberator actually expands the four possibilities to eight. If each commonplace also generated one solution for each problem, there would be four possible solutions for each. The solutions for each problem could be doubled (from 16 to 32) by working on the utopian *vs* realistic distinction. The *minimum* of four problems, each with four solutions gives us twenty distinct formulations (four problems plus 16 solutions), though this may be weighted too heavily at the solution end. Nonetheless it would serve to fragment global mentality. Nor, when the richness of the problematic situation begins to take on meaning and interest, will this number seem out of line. Siegel's single-person deliberation on an imagined situation produced 101 possible ways to teach *Hamlet* to one group of students. This was a curricular *tour de force* which, nevertheless, carried a lesson on outer limits.[34]

Habits impeding the deliberative process

This theoretically-postulated number of twenty suffers from a certain starchiness. Its formalism fails to take into account the weaving of the various commonplaces into diverse problems and solutions while skipping back and forth between problem and solution stages. The impeding difficulties here involve backtracking – a crucial movement in the process, already seen in our diversion of the rush to the solution back into the problematic situation. One impeding habit concerns the 'expectation of linear progress'; the other involves the 'intolerance of uncertainty'. The two are related.

Deliberation is not a serial process which moves from stage to

stage in a neat manner. Rather it is a *spiral discovery of meanings*.
For example, let us take a problem of student reading difficulties.
Our formulation suggests several solutions arising from alternative
views of subject matter content. We oppose a mythic structure to
an Aristotlean one. We further postulate that stressing the relation
of story content to student experience might be an improvement
over purely structuralist approaches. These solutions are written
down, discussed, clarified. We return to the situation for another
way of shaping the problem – hitting on teacher values, the
internal problem of bias towards one or another of the structures
of literature. This second problem formulation suggests a third –
school class milieu. Uniform scheduling imposes time periods
which are mismatched to student attention spans. The two new
problem posings are compared to each other and to the first one.
A solution from the first problem is detached and modified to
work with the third one as we estimate how the relation of story
and student might work if the teachers converted the classroom
milieu to group discussion methods instead of alternating
one–on–one instruction with lecture. Devil's advocacy from the
student commonplace, i.e. training students to use classroom time
better during one–on–one instruction, supplies a competing
solution. As the shifting relations between problem posings and
solution settings continue, additional details and new meanings in
the situation occur to the deliberators. They begin the movement
from confronting a problematic situation to developing a situation
of problems and solutions.

But as the process itself moves in an uncertain spiral manner
with attendant delays and postponement of result, the most
dangerous moment arrives. Uncertainty and the felt lack of
progress can push curriculum students to an aborted conclusion.
The counsel of patience needs a rationale. It will be insufficient to
assert that the attempted escape from obscurity and confusion by
hasty conclusion only leaves the perplexities awaiting a new effort.

The arts of the deliberative process

At this crucial point in the deliberation some discussion of the
sources of confusion is in order. We need to lay out the
time-consuming terms of the process of deliberation. These are the

arts of critical reflection, backtracking, and review and revision. They have been implicit in the developing description of how to treat the impeding habits. They are also intrinsic to the character of the process.

Critical reflection needs to operate on the process as a whole as well as the impulses of the deliberators. One aspect of it is self-criticism, which operates when deliberators take the time to perceive, criticize and alter their own deeply felt preconceptions of the situation revealed in their pet or global formulations. In order to be effective, this self-criticism must operate when the situation impinges upon the deliberator's feelings, leading her/him to ignore some of the perceivable details. Critical reflection also operates on the process as a whole, with questions such as: Were the formulations sufficiently numerous and varied to do justice to the situation? Were the commonplaces treated in a coordinate way so that none was ignored or slighted? Did the solutions take into account the possibility of further coordination with future deliberations?

Such questions lead to the arts of review and revision, which are an extension of the arts of critical reflection to the process as a whole as well as to the monitoring of its outcomes. These arts are necessary to discover how the attempted solutions are working, to rectify errors in its formulation, or to adjust miscalculations in its execution revealed through further experience of the problematic situation.[35] Finally review and revision connects the efforts to solve the selected problems and solutions with other problems in the situation. Thus we make explicit the movement in the understanding of the deliberators inherent in the initial assignment of possible meanings from 'problematic situation' to 'situation of problems', as more aspects of the situation are formulated and additional solutions related.

Review and revision tend to come into play as a deliberation completes itself, and practically constitutes its own stage after action. In order to do its job, however, it must take seriously the 'review', which means moving back over the process. Here it resembles the third of our triad of terms concerned with the process of deliberation – backtracking. *The arts of deliberation are not stages which constitute the beginning, middle and end of deliberation.* As we have pointed out, the expectation of linear process ignores the skipping about the stages so that the arts of deliberation enhance and reinforce one another. Two examples may be relevant.

In my curricular deliberation cited earlier[36] I entertained philosophical readings as an alternative solution to using literary works for remediation of black students' impulses to stereotype white society and their role in it. Though reading philosophy proved too difficult, given the students' skills level, the entertainment of this resource led to the recognition of a disposition in the students' classroom behaviour. This was their outspokenness – an aspect of their impulsivity which many teachers found disruptive to lecturing since it took the form of interruptions for both questions to teachers and side conversations with fellow students. This problematic characteristic, however, proved an asset when channeled into discussion method as part of the solution for including student experience. The formulation of this additional way of looking at the problem led me to adapt discussion methods for use with short stories, the subject matter solution hit on earlier.

Getzels gives another example involving educational administrators. This time backtracking returned to dilemmas in the problematic situation itself instead of, as above, moving from attempted solution to additional problem-posing to enhanced solution setting. Getzels points out:

Although it seems more normal to go from a dilemma to formulating a problem for solution, the interviews in this study revealed that the administrator must often proceed in the opposite direction, following an already formulated problem brought to him for solution back to the dilemma that someone else had transformed into the problem that the administrator is required to solve.[37]

One of Getzel's examples of this is instructive:

Asked to describe a difficult decision that he had to make, one superintendent of schools gave this account: One school in his district had become overcrowded, and the larger building to replace it would not be completed for two years. In the meantime, seventeen mobile classrooms filled the playground and the parking lot, but they were insufficient for the expected influx of children in the fall.

The Dilemma was obvious – overcrowding. Discussion among the principal, superintendent and president of the board of education centred on two problems: whether to get more mobile classrooms and where to put them, or whether to move the excess children to other, less crowded schools and how to transport them there. Typically, one dilemma was transformed into two different problems. The decision was left up to the superintendent, and it was to depend on the problem that lent itself to the easiest solution. As the superintendent tells it, in due course it occurred to him that the problem was really not whether to get more mobile classrooms and where to put them or whether to get rid of the excess children and how to transport them, but simply how to get more space!

Once this problem was formulated, the solution proved not at all difficult. It was possible to build a temporary classroom structure that could later be converted to commercial use, and this is what was done.[38]

Revised model for deliberation

The discussion of the three terms – critical reflection, review and revision, and backtracking – require a third model for deliberation. This revision of the first two models shows how the deliberative process develops through interactions between the stages:

CRITICAL REFLECTION BACKTRACKING	1. Assignment of meaning to details in the problematic situation 2. Formulation of meaningful details into discrete problems 3. Weighing and choosing among problem formulations 4. Formulation of solutions to chosen problems 5. Rehearsal of consequences of solutions 6. Weighing and choosing solutions 7. Termination and action 8. Review and revision	by a group using the commonplaces of education

Acknowledgement of backtracking has led to rewording of numbers 4 & 6: solutions are now formulated to the various problem*s*, not just one; and more than one solution may be chosen and coordinated. Here the earlier terms of deliberation – the commonplaces, details of the problematic situation, problem posings and solution settings, etc. – concern the content of deliberation and are in some sense its concrete results. The new terms involve the process. Two of these, backtracking and critical reflection, enter into the process at every point. Backtracking involves the movement between stages, while critical reflection attempts to keep the terms from becoming unbalanced either by bias towards some of the commonplaces or by insufficient number and quality of formulations. Review and revision, while clearly a stage after termination of a given deliberation, is not detached from it, and could be called the spirit of the process since it involves both backtracking and critical reflection.

The revised outline also suggests an impeding habit which can arise out of an excess of the virtues just expounded. This is an 'inability to decide' plaguing those individuals or groups with an overabundance of patience for looking at all sides of the question. These continue to pull in different directions without concensus. Sometimes the cause is akin to the timid, non-deliberating administrator's fear of consequences or mistakes. Sometimes the vice is an infatuation with the process itself. In either case the best cure for habitual indecision is reflective awareness that no deliberation is final or perfect. Mistakes are, as indicated 'guaranteed,' particularly at the onset.

The remedy for over-indulgence of the process leading to interminable deliberation has already been suggested. Curriculum deliberation is not like parenting or a good dean's search committee. Such roles are normally abandoned as soon as one becomes good at them. Instead, termination and action should be but one stage in the ongoing life of a curriculum group which develops and monitors its changing situation of problems.

Conclusion and recommendations – the need for a recording angel

Success in deliberation concerns how well the resultant actions remedy the difficulties. It also involves how well the deliberators formulate the troublesome situation. These two aspects are, ironically, not inevitably correlated. Poor deliberators can hit upon a workable change in curricular practice. Good deliberators can fall prey to unforeseen contingencies. The former, however, will soon find themselves beset again when they fail to monitor their 'final' solutions, which are the inevitable breeding ground for further difficulties. This is why we need the process of review and revision to continue reformulating the problematic situation into a situation of ongoing coordinate problems. Thus we look for how the action taken reveals further details in the circumstances worth formulating, how it might work with other solutions to a related problem, and how unforeseen problems impede implementing the solution. Our hope is that successful critical reflection upon the character of the process will enable us to do it even better. Seen from outside, this requirement that curriculum deliberation in schools be ongoing and continuous may seem extraordinarily burdensome. The reverse, however, is the truth. It is the start-stop-start again character of impeded deliberations which are the most burdensome. Habits that further deliberation render it much more fulfilling, rewarding and even enjoyable, though no less necessary.

The recommendations from this study concern three interrelated activities – involving the conducting, teaching and recording of curricular deliberations. Concerning conducting, it is obvious that the dearth of concrete deliberations is itself an impediment to adequate grasp of its terms and processes. This lack creates the impression that deliberation is an idealized type of discourse in which its stages and operations are to be studied apart from the various interfering factors. I have tried to show instead how factors impeding deliberation, like the habitual difficulties discussed here, are best studied and acted upon as part of the process. When more deliberations are undertaken and recorded the process itself as a nonprocedural practical enterprise will doubtless take more varied forms. In particular the absence of the classroom type of deliberation is vexing. As Schwab puts it, '...almost every classroom episode is a stream of situations requiring discrimination of deliberative problems and decisions thereon'.[39]

Concerning teaching, since deliberation is only really understood by those who do it, we need to persuade more educators to undertake and record their deliberative endeavours.

This we must do by teaching curricular students some such story as I have just related concerning the impeding habits and requisite arts when we take them through the process, real or simulated. Moreover, the more models we have of successes and failures the more persuasive will be our case. Therefore both teaching and conducting deliberations can benefit from the last recommendation.

Concerning recording, deliberators can monitor themselves through the arts of critical reflection. They can also publish the results of deliberation, e.g. a new college catalogue. But we need more than retrospective reflections or packaged results; we need to see how the package was produced, most preferably from the viewpoint of a Recording Angel. Short of this, we will have to fall back on an addition to Schwab's ideal curriculum group.[40] In his version this included representatives of the four commonplaces plus a curriculum expert. The requisite addition is a knowledgeable but impartial recorder to tape the deliberations, request clarification of positions and inquire concerning rationales. The parallel inquiry from another area would be the tape recorded jury deliberations in the University of Chicago Law School study, though here with the added role. Graduate students might be persuaded to look into this problem for their theses, while ethnographers might profitably look for and inquire into signs of deliberative activity by teachers in classrooms.

References and notes

1.   SCHWAB, J.J. 'The practical: A language for curriculum.' In: WESTBURY, I. & WILKOF, N.J. (Eds.) (1978). *Science, Curriculum and Liberal Education: Selected Essays of Joseph J. Schwab.* Chicago: University of Chicago Press. This paper was originally published in 1969. REID, W.A. 'The deliberative approach to the study of curriculum and its relation to critical pluralism.' In: LAWN, M. & BARTON, L. (Eds.) (1981). *Rethinking Curriculum Studies.* London: Croom Helm. WESTBURY, I. (1972). 'The Aristotelian art of rhetoric and the "art" of curriculum,' *Philosophy of Education;* ORPWOOD, G.W.F. (1983). Deliberative inquiry: The study of politics and practice in Canadian science education. Paper given at the annual meeting of the American Educational Research Association, Montreal, 1983; PEREIRA, P. 'Deliberation and the arts of perception,' *Journal of Curriculum Studies,* in press. See also

COREY, S.M. (1953). *Action Research to Improve School Practices.* New York: Bureau of Publication, Teachers College, Columbia University. SMYTH, J. (1982). 'A teacher development approach to bridging the practice-research gap,' *Journal of Curriculum Studies* 14; SCHON, D. (1983). *The Reflective Practitioner.* New York: Basic Books; ALLISON, G. (1971). *The Essence of Decision: Explaining the Cuban Missile Crisis.* Boston: Little Brown.

2. See, for instance, SKINNER, B.F. (1971). *Beyond Freedom and Dignity.* New York: Knopf.

3. See, for example, DEWEY, J. (1957). *Human Nature and Conduct.* New York: Random House.

4. SCHWAB, J.J. 'The practical: Arts of electic.' In: WESTBURY, I. & WILKOF, N.J. *Op. cit.* p. 326. (See Note 1.)

5. SCHWAB, J.J. *College Curriculum and Student Protest.* Chicago: University of Chicago Press, pp. 167ff.

6. SCHWAB, J.J. 'The practical: Translation into curriculum.' In: WESTBURY, I. & WILKOF, N.J. *Op. cit.* (See Note 1.) See also SCHWAB, J.J. 'The teaching of science as inquiry.' In: SCHWAB, J.J. & BRANDWEIN, P.F. (1964). *The Teaching of Science.* Cambridge, Ma: Harvard University Press.

7. ROBY, T.W. (1978). 'Problem situations and curricular resources at Central College: An exemplification of curricular arts,' *Curriculum Inquiry* 8.

8. SCHWAB, J.J. 'The practical: A language for curriculum.' (See Note 1.)

9. SCHWAB, J.J. *College Curriculum and Student Protest*, pp. 3ff. (See Note 5.)

10. TOWNSEND, R.G. One way to Train for the Problems of Administrators. Revision of a paper given at the annual meeting of the American Educational Research Association, Los Angeles, 1981. ERIC ED 208 473.

11. SIEGEL, J.S. (1973). Curricular deliberation and Hamlet: An Exercise in the Practical Doctoral dissertation, University of Chicago.

12. ROBY, T.W. (1973). A Use of Literary Materials Toward Characterial Change. Doctoral dissertation, University of Chicago. See also ROBY, T.W. (1984). Deliberation and the arts of teaching. Paper given at the annual meeting of the American Educational Research Association, New Orleans.

13. The specific habits set forth here do not represent an exhaustive taxonomy. Rather, they are a set of 'modest generalizations' drawn from the responses of the curriculum students mentioned earlier. I imagine that readers will find them familiar. These may also suggest variants of those given, others not named, or even a different organization as teachers involve different groups of curriculum students in the deliberative format and process. Of course not every curriculum student exhibits every habit. For a discussion of the

development and use of 'modest generalizations' see PEREIRA, P., 'Deliberation and the arts of perception' (See Note 1).

14.   Pet solutions are one form of pet formulations. Schwab points out that in their subject matter form pet solutions result in tunnel vision, the limitations imposed by the univocal subscription to a single theory of the subject from the available alternatives.

15.   The indefinite reference masks a real example.

16.   SHAKESPEARE, W. *All's Well That Ends Well*, 11.ii.15ff

17.   BLOOM, B.S. (1981). *All Our Children Learning: A Primer for Parents, Teacher, and Other Educators*. New York: McGraw-Hill.

18.   'Mastery learning aims at reading progress,' *Covering Education*, 1 (1982). (Chicago Board of Education, Chicago, Illinois.)

19.   REID, W.A. (1981). 'Core curriculum: Precept or process?' *Curriculum Perspectives*, 1.

20.   SCHWAB, J.J. 'The practical: A language for curriculum,' pp. 315–18 (See Note 1).

21.   In a series of articles in various journals (*History of Education Quarterly, School Review, Journal of the Midwest History of Education Society*) Harold B. Dunkel has explored the checkered histories of educational movements. Much of this material has been reworked in *Writ in Water: the Epitaph of Educational Innovation* (in manuscript). See also DUNKEL, H.B. (1970). *Herbart and the Herbartians*. Chicago: University of Chicago Press; and 'Voices from the past'. *Elementary School Journal*, 75 (1975) in which some of these parallels are suggested: e.g. the strengths and weaknesses of Mastery Learning can be paralleled to those of the Winnetka Plan; or we can estimate possibilities of success for voucher plans by comparison to those Harris opposed in St. Louis. What parallels are to be brought into play depend, of course, on the students' sense of innovation and the teachers' sense of history.

22.   PLATO. *The Republic*. Loeb Classical Library. Cambridge. Mass. (1956). SKINNER, B.F. (1962). *Walden II*. New York.

23.   For the pedagogical uses of devil's advocacy, see ROBY, T.W. The other side of the question: Controversial turns, the devil's advocate, and reflective responses. Paper given at the annual meeting of the American Educational Research Association, Montreal, 1983.

24.   PEREIRA, P. Curriculum students and their discontents. Paper given at annual meeting of the American Educational Research Association, Los Angeles, 1981. ERIC ED 201 635.

25.   See, for example, ROBY, T.W. *The Use of Literary Materials* (See Note 12).

26.   TOWNSEND, R.G. *Op. cit.* (See Note 10.)

27.   See also HEGARTY, E.H. (1977). 'The problem identification phase of curricular deliberation: Use of the nominal grid technique,' *Journal of Curriculum Studies* 9. Ilene Harris, University of Minnesota, reports that the use of this technique is helpful for focussing on the details of the problematic situation, identifying all the aspects of a problem and determining priorities of

those aspects. A version of this procedure might be successfully employed at the problem identification stage as a supplement to the Pereira (See Note 1) and Townsend (See Note 10) approaches referred to above.

28. SCHWAB, J.J. 'The practical: Translation into curriculum' (See Note 6). See also SCHWAB, J.J. 'The practical 4: Something for curriculum professors to do,' *Curriculum Inquiry* 13 (1983).

29. PEREIRA, P. 'Deliberation and the arts of perception' (See Note 1).

30. SCHWAB, J.J. (1973). 'The practical 3: Translation into curriculum,' *School Review* 81, p. 503. The line about the 'chinese boxes' was cut from the version of this paper published in WESTBURY, I. & WILKOF, N.J. *op. cit.*, p. 366 (See Note 1).

31. ROBY, T.W. 'Problem situations and curricular resources.' (See Note 7.)

32. SCHWARTZ, D.M. (1977). A Study of Interpersonal Problem Solving. Doctoral dissertation, University of Chicago.

33. The suggestions in this section are my embellishments on Pereira and Townsend freely adapted from the notions of curriculum group deliberation offered by J.J. Schwab in 'The practical: Translation into curriculum' (See Note 6) and 'The practical 4' (See Note 28).

34. SIEGEL, J.S. *Op. cit.*, (See Note 11).

35. Curriculum deliberation is a sufficiently complex enterprise to 'guarantee' miscalculations, misunderstandings and errors. Mere 'curriculum implementation,' on the other hand guarantees that they cannot be corrected. The trick is not to waste time searching for the error free El Dorado of curriculum development. A case in point would be the 'teacher proof' curricula which failed to penetrate beyond the classroom door. It is safer to assume that if all seems to be going well, something must be going wrong or could be done better. Thus we need to convert curriculum students counsels of perfection into a drive for improvement.

36. ROBY, T.W. 'Problem situations and curricular resources,' p. 115 (See Note 7).

37. GETZELS, J.W. (1982). 'The problem of the problem.' In: HOGARTH, R. (ed.) *New Directions for the Methodology of Social and Behavioral Science: Question Framing and Response Consistency,* 11, p. 46. San Francisco: Jossey–Bass.

38. *Ibid.,* pp.45–6.

39. SCHWAB, J.J. 'The practical: A language for curriculum', p. 321 (See Note 1).

40. SCHWAB, J.J. 'The practical: Translation into curriculum' (See Note 6).

Part Two

Curriculum History

The history of education has a long tradition and many practitioners. Curriculum history on the other hand is neglected and has few practitioners and those only recently at work. Why is this? Reid, in his paper, gives several reasons. 'On the whole', he says, 'curriculum scholars have been raised in other disciplines.' He cites their grounding in psychology, sociology and anthropology, the theories and methods of which they employed in dealing with curriculum issues and problems. And the curriculum literature of the past quarter of a century is witness enough to the validity of this observation.

But Reid points to other causes. The 'meliorism' of the field of curriculum studies; that concern to make things better in education, which has motivated and preoccupied so many curriculum scholars, turning them into prophets of a new millenium in schooling. He also instances the view more recently held that curriculum problems are rational-technical ones requiring only the application of the right method for their solution.

Hamilton's paper, as he says:

Analytically . . . adopts the standpoint that educational practice lies at the intersection of economic history and the history of ideas. That is the pedagogical practices of an epoch are expressions of both material and ideological resources.

He focusses on the emergence of the classroom as an educational means nested within the physical setting of the school. He traces its emergence in the 1930s in relation to the ideas of Adam Smith, Robert Owen, Andrew Bell and Joseph Lancaster, and the growing national concern with free trade and the belief that self-interest was in the best interest of the Nation.

In so far as the classroom could be shown to be efficient, in the interest of the individual pupil and the age group, it was arguably a reflection of a desirable social state of affairs. It is in tracing these arguments and the practices that they promulgated that Hamilton's paper makes a valuable contribution to curriculum history.

The paper by de Castell and Luke addresses a broader canvas: the changing concepts of literacy; a concept at the very core of the curricular enterprise wherever it is to be found. The setting for their study is North America. Their method is to trace the changing models of literacy over time; over more than one hundred years and *to show, much as Hamilton does, that models of literacy are largely socially determined. Literacy is not a matter of fact. It is defined by educational systems in their social and ideological settings. As these settings change, so will the meaning of literacy.*

But de Castell and Luke's paper is more than an exercise in curriculum history. It is concerned to judge whether current models of literacy are educationally sound. In the end this must be the role of curriculum history: to enable us to make judgements about what ought to be the case in curricular practices.

Further reading

BALL, S.J. (1982). 'Competition and conflict in the teaching of English.' *Journal of Curriculum Studies,* 14, 1, 1–28.

BURLINGHAM, M. (1982). 'The U.S. government and the public school curriculum: an interpretation of the post-Second World War decades,' *Journal of Curriculum Studies,* 14, 4, 313–29.

GIAQUINTA, J.B. and KAZLOW, C. (1980). 'The growth and decline of public school innovations: a national study of the open classroom in the United States,' *Journal of Curriculum Studies,* 12, 1, 61–73.

GOODSON, I. (1983). 'Subjects for Study: Aspects of social history of curriculum,' *Journal of Curriculum Studies,* 15, 4, 391–408.

KLIEBARD, H.M. (1979). 'The drive for curriculum change in the United States. 1890–1958. 1. The ideological roots. 2. From local reform to national preoccupation,' *Journal of Curriculum Studies,* 11, 3, 191–202 and 11, 4, 273–86.

Curriculum Theory and Curriculum Change: what can we learn from History?*

William A. Reid

Curriculum, as a focus of academic activity, was first institutionalized in North America as a means of supplying school districts with educational leaders who understood how curricula could be improved, updated or reformed. Such aspirations are still at the heart of the curriculum enterprise. But to understand how to change a curriculum is to understand an activity of great complexity. In order that formalization and communication of the relevant knowledge can take place ideas have to be structured, conceptions elaborated and theories advanced. Typically, the source of such conceptualizations has been the disciplines which curriculum scholars have recognized as ancestral to their own, and especially the social sciences. Thus House, in his 1979 paper 'Technology versus craft: a ten year perspective on innovation'[1], cites a variety of studies which, with rare exceptions promote change theories grounded in sociological, anthropological or psychological traditions. The exceptions are studies which adopt a political perspective. Yet it would appear that History, which is directly concerned with accounts of change as it has actually occurred, should also be a prime source of ideas on how it comes about and how it can be managed and controlled. Why has History been neglected?

One reason for this neglect has already been suggested: on the whole, curriculum scholars have been reared in other disciplines. When colleges and departments of education sought status within

*Paper presented at the Symposium 'History of Education and Curriculum Theory', AERA Annual Meeting, New Orleans, LA, April 1984.

universities, they did so by embracing those academic disciplines which were associated in the popular as well as the academic mind with progress, modernity and the shaping of social policy.[2] The ideological commitments which guided such preferences have been explored by Kliebard who points to the fact that workers in the curriculum field have on the whole been deeply committed to 'meliorism': the notion that current states of affairs are unacceptable and that things can and should be made better.[3] As Westbury explains: 'all too often our stances imply a condemnation of what schools do, with the consequence that we have difficulty in accepting even the possibility that the schools have in fact succeeded in doing many of the things that they set out to achieve.'[4] Thus, curriculum study has, in general, been doggedly ahistorical – unwilling to sacrifice the vision of a better future to the study of a past which is seen as a dark age. 'The major researches in the field,' says Kliebard, 'are basically efforts to establish the primacy of the forces of good over the forces of wickedness and reaction.'[5] But under what conditions might such an ideological prejudice be overcome and what benefits might result?

The gains we might envisage from explorations of History are contingent on the view we take of curriculum itself. Kliebard's point is that if we hold to a rational-technical conception of curriculum then, from a practical point of view, History is simply a source of parables about the less than satisfactory world we are engaged in rebuilding. Monitorial schools, Herbartianism, and the platoon system will furnish us with cautionary tales of misguided practice comparable to those offered to the 'normal' scientist by phlogiston theory, the flat earth, and the ether. But if we consider (following Schwab[6]) that the concerns of curriculum are primarily practical and only secondarily technical then our attitude to History will be very different. The knowledge that it can afford will be attractive on account of three central features of the practical conception of curriculum:

(i)   its depiction of curriculum change in terms of actions rather than plans, for the point and significance of action arises from the historical context within which it is taken.

(ii) its focus on the particularity of situations rather than on generalizations, for the capacity to deal with the particular stems from understanding based on human arts and only to a lesser degree on explanations offered by social science.

(iii) its demand that the products of theory, in so far as they can provide a guide to action, be evaluated against practical contexts, for the data of History can be a source of such contexts.

Change as action

A practical view of the curriculum holds that curriculum activity is aimed at the resolution of uncertain problems, and that this resolution consists in the taking of action.[7] Its concern is therefore with people doing things rather than with abstract notions such as programme design or curriculum implementation. Further, what has to be done is something that will affect the lives of others. On both counts, the quality of action is something to be understood in terms of the stuff of History – personal careers and collective traditions. Change takes place in an historical context which on the one hand defines and limits a field of action, but on the other hand provides a rhetorical ground from which arguments about needed change can proceed.[8] The actions we engage in have meanings which are shaped by our histories and only become accessible to others through their understanding of those histories. As McIntyre suggests: 'Narrative history of a certain kind turns out to be the basic and essential genre for the characterisation of human actions.'[9] Deliberation – the method of the practical – as described by Schwab and others is to an important degree the discovery and articulation of those traditions and biographies which constitute the ground for justifiable and intelligible courses of action.[10] As Brann asserts: 'An engagement with the tradition is the only means of discovering that collective past which is active in our present'[11] – a remark which needs to be joined with Ricoeur's observation that 'Histories of the past uncover the buried potentialities of the present'.[12]

We need, through deliberation, to discover the past not only in order to understand within what parameters proposals for action have to be discovered, but also in order to appreciate the potential which traditions offer for renewal, invention and redirection. If our concern is the curriculum of a single classroom, the span of our historical attention may be short – so short that the archival activity associated with History may not be needed. But if the object of our deliberation is the curriculum of the US high school or the English sixth form, then the extent to which current practice is sustained by traditions laid down over decades or even centuries should impel us towards a more extended voyage of historical discovery.[13] Without that exploration, initiatives for change may miss the mark because the actions associated with them are perceived as arbitrary, contradictory or meaningless.

Change as the modification of the particular

Practical action always has to deal with the particular rather than the general. It is taken with a view to modifying the practice of particular classrooms, schools or school systems. Therefore it is never possible to determine or justify action simply by reference to theories, explanations or generalizations: these are produced as answers to theoretic questions and are of only limited use in the treatment of practical ones. Theories gain their power by their narrow disciplinary focus and by assuming their subject matter to be 'universal or extensive or pervasive'.[14] But these very qualities render them unfitted as prime determinants of practical action which has to be grounded in understanding rather than explanation. Understanding, since it is concerned not with 'grasping a fact but with apprehending a possibility of being', can serve to 'orient us in a situation'[15] and provide the means of discerning and choosing among courses of action.

Such a view of curriculum change is, of course, in direct opposition to one which sees it as a technical problem and the implementation of change as a matter of management. Managers do choose and justify plans on the basis of the kinds of generalizations and explanations which the social sciences claim to offer.[16] But action based on practical problem solving finds a better underpinning in those human arts, such as History, which aim to promote understandings based on the examination of particular traditions, careers and accomplishments. Where explanations are given they are used as means to this end, rather than as an end in themselves.[17]

The confrontation of the need for specific curriculum change affecting particular people and institutions may be better served by studies such as McKinney and Westbury's curriculum history of the Gary Schools[18] than by models and paradigms of change proposed by sociologists as generalized explanations. Historical work promotes understanding through the opportunity it offers to reflect on the interplay of particular people, traditions, places and epochs in situations where both the antecedents and the consequences of action are open to disciplined scrutiny.

The eclectic use of theory

At this point, some redressing of the balance is needed. The argument is not that models, theories or hypotheses should be totally neglected. Indeed, the McKinney and Westbury paper makes extensive reference to sociological work on curriculum change. What the practical perspective enjoins on us is the need to have regard to the partiality and temporality of theories when we estimate the weight and purpose they can be given in the much wider collection of data that curriculum deliberation should take into account. Here we are dealing with what Schwab terms 'arts of eclectic'.[19] The purpose of these is to ready the products of theorizing for use in practical reasoning, adapting and joining together the generalizations of social science to confront the problems of education which 'arise from exceedingly complex actions, reactions and transactions of men (constituting) a skein of myriad threads which know no boundaries separating, say, economics from politics, or sociology from psychology'.[20]

Here, too, History can come to our aid. Theories derived from a consideration of synchronic and uniform data sets chosen for the convenience of disciplinary modes of social science inquiry can be projected on the diachronic and multifaceted accounts of curriculum change offered by historical research.

In this way we can test the 'range of convenience' of a change theory. Does the confrontation with historical evidence reveal severe limitations occasioned by implicit assumptions inherent in the time and place of its conception? For example, does the theory depend on the existence of a particular style and structure of educational provision? Does an historical perspective show that the theory works as long as 'innovatory mechanisms' are in place, but that, in the longer term, careers and traditions continue much as before? Or that the effect on career and tradition is not the intended one? Do the complex data of History point to the crudity of the theory, or do they show how its simplicities can be profitably elaborated to produce a conception which is perhaps from a disciplinary point of view less elegant, but from a practical one more serviceable?[21]

We have considered three ways in which explorations of History can be beneficial to a practically–based conception of curriculum change. It can illuminate possibilities for action, provide understandings of the unique contexts within which action has to be taken, and play a part in the eclectic incorporation of theoretic knowledge in deliberation about change. Such beneficial results are, however, contingent not only on the adoption of a particular view of curriculum but also on a particular view of History. Few historians of education would agree that their discipline has, as a central purpose, to assist us towards 'apprehending a possibility of being'; few that it can provide understandings which go beyond illumination of the specific historical questions which are the object of study; few that History can be a 'test bed' for social science theories. When we bemoan the lack of interest in History on the part of curriculum theorists and curriculum workers we must also recognize that, if they were to adopt a more welcoming stance towards History, they might find little sustenance in what the majority of Historians of Education produce. Their work may not be pursued in the manner of the social sciences in the sense that it does not address itself to the generalities of social processes with a view to the production of explanatory theories; but neither does it take seriously McIntyre's critique of History as accepting a false dichotomy between 'two pasts, one populated by only actions, and the other only by theories'[22] or Ricoeur's comment that 'We belong to history before . . . writing history'.[23] Historians of education typically regard the past as separable from the present and the events of the past as occurring in parallel with, rather than in concert with the evolution of the theories and conceptions by which men have made sense of their world.

Thus, to a large extent, History of Education has fulfilled a similar function to the social sciences in relation to the managerial view of curriculum. Though it has not offered explanatory theories, it has projected the development of education as a narrative of successful managerial and executive activity through central and local agencies of government, highlighting the antecedents of currently favoured practice and discrediting or ignoring others which are seen as aberrations or blind alleys. Harold Silver, for example, points to neglect on the part of English historians of education of the monitorial schools of the nineteenth century. By adopting a managerial language of 'innovation, progress, and reform' they have, he says, 'ensured certain kinds of neglect. The historians of nineteenth century education have presented the monitorial system as a wraith, and discussed it as if it were flesh.'[24] Even revisionist historians of education have not effected a shift of focus. Managerialism is still centre stage, but now as villain rather than hero.

It is for these reasons that I suggest it is useful to try to invest the term 'Curriculum History' with a special significance to signal a style of historical writing which is not just claiming a particular focus of interest but also a relevance to curriculum practice. The basic orientation of such a form of History is set out by Hamilton in his 'Adam Smith and the moral economy of the classroom system' where he says:

> (this) paper adopts the standpoint that educational practice(sc. curriculum) lies at the intersection of economic history and the history of ideas. That is, the pedagogical practices of an epoch are expressions of both material and ideological resources. Taken independently, neither technologies (material resources) nor beliefs (ideological resources) are sufficient to account for the practices of schooling.[25]

This seems to me a good statement of the means that should be employed in the construction of Curriculum History. To it needs to be added something about ends. It will be History which concerns itself not only with past events but also with present action and potentialities for action:

> For to recognise the values of the past in their *differences* with respect to the present is already to open up the real towards the

possible. . . . Croce said that there is only a history of the present. That is true provided we add: *there is only a history of the potentialities of the present.*[26]

Curriculum History will not be objective in the way that History has conventionally claimed to be: but surrendering that spurious objectivity it may become a truer guide to the understanding of curriculum change.

Notes

1. HOUSE, E.R. (1979). 'Technology versus craft: a ten year perspective on innovation', *Journal of Curriculum Studies*, 11, 1, 1–15.
2. See for example, WHITE, Woodie T. (1982). 'The decline of the classroom and the Chicago study of education', *American Journal of Education*, 90, 2, 144–74.
3. In 'Persistent curriculum issues in historical perspective', pp. 39–50 in PINAR, W.F. (Ed.), *Curriculum Theorizing: the Reconceptualists*, Berkeley: McCutchan, 1975.
4. WESTBURY, I. (1973). 'Conventional classrooms, "open" classrooms, and the technology of teaching', *Journal of Curriculum Studies*, 5, 2, p. 99.
5. *Op. cit.*, p. 42.
6. SCHWAB, J.J. (1969). 'The practical: a language for curriculum', *School Review*, 78, 1, 1–24
7. REID, W.A. (1978). *Thinking about the Curriculum*. London: Routledge and Kegan Paul, Ch.4.
8. REID, W.A. and FILBY, J.L. (1982). *The Sixth: an Essay in Education and Democracy*. Lewes: Falmer Press, Ch.12.
9. McINTYRE, Alasdair (1982). *After Virtue: a study in moral theory*. London: Duckworth, p.194.
10. The mention of biography reminds us how close some reconceptualist positions are to the conception of curriculum discussed here.
11. BRANN, E.T.H. (1979). *Paradoxes of Education in a Republic*. Chicago: University of Chicago Press.
12. RICOEUR, Paul (1981). *Hermeneutics and the Human Sciences*. Cambridge: CUP.
13. Reports on English secondary education in the interwar years typically began with an extended historical introduction.
14. SCHWAB, *op. cit.*
15. RICOEUR, *op. cit.*, p.56.
16. McINTYRE, *op. cit.*, p.84ff.
17. RICOEUR, *op. cit.*, p.17.

18. McKINNEY, W.L. and WESTBURY, I. (1975). 'Stability and change: the public schools of Gary, Indiana, 1940–70'. In: REID, W.A. and WALKER, D.F. (Eds.), *Case Studies in Curriculum Change*. London: Routledge and Kegan Paul.
19. SCHWAB. J.J. (1971). 'The practical: arts of eclectic', *School Review*, 79, 4, 493–542.
20. SCHWAB, *op. cit.*
21. My own investigations of Meyer's theory of institutional categories and organisational forms has led me, through consideration of historical data, to see it as one which is readily capable of being elaborated to suit it for incorporation into deliberation on change (MEYER, John W. (1980). 'Levels of the educational system and schooling effects'. In: BIDWELL, C.E. and WINDHAM, D.M.(Eds.) *The Analysis of Educational Productivity*, Vol.2 *Issues in Macro–Analysis*, Cambridge, Mass.: Ballinger, and REID, W.A. 'Curriculum change and the evolution of educational constituencies: the English sixth form in the nineteenth century'. In: GOODSON, I.(Ed.) *Subjects for Study: Case Studies in Curriculum History*. Lewes: Falmer Press, forthcoming.
22. McINTYRE, *op. cit.*, p.58
23. RICOEUR, *op. cit.*, p.294
24. SILVER, Harold (1977). 'Aspects of neglect: the strange case of Victorian popular education', *Oxford Review of Education*, 3, 1, p.58
25. HAMILTON, David (1980). 'Adam Smith and the moral economy of the classroom system', *Journal of Curriculum Studies*, 12, 4, p.282 and this volume, pp.84 *et seq.*
26. RICOEUR, *op. cit.*, p.295

Adam Smith and the Moral Economy of the Classroom System

David Hamilton

Domestic education is the institution of nature: public education, the contrivance of man (Adam Smith[1])

On 11 May 1762, a meeting of the Faculty of Glasgow University decided to convert a College 'Chamber' (living room) into a 'classroom' for civil law. The appearance of the term classroom in the Faculty minutes is historically noteworthy: indeed, its use is perhaps unprecedented in English language sources. The term does not reappear in the minutes until 1774 yet, by the time the college opened a new suite of teaching rooms in 1813, the comparable Medieval and Renaissance labels – 'school' and 'class' – had virtually disappeared.[2]

In 1762 Glasgow was a centre of educational and intellectual innovation. The 11 members of the May Faculty meeting included Joseph Black, whose discovery of latent heat enabled James Watt to revolutionize the steam engine; John Anderson, whose educational and social ideas helped to shape popular adult education in the 19th century; and not least, Adam Smith, whose writings did much to establish the science of political economy.

Although Black, Anderson and Smith achieved fame well beyond the boundaries of Glasgow University, their work also had an important local impact. Anderson's use of practical demonstrations in physics was sufficiently notorious to earn him the nickname 'Jolly Jack Phosphorous'. Smith's service as college quaestor (book–keeper) in the late 1750s coincided with a rapid growth of the University library. And Black's earliest communications on latent heat were given a month before the May Faculty meeting to a college gathering of the Glasgow Literary Society.[3]

The presence of 'several gentlemen of the City' at the Literary

Society's meeting and its subsequent change of name to the 'Literary and Commercial Society of Glasgow' underline the fact that the local trade in philosophic, economic and social ideas embraced both town and gown.. Further, the same 'commerce intellectual' continued through time – linking members of the 1762 Faculty with influential 19th-century figures such as Robert Owen of New Lanark (who helped to introduce Pestalozzian ideas into British schooling); William Hamilton of Edinburgh (who encouraged public support for a state–run system of education along Prussian lines); and David Stow of Glasgow (who founded a 'normal seminary' which served as a prototype for teacher training in England and elsewhere).

This paper examines the general ferment of educational and social ideas that, in Glasgow and beyond, was associated with the work of reformers like Smith, Owen, Hamilton and Stow. Specifically, it is activated by three related assumptions. First, that the educational practices of Glasgow University had a direct influence on those adopted in the elementary schools of the 19th century. Secondly, that the change from class to classroom reflected a more general upheaval in schooling – the ultimate victory of group–based pedagogies over the more individualized forms of teaching and learning that had dominated previous centuries. And thirdly, that the shift from class to classroom in the early days of the Industrial Revolution was as important to the administration of schooling as the concurrent shift from domestic to factory production was to the management of industry.[4]

Analytically, the paper adopts the standpoint that educational practice lies at the intersection of economic history and the history of ideas. That is, the pedagogical practices of an epoch are expressions of both material and ideological resources. Taken independently, neither technologies (material resources), nor beliefs (ideological resources) are sufficient to account for the practices of schooling. For instance, the technological basis of chalk–and–talk teaching – the blackboard – did not become a commonplace item of school furniture until the 19th century, which is nearly 150 years after it had appeared in Comenius's *Orbis Pictus* (1658). One explanation for the delay is that, prior to the 19th century, open–ended chalk–and–talk teaching was a much less acceptable mode of popular instruction than more closed forms of tuition such as catechesis.[5]

As an architectural unit, the classroom came to prominence in Britain after the 1830s with the gradual spread of state–supported (and state supervised) schooling. By the 20th century, the batch–production rhetoric of the 'classroom system'[6] (for example lessons, subjects, timetables, grading, standardization, streaming) had become so pervasive that it successfully achieved a normative status – creating the standards against which all subsequent educational innovations came to be judged. Indeed, the widespread penetration of the classroom system had another important ideological effect. It obscured the fact that, before about 1800, schooling had been organized around a quite different vocabulary, and quite different assumptions, resources and practices.

This paper, then, has been written to excavate such differences. Its backcloth is the post–Medieval context of education. Its foreground is the reformulation of ideas about universal (or mass) schooling that, with the shift from individualized to group mass instruction, came to a head in the late 18th and early 19th centuries. Like the associated shift in industry from tools to machines, the time–span of this pedagogical transformation is measured in decades rather than years. Nonetheless, schooling, like industry, eventually yielded to the dominance of new instruments of production (the mass–produced steel–nibbed pen for example), new patterns of organization (for example the multi–room school) and new forms of management (for example payment by results). In short, the production and distribution of the educational 'goods' or 19th–century popular schooling came to be governed by a new set of principles – the 'moral economy'[7] of the classroom system.

> Systems in many respects resemble machines . . . A system is an imaginary machine, invented to connect together in the fancy those different movements and effects which are already in reality performed. (Adam Smith[8])

Insofar as the classroom system operated as a unified discipline of schooling, it was both a system of thought and a system of practice. Indeed, the fact that it was designated as a 'system' is, itself, historically significant.

The assumption that any group of phenomena can be

systematized dates back at least to the late Renaissance when philosophers like Francis Bacon (author of the *Novum Organum*, 1620) sought to formulate the disparate teaching of the period into a unified science. Basically, the term 'system' came into use (for example in Hartlib's translation of Comenius's *A Reformation of Schools*, 1642[9]) at about the same time as mechanistic views of the universe superseded more animistic ideologies.[10] Isaac Newton was a major figure in this general philosophical transformation. His eventual success in explaining the law–like workings of planetary and terrestrial motion (in the *Principia*, 1687) served both as a model and a motivation for thinkers in other fields.

Shortly after the appearance of the *Principia*, one of Newton's colleagues, John Locke, published an early venture in the systematization of the social world (*viz. An Essay on Human Understanding*, 1690)[11]. If Bacon's *Novum Organum* was about the systematization of scientific method (via an appeal to the priority of externally–derived sense experience), Locke's *Essay* was about the systematization of scientific analysis (via an appeal to the inner light of 'natural reason'). Collectively, philosophers like Bacon, Newton and Locke strengthened the inner and outer workings of the mechanistic world view. In the process, the new levels of sophistication which they brought to human inquiry did much to validate the belief that nature was accessible, knowable and controllable.

During the century that followed, such power–laden ideas about reason, nature and law–like behaviour had a considerable influence upon those, like Adam Smith, who grappled with the social changes brought about, variously, by the extension of international trade, the improvement of agriculture, and the development of industry. Whereas Newton pivoted his natural universe around the unifying concept of gravity, Smith set out to construct an analogous ethical and economic cosmology around what he deemed to be the unchanging ethical and economic relationships of human life. His ethical system – *A Theory of Moral Sentiments* (first edition, 1759) – was built around the 'natural principle' of 'sympathy' (or 'fellow feeling'); his economic system – *The Wealth of Nations* (first edition, 1776), was shaped around the human 'propensity' to 'truck, barter and exchange'.[12] Smith's works consciously advanced elements of a general or Newtonian system of social philosophy and political economy.

Their construction, however, was far from 'natural'. In his choice of concepts, Smith deliberately highlighted the virtues of economic liberty over those of trading restraint. Most notably, *The Wealth of Nations* harnessed the self–interested pursuit of gain to the belief that such activity would also benefit society at large.

Smith's ideas, of course, were the answer to every enterpreneur's prayer. They gave legitimacy, even sanctity, to the (then) marginal members of society, who, outside the restrictive practices of the established merchant and craft guilds, were actively developing new forms of industrial production (for example the factory spinning of cotton fibre).

As shown in a later section of this paper, Smith's harmonization of the ideas of self and collective interest was also crucial to the development and legitimation of simultaneous instruction.

> There is a faculty inherent in the human mind . . . which constitutes the Madras System, the organ desiderated by Lord Bacon, for the multiplication of power and the division of labour . . . which like the principle of gravitation in the material world, pervades, actuates, invigorates, and sustains the entire scholastic system. (Andrew Bell[13])

One of the most successful Glasgow enterpreneurs was David Dale who, in 1786, entered into partnership with Richard Arkwright (inventor of the water–frame) to build a water–powered cotton mill on a fast flowing stretch of the River Clyde near Lanark, about 25 miles upstream from Glasgow. Dale provided the appropriate finance and Arkwright supplied the relevant technical support. By 1800, the New Lanark mill was the largest in Scotland.

Early cotton mills such as New Lanark were a mechanical embodiment of the systematic ideas of Bacon, Newton, Locke and Smith. Their production was *organized* around a series of separate processes, powered by a single energy source, and harmonized by a disciplined army of drive shafts, pulleys, gears and 'hands'. Under optimum conditions – a surplus of water, raw materials and labour – the production of cotton yarn was administered, quite literally, like clockwork.

Just as the first factory system began to replace the domestic (i.e. hand–spinning) production of cotton yarn, so the rhetoric and ideals of systematization began to penetrate other spheres of life. Some of the educational consequences of this accelerating social transformation can be readily traced out in the single–volume *Complete Works*[14] of Andrew Bell, the self–styled 'discoverer' of the monitorial system. In 1789 Bell, a Church of England Minister born and educated in Scotland, was appointed superintendent of the East India Company's Orphanage (or 'military male asylym') near Madras. His published writings commence in 1796 with a report to the Directors of the Company documenting the modifications that he had made to the form of schooling offered by the asylum. On the basis of Bell's testimony, it seems that the Madras Orphanage had originally been modelled on the forms of charity (or pauper) schooling that had blossomed in early 18th–century England alongside the workhouse movement.

Socially and pedagogically, such charity schools were a transitional form of educational life. On the one hand they were an integral part of the domestic or craft economy of the 16th and 17th centuries; yet, on the other hand, they were also a response to the spread of wage labour (and its *alter ego,* unemployment). From the first perspective, charity schools pre–date the factory system. They were a surrogate of family life, not an alternative mode of existence. By the end of the 18th century, however, the second perspective dominated. Workhouse charity schools could no longer cope, educationally or financially, with the increasing numbers of indigent poor children who populated areas of urbanization and industrialization.

In this context of crisis, Bell's novel intervention in the affairs of the Madras asylum was as simple as it was time–honoured. He elevated to the level of a major educational principle the practice of employing pupils as teaching assistants. If the financial implications of such a strategy were not immediately evident, Bell was careful to draw attention to them. 'After this manner,' he wrote, 'THE SCHOOL TEACHES ITSELF'.[15]

In the early 19th century Bell was encouraged to prepare his ideas for a wider audience. In the process, his writings gradually assimilated the language of the Industrial Revolution. For instance, the title–page of *Elements of Tuition* (1807) not only included the word 'system', but also echoed Adam Smith in noting that Bell's discovery achieved a 'multiplication of power and a division of labour' in the 'moral, religious and intellectual world'.

In the 1820s, Bell also attempted to turn his ideas from a technology into a science. The *Brief Manual of Mutual Instruction and Moral Discipline* (1823–1827), for instance, refers to the 'code of laws' – founded on the 'constitution of man'[16] – which, Bell argued, gave coherence to the 'Universal principle' of 'mutual tuition'.[17]

Bell's dual perspectives on mutual instruction – technological and scientific – survived into his last writings. In the seventh edition of *Mutual Tuition and Moral Discipline* (1832), Bell portrayed the mutual system as an *entire economy*. At the same time, however, he characterized the workings of the system as a kind of muscular pedagogy. Its primary purpose was to *prevent the waste of time* by *calling forth* the *exertion* and fixing the *attention* of the students.[18]

If Bell's later writings mask the charity school origins of the monitorial system, a less clouded view can be gained from the early writings of his nonconformist counterpart, Joseph Lancaster. Although the systems of Bell and Lancaster shared the same 'mechanical part[s]'[19] the rhetoric of the machine is much less obstrusive in Lancaster's prose. In fact, *Improvements in Education* (1806) reflects a much older source of Lancaster's ideas. It is saturated, particularly in its early pages, with notions of militant piety and ascetic discipline that, like the concept 'division of labour', [20] emerged in the Reformation and counter-Reformation of the 16th and 17th centuries.

Like Andrew Bell, Joseph Lancaster started his experiments before the end of the 18th century. As a young man in Southwark he set up a small school in his father's house, later receiving financial support from a network of local Quakers.[21] Although *Improvements in Education* gives no explicit indication of the source of Lancaster's ideas, the methods he used, like those of Bell, were firmly rooted in the urban charity school tradition, which, in turn, was influenced by continental educational ideas brought over by Catholic and Protestant refugees.[22]

Although Lancaster may not have been aware of the connection, *Improvements in Education* had much in common with *The Conduct of Schools* (1720), an educational treatise written (in French) by Jean Baptiste de la Salle (1651–1719), founder of the Christian Brothers.[23] De la Salle's efforts in Northern France were directed to the same ends as those of Bell and Lancaster; namely, the reorganization of pre–existing charity schools to cope more adequately with the salvation of the growing population of urban poor.

Like his British successors, de la Salle provided a system of vernacular and elementary instruction. His most noted contribution, however, was in the realm of school administration. As enrolments grew de la Salle chose not to form new schools by a process of fission but, rather, to reorganize existing schools into a hierarchy of smaller administrative units of 'anything up to a hundred boys'[24] – known as 'classes'.

De la Salle's adoption of the Renaissance term 'class' brought a new metaphor to charity schooling. If a sense of order was invested in schooling in the industrial revolution through the notion of the 'machine', it was brought to earlier forms of schooling via the notion of the 'ladder'. By the 19th century, schooling in Scotland had assimilated both these metaphors. Each reinforced the sense of order – structural or sequential – advanced by the other; and, as shown in the next three sections, each was an essential element in the ideological underpinning of the classroom system.

It is a common practice for one class to try to excel another. The highest class, as to proficiency in learning, occupies the most honourable place in the school: a place no otherwise distinguished from the rest, than that it is the customary seat of that class. When an inferior excels a superior class, the superior class quits its station, and goes down to the seat of the inferior. When this happens, the superior class finding itself excelled, and not liking the disgrace, usually works very hard to regain its former seat.' (Joseph Lancaster)

One of the earliest known uses of the word 'class' appears in an account of life at the University of Paris printed in 1517. Before that time (and particularly during the early days of Medieval foundations such as Bologna), university students followed a self–directed set of studies. That is, degree programmes took shape, year–by–year, according to the availabilty of students, teachers and texts. By the beginning of the 16th century, however, the larger colleges at the University of Paris had adopted a different system. Their teaching was organized around groups (which gradually became known as classes), each of which comprised the students of one year and each of which was taught by a regent who accompanied the students through the different stages of the Master of Arts degree. This pedagogic form, known as the *modus et ordo Parisiensis,* became a prototype for both the establishment of new universities and for the reformation of Medieval foundations.

In 1577, for instance, Glasgow University received a new Charter (the *Nova Erectio*) which supplanted its original, Bologna–derived constitution of 1451. The new foundation was consciously framed to advance the more 'definitely Protestant end[s]'[26] of the Scottish Reformation. Residence in college was made compulsory for the Principal; courses were reduced in length; teaching was planned according to a 'rigid programme';[27] examinations were more closely regulated; and teachers and students were expected to profess the Protestant faith and attend compulsory worship.

As the evidence of Paris and Glasgow suggests, the notion of classes came into prominence with the rise of sequential programmes of study which, in turn, resonated with various Renaissance and Reformation sentiments of upward mobility. In Calvinist countries (such as Scotland) these views found their expression, theologically, in the doctrine of predestination (the belief that only a pre–ordained minority could attain spiritual salvation) and, educationally, in the emergence of national but bipartite education systems where the 'elect' (i.e. predominantly those with the ability to pay) were offered the prospect of advanced schooling, while the remainder (predominantly the rural poor) were fitted to a more conservative curriculum (the appreciation of religious knowledge and secular virtue).[28]

In many respects, the Reformation coexistence of conservative and meritocratic sentiments (i.e. of sponsorship versus maintenance of the *status quo*) survived in the pattern of charity schooling that emerged in the 17th and 18th centuries.[29] In Glasgow, for instance, the earliest charity school (Hutcheson's Hospital, founded 1641) was set up deliberately to advance the orphan sons of 'burgesses'.[30] At a later date charity schools with more limited goals were also set up in rural areas (for example the S.S.P.C.K. opened its first school – for the 'salvation of souls'[31] – on St. Kilda in 1711). And the first urban charity school for paupers (*viz.* the Town's Hospital of Glasgow, founded 1733) was set up to both improve and civilize its inmates.[32]

These ideological variations, which were echoed in England and Europe,[33] also survived into the era of the monitorial school. Bell and Lancaster, for instance, were both concerned to inculcate virtue (for example through good school attendance) but only Lancaster's use of an elaborate system of prize–giving gave full expression to the meritocratic ethic.

The reasons for this differential emphasis of sponsorship and conservatism are not difficult to uncover. Bell's system, supported predominantly by the established church and the landed classes, was more concerned with retaining the *status quo.* Its functioning and rhetoric were dedicated to the efficient maintenance of the social machine, rather than to the improvement of its human product. On the other hand, Lancaster's system, which stressed industry and achievement as much as virtue and salvation, was supported by the dissenting churches and financed by wealth derived from industry rather than from inheritance.

In turn, Bell's ideas hinged on a vision of an ordered, static, agricultural society; whereas Lancaster's system was built around a future–oriented technological and Utopian vision of the new moral world. Bell and his supporters sought to stem the flow of history; Lancaster and his colleagues struggled to channel its social energies along more profitable lines. For Bell, education was a static steam–engine; for Lancaster it was a locomotive.[34]

In general, the larger the classes the greater the improvement.
(Andrew Bell[35])

In 1751 Adam Smith became Professor of Logic at Glasgow University. His appointment was a direct reflection of a modernizing climate in Scottish life. To secure the services of this already–noted scholar, the Glasgow Faculty suspended the regular logic syllabus and allowed Smith to repeat a series of lectures on literature and economics given in Edinburgh between 1748 and 1751. Although Smith's modern notions were not to the liking of all Faculty members, it was generally agreed that they would revive the flagging fortunes of the university by attracting students from 'industry and commerce' – a relatively new and untapped constituency.[36]

Adam Smith spent only one year as Professor of Logic. In 1752 he was transferred, following the death of the incumbent, to the Chair of Moral Philosophy, a position that accorded more reasonably with the content of his Edinburgh lectures. Gradually, Smith's moral philosophy course took shape in four parts: natural history, ethics, jurisprudence (legal theory) and political economy. The conceptual apparatus erected in the lectures had a direct influence on education, as it did upon other spheres of life. Specifically, Smith's ideas on the 'division of labour' (elaborated in *The Wealth of Nations*) and 'fellow–feeling' (elaborated in *A Theory of Moral Sentiments*) were to furnish a more sophisticated justification for the deployment of 'classing' in education.

Both the *Theory of Moral Sentiments* and the *Wealth of Nations* began with a discussion of the origin of the 'distinction of ranks'. In the first of these works, Smith drew upon static images of social structure to describe the place of the individual in society. He used such terms as 'distinction', 'rank' and 'station'.[37] By the publication of *The Wealth of Nations,* however, Smith had refined his views on rank in three respects.

First, his discussion of 'the division of labour' (in the early chapters of *The Wealth of Nations*) brought into focus the idea that society could be divided, not into many ranks, but into a smaller number of groupings (i.e. divisions). To identify such groupings, later writers (but not apparently, Smith[38]) borrowed the word 'class' from education where, as noted, earlier, it had been used since the Renaissance to refer to cohorts of students at different levels on the same course of study.

Secondly, Smith advanced the claim that the distinction of ranks was due not to 'nature' (as was his argument in respect of 'species' differences) but, rather, due to differences in 'habit, custom and education'.[39] By apportioning the effects of heredity and experience in this way, Smith resolved a problem of social taxonomy. Inter–class/division/species differences were thus identified as fixed (and unalterable); while intra–class differences were identified as fluid (and open to influence).

Thirdly, Smith pointed out that the clustering of ranks also had consequences for the mutual social and economic advancement of society. He argued that members of a social group (however labelled) shared a 'common stock' of 'talents' wherein even the most 'dissimilar' genius could, by 'barter, and exchange', purchase 'whatever part of the produce of other men's talents he has occasion for'.[40] In actuality, of course, Smith's ideas related principally to the economic exchange of commodities in the market place. Yet, the rhetoric of 'talents' and 'genius', together with Smith's predictions about the benefit of sharing the 'common stock', was easily translated from the economic to the academic market–place.

Overall, Smith's philosophy was both collectivist and market–oriented. The collectivism expressed both educationally through the view that classing increased learning; the market orientation expressed itself through the view, discussed in the next section, that mutual educational benefit could only be realized through the association of classing with a meritocratic system of individual advancement.

> Three children . . . cannot by any possibility make the same progress as if there were thirty, and the reason is obvious; each one of the thirty sympathizes with those of the same age, and the example of each operates mutually . . . This principle operates equally in regard to children of whatever rank in life. Sympathy and example are the most important auxiliaries of the infant system. (David Stow[41])

Besides highlighting the differences between divisions and ranks, Smith also challenged the associated belief that society could be regarded as a static entity. His attack took two forms – both typical of the general historical bias of the Scottish Enlightenment.[42] First, Smith offered an account of the changes that had taken place in human society since its origins (thus demonstrating the mutability of social forms); and second, he speculated about the forces that lay behind the dynamics of social evolution. This latter thrust was to prove very influential in education since the mechanisms proposed by Smith to account for the progress of the individual in society were equally applicable to the advancement of the individual through schooling. In both instances, promotion was deemed to occur not through isolated effect, but rather, through the group–based mechanisms of mutual 'sympathy' and 'emulation'.

As noted earlier, 'sympathy' (or 'fellow–feeling') was the pivotal concept of *A Theory of Moral Sentiments*. Smith believed it to be the ethical relationship that existed among all members of society, irrespective of their wealth or rank. Previously, sympathy had been regarded by moral philosophers as some kind of spiritual essence that well–endowed people distributed, like alms, to the less fortunate (cf. 'sympathy for'). In Smith's revised usage, sympathy became something that is shared, like common property (cf. 'sympathy with'). To the extent, therefore, that individuals were in sympathy with each other, they could be regarded, in Smith's terms, as morally equal (cf. the presumed economic equality of buyer and seller under conditions of free trade).[43]

If the concept of sympathy accorded all humans the same initial natural or moral status, then Smith deployed the concept of emulation to account for any subsequent differentiation. He argued that, through an appreciation of (or sympathy with) the achievements of the successful, the poor would be motivated to further their own self–improvement. In these terms, Smith and his supporters believed that the ethical sentiment of emulation, like the analogous economic sentiment of enlightened self–interest, would advance the collective interests of the rational, plentiful and equitable society.

In Smith's cosmology, then, sympathy and emulation were to be regarded as collectivist principles – referring in the first instance to the basis of society's social cohesion and, in the second instance, to the source of society's continuous progress. Although later writers were prone to conflate competition and emulation, Smith regarded them differently. Emulation was not about rivalry, but about self–improvement. Further, sympathy and emulation were not held to be in opposition like cooperation and competition. Rather, Smith assumed that without sympathy there could be no emulation. In a manner consistent with the early optimistic days of the industrial revolution, sympathy and emulation were seen as devices for the levelling up rather than for the differentiation of human beings.[44]

Despite its novel features, Smith's analysis of sympathy and emulation also served to refocus a long-standing debate about the merits of classing in education. In 1512, for instance, Erasmus's *De Ratione Studii* had drawn attention to the fact that group teaching (as opposed to individual tutoring) could be beneficially used to arouse a 'state of mutual rivalry'[45] among groups of scholars.

Bacon and Locke advanced similar views in the 17th century. At that time, the supposedly sterile (Medieval) methods and curricula of the grammar schools had led many wealthy parents to resort to home tuition. Locke was equally critical of Medieval methods but also noted that if students were sent 'abroad' (i.e. away from home), they might be motivated, through the 'emulation of [their] school fellows', to put 'life and industry' into their learning.[46]

By the time of Adam Smith, the debate about grouping had, as shown earlier, become merged with the other issues. In turn, Smith's 19th–century disciples tended to pull apart the concepts of sympathy and emulation and, presumably under the influence of Malthus, confuse them with notions about competition and cooperation.[47] For instance, the individualized pedagogies of Bell and Lancaster placed greater emphasis on emulation and competition; whereas the Glasgow–linked pedagogies of Owen and Stow (whose sophistication leaned more to group teaching) placed more store by the concept of sympathy. Indeed, both Owen and Stow specifically eschewed the monitorial practice of prize–giving, preferring the alternative pedagogic strategy of using the *sympathy of numbers* to 'animate and invigorate'[48] their pupils into 'friendly emulation' and *going forward with their companions.*[49]

In these terms, the connection between Adam Smith and the legitimation, adoption and dissemination of group teaching is more than merely coincidental. Yet, in the event, Smith's conceptual system came to be revised as the Industrial Revolution turned on periods of famine, slump and social discontent. Just as it is certain that the ideas of Smith and his contemporaries were never fully articulated in educational terms, it is equally the case that many people took elements from them and built their own pedagogic systems. But association does not prove causality. How, then, did the constellation of pedagogical concepts that prefigured the classroom system enter the commonsense world of education? What specific intellectual genealogies, social networks and cultural catalysts served to translate ideas into practice?[50]

In a chronological sense, it is true that Owen and Stow succeeded Bell and Lancaster. Pedagogically, however, there is a sense in which the methods of group instruction did not evolve from within the monitorial system but, rather, from a different tradition. If Owen and Stow explicitly rejected the individualizing and competitive ethos of the monitorial system, what was the source of their alternative perspectives? Again, there are good grounds for looking towards events at the Scottish Universities.

> In a classroom . . . emulation and energy are found to result from the simple circumstance, that a number of young persons similarly situated as to age and advantage, are engaged in listening to the same things, and in receiving the same impressions. A sympathetic animation pervades the whole; the glow of zeal, and an expression of curiosity are perceived in almost every countenance; and the faculties of the mind are exerted, and powers unused before, are awakened into life and activity. (George Jardine[51])

In the early 18th century, university teaching methods were still largely Medieval in origin and style. The professors and lecturers at Glasgow University dictated their lectures in Latin, and examined their students through a version of the oral disputation. Their pedagogy assumed scarcity of texts, placed little emphasis on extempore writing and reflected Medieval assumptions about the nature of knowledge, the establishment of truth and the philosophy (or psychology) of teaching and learning.

The 18th century saw a number of developments which foreshadowed a shift in the pedagogy of Scottish university teaching. The wider dissemination of printing increased Glasgow University Library's holdings (and opened up class libraries to undergraduates); the systematization of knowledge led to specialization among university teachers (*viz.* the rise of subject professors over generalist 'regents'); the emergence of new ideas that could not easily be expressed in old languages gradually led to the substitution of English for Latin as the dominant medium of tuition;[52] and, finally, various factors led certain teachers, like Adam Smith, to adopt relatively extempore methods of teaching and examining.

Some of the most significant changes came at the end of the century and were developed by former pupils and successors of Adam Smith – John Millar (Professor of Law, 1761–1801); James Mylne (Professor of Moral Philosophy, 1797–1839) and most notably, George Jardine (Lecturer and Professor of Logic from 1774–1827).[53]

Towards the end of his career Jardine recorded – in *Outlines of Philosophical Education* (first edition, 1819) – some of the developments that had taken place over his 67–year connection with Glasgow as student and teacher. Jardine's particular contribution was to complete the transformation of the logic class set in train by Adam Smith and, in the process, to provide a pioneering rationale for what came to be known as 'simultaneous instruction'. Drawing on the ideas and direct influence of Smith, Hume and Helvetius (whom Jardine had met through an introduction from Hume), Jardine's revision of the logic class encompassed both its content and organization. The new course, like the old one, focussed on the processes of human thought but used ideas from the nascent field of psychology rather than from the traditional discipline of syllogistic logic. In turn, Jardine not only regarded learning as an active process he also used the same psychological ideas as the basis of his teaching methods. In his own lectures, that is, he sought to cultivate 'all the powers of the intellect and taste' by calling them 'severally into action'.[54]

The first part (or 'division') of Jardine's lectures to the logic class was devoted to the 'study of mind' – the *'mother science* . . . from which all others derive at once their origin and nourishment'.[55]

Jardine chose the 'powers of the understanding' as his first topic and lectured, initially, on the 'faculties' of 'perception' and 'attention'.[56] Such a selection was probably deliberate. Jardine regarded perception as the primary mechanism of thought – the 'first and wonderful communication between mind and matter'[57] – and 'attention' as the focussing device which helped to discriminate among sense impressions.

Perception and attention also figured prominently in Jardine's educational practice. They were not new ideas, being an important element in Comenius's philosophy of education[58] but Jardine gave them a new lease of life by linking them to late 18th–century notions about improvement and industry. For instance, echoing Adam Smith's ideas about emulation and the division of labour, he believed that, by 'deep and perservering attention to one subject' persons of 'moderate abilities' could attain 'remarkable degrees of eminence'.[59]

If the first part of Jardine's 'practical system of discipline'[60] embodied a philosophy of learning, the second part articulated a psychology of teaching. Notably, Jardine chose to bring together the processes of teaching and assessment which, hitherto, had been conducted separately. Together with his colleagues, Jardine gradually incorporated into (and alongside) his lectures an extempore system of questioning. According to Jardine's own account, such questioning gradually developed into a pedagogic system that consciously blended the requirements of both individual and group teaching. That is, questions were not 'put indiscriminately'[61] but, instead, tailored to the 'particular circumstances of each individual'.[62] Nevertheless, such a pedagogy also had consequences for the group. Its 'active discipline',[63] as Jardine recognized, placed 'constant demands' upon the 'attention' of all students.[64] Like Erasmus, Bacon, Locke and Smith, Jardine believed that classing could, at the same time, serve the interests of the individual student.

External evidence for the introduction of a new group–based system of teaching at Glasgow can be gleaned from the gradual spread of endowed prizes, following their initiation in 1776. Prizes given solely for achievement had been known since the Reformation (if not earlier) but Jardine pioneered a broader approach which rewarded effort ('regular and spirited exertion')[65] as well as achievement ('genius or proficiency').[66] By bringing prizes within the 'reach of every degree of talent and industry',[67] Jardine hoped to promote a general 'spirit of emulation'[68] and, thereby, activate all the members of the logic class.

Jardine's system of prize–giving, unlike earlier variants in Glasgow, emphasized the homogeneity of the student group. His classes, that is, were analogous to Smith's 'division'.[69] Overall, Jardine and his colleagues transformed the Medieval lecture. In its new form it was to be construed not as a 'dictate' (as it had been known earlier) but as a vernacular discourse – an 'easy dialogue'[70] between a teacher and a group of 'not more than thirty or forty' students.[71] Although the term 'lecture' was retained, Jardine's teaching represented, as he acknowledged, a convergence of tutorial and lecturing methods. Thus, despite their different labels, Jardine's university lectures, 'properly so called',[72] and the 'simultaneous' instruction of 19th-century elementary schools exhibited certain marked similarities.[73]

Certainly, to anyone schooled within the classroom system, most of Jardine's ideas would seem commonsensical. Yet, the fact that his *Outline* covered more than 500 pages and ran to two editions, suggests that they contained much that was both new and acceptable. Jardine's blending of naturalistic philosophy and political economy advanced a powerful case for the superiority and efficiency of simultaneous class teaching. Through the agency of colleagues (like John Millar), fellow members of the Glasgow Literary and Commercial Society (like Robert Owen), and pupils (like William Hamilton), Jardine's ideas took on a life of their own and successfully penetrated into the wider educational debates of the early 19th century (for example university reform, education for the working class, state control of schooling).

Their penetration, however, was far from inevitable. There was still a large gulf, socially and ideologically, between the 'classes' of Glasgow University and the 'classrooms' of a model 19th–century elementary school. In particular, why would a form of schooling directed to the promotion of 'learning' have any relevance to elementary schooling – an institution that, historically, went back to the Reformation ideas of schooling–for–virtue? What were the changes in educational climate that allowed such a connection to be made? And who were the educational entrepreneurs who brought them to life?

> Many well–intentioned individuals, unaccustomed to witness the conduct of those among the lower orders who have been rationally treated and trained, may fancy such an assemblage will necessarily become a scene of confusion and disorder; instead of which, however, it proceeds with uniform propriety; it is highly favourable to the health, spirits, and dispositions of the individuals so engaged; and if any irregularity should arise, the cause will be solely owing to the parties who attempt to direct the proceedings being deficient in a practical knowledge of human nature. (Robert Owen.[74])

At first glance, George Jardine seems to have had very little involvement in the schooling of the urban proletariat. Most of his energies were directed towards the reform of Glasgow University and its preparatory institution, Glasgow Grammar School. Nevertheless, there is evidence that, if Jardine did not so much give his ideas to elementary schooling, others were ready to take them. A key figure in this respect was Robert Owen. Besides their concurrent membership of the Glasgow Literary and Commercial Society, Jardine was present in 1812 when Owen made his first major pronouncements on education (at a banquet in Glasgow held to honour the visit of Joseph Lancaster). Jardine's influence is most evident in the organization of Owen's 'New Institution for the Formation of Character' (which was opened at New Lanark after Owen had broken with the monitorial system). Not only was the Institution built with a 'lecture room' as well as various schoolrooms, but older children were taught advanced subjects (natural history for example) by means of 'familiar lectures' based on 'sensible signs and conversation' and 'delivered extempore' to classes of from 40 to 50'.[75]

The link between the systems of Jardine and Owen derives from the fact that, despite their apparent differences, both were organized to foster intellectual growth. Unlike Bell and Lancaster, Jardine and Owen were more interested in teaching their students a mental rather than a corporal discipline. If Bell aimed to promote 'virtue' by keeping students 'unceasingly, busily, happily and profitably employed',[76] Owen sought to instil 'character' by more rationalist methods. As far as Owen was concerned, the 'beginning and end of all instruction' was that pupils should understand, as clearly as the 'demonstrations of Euclid',[77] the 'inseparable connection' between the 'interest and happiness of each individual and the interests and happiness of every other individual'.[78] For this reason, mentalist concepts like 'understanding', 'perception', and 'attention' found a more important place in the rhetoric of Owen and, to a lesser extent, Stow, than in the writings of Bell and Lancaster.

The rationalist thrust of Owen's thinking was part of an important educational groundswell in the early 19th century. Philosophic radicals, like Owen, argued that rationality was as appropriate an educational goal for the lower classes as it was for the upper strata. Unlike the conservatives of the day who assumed that the virtue of the working class could be assured through forms of bodily discipline, the philosophic radicals claimed that a more 'durable' character would be formed when, in Owen's words, 'the mind fully understands that which is true'.[79]

For such reasons as these a range of 'intellectual' systems of working–class schooling began to appear in the 19th century.[80] Thus, if the history of urban elementary schooling in Britain before 1815 pivots around charity school ideas about the relationship between piety and virtue, the period after that date is marked by the penetration of the new ideas about the relationship between rationality and virtue. In the event, it was from Jardine, Owen and the Swiss educationalist, Pestalozzi, that post–1815 educators took their pedagogic models. Conservative notions of piety, of course, did not die out; as in the different versions of the monitorial system they existed uncomfortably with the meritocratic social–engineering views of the rationalists. Overall, however, the educational rationalists forced the pace in the years after 1830. As political suffrage was extended to larger sections of society, ideological arguments about the ultimate civilizing value of teacher training and higher teacher/pupil ratios carried the day.[81] Forms of (relatively) small–group instruction were officially endorsed that, in time, were to become the pedagogic mainstay of the classroom system.

> When we contemplate the amazing diversity to be found in the laws of different countries, and even of the same country at different periods, our curiosity is naturally excited to enquire in what manner mankind had been led to embrace such different rules of conduct, and at the same time it is evident that, unless we are acquainted with the circumstances which have recommended any set of regulations, we cannot form a just notion of their utility, or even determine in any case, how far they are practicable. (John Millar[82])

This paper has tried to go beyond appearances and identify some of the new ideological props that enabled simultaneous instruction to supersede the hitherto dominant forms of individualized domestic production in schooling. For the sake of coherence, the ideas of Adam Smith, Andrew Bell, Joseph Lancaster, George Jardine and Robert Owen have received particular attention. But, as has been indicated, the development of 19th–century elementary schooling was neither restricted to Glasgow nor was it the responsibility of individual thinkers.[83]

Nevertheless, the relation beteen Glasgow and elsewhere remains problematic. At one level this paper can be regarded as a case study of a more general phenomenon – the extension of mass schooling. Within such a framework, then, the choice of Glasgow is purely arbitrary: Manchester, Liverpool or London would have served the same purpose.

At another level, however, the choice of Glasgow is less than arbitrary. The early appearance of the word 'classroom' in that city allows an alternative reading – that Glasgow's importance as an intellectual and economic centre enabled it not only to invent a solution to the problem of urban schooling, but more important, to export such ideas to all parts of the world. In these terms, then, the ideas of Jardine and Owen were not unique; they merely had a trading advantage over equivalent notions that, elsewhere (for example The Netherlands and Switzerland), were also emerging from the common European heritage of charity schooling and Enlightenment philosophy.[84]

There is also a third level of analysis embedded in this paper – the attempt to link schooling and production. Specifically, it is argued that the transition from individualized mass–production (the domestic system) to batch mass–production (the early factory system) can also be followed in the history of schooling and pedagogy. From this perspective, then, the disjunction between monitorial and classroom methods is explicable in the sense that the former were not so much the harbinger of factory production as the last gasp of the domestic system in education.

Overall, this paper should be read primarily as an essay in the history and theory of pedagogy. It tries to explore, in a complementary fashion, topics that seem to be missing from standard accounts of 18th and 19th–century schooling.[85] It is hoped in due course to provide a more rounded analysis. In the meantime, these notes may serve as a preliminary ground–clearing exercise.

References and notes

1. SMITH, ADAM. *A Theory of Moral Sentiments*. In: RAPHAEL, D.D., and MCFIE, A.L. (Eds) (1976). Oxford: Clarendon Press. p.222.
2. Examination of secondary sources suggests that, among the British universities, only Glasgow used the term 'classroom' in the 18th century. The most likely rival contender is Edinburgh: but there is

no such usage in the Edinburgh University Senate minutes for that period. An early printed reference to classroom occurs in GIBSON, J. (1977). *The History of Glasgow* (printed for R. Chapman and A. Duncan, Glasgow,) p.143. Wider use of the term in education seems to have followed its popularization by Samuel Wilderspin in the 1820s (see *On the Importance of Educating the Infant Children of the Poor* [Goyder, London, 1823] pp. 18 and 26).

3. Adam Smith's wider contribution to Glasgow College life is documented in SCOTT, W.R. (1937). *Adam Smith as a Student and Professor.* Glasgow: Jackson, Son & Co. Joseph Black's attendance at the Glasgow Literary Society is described in READ, J. 'Joseph Black M.D.: the teacher and the man'. In: KENT, A. (Ed) (1950). *An Eighteenth Century Lectureship in Chemistry.* Glasgow: Jackson, pp. 78–98.

4. The distinction used in this paper between domestic and factory production is taken, ultimately, from UNWIN, G. (1904). *Industrial Organisation in the Sixteenth and Seventeenth Centuries.* Oxford: Clarendon Press. In a future paper it will be argued that Unwin's economic forms have direct pedagogical analogues: that the dominant pedagogic form which preceded the classroom system was akin to the domestic (or workshop) system of production and that the origins of the subsequent dominant pedagogic form (technological progressivism) can be tied into the revolution in scientific management and production that took place in the late 19th and early 20th centuries.

5. For a discussion of some of the political, social and theological disputes over open–ended lecturing versus closed catechesis in the 16th century, see HILL, G. (1969). *Society and Puritanism in Pre–Revolutionary England.* London: Panther Books, Chapters 2 and 3.

6. The expression 'simultaneous instruction' appears in the *Minutes of the Committee of Council* (1839–1840) pp. 26–32. 'Classroom system' was a later invention. By the end of the 19th century, however, the terms were used interchangeably (for example 'the simultaneous or class room system'), LANDON, J. *School Management* [Kegan Paul, London, 1883] p. 150).

7. For the term 'moral economy' see STOW, D. (1850). *The Training System.* London: Longmans, p. 22. Stow took the term from his Glasgow patron, Thomas Chalmers. E.P. Thompson's more recent usage ('The moral economy of the English crowd in the eighteenth century,' *Past and Present,* 50 [1971], pp. 76–136) is virtually synonymous.

8. In SMITH, ADAM (1795). *Essays on Philosophical Subjects.* London: T. Cadell and W. Davies, p. 44.

9. COMENIUS, J.A. *A Reformation of Schools,* facsimile of S. Hartlib's original translation, 1642 (Scolar Press, Menston, 1969): The earliest use of 'system' reported in the *Oxford English Dictionary* is 1638.

10. For a study of the changing belief systems of the 16th and 17th centuries see THOMAS, K. (1978). *Religion and the Decline of Magic.* Harmondsworth: Penguin.

11. A discussion of the influence of Newton and Locke appears in BUCHDAHL, G. (1961). *The Image of Newton and Locke in the Age of Reason.* London: Sheed & Ward. The scientific revolution marked by Newton's work was only one of the educational outcomes of the 17th century. For complementary studies see HILL, C. (1975). *The World Turned Upside Down: Radical Ideas during the English Revolution.* Harmondsworth: Penguin; and WEBSTER, C. (1975). *The Great Instauration: Science, Medicine and Reform, 1626–1660.* London: Duckworth.

12. 'Sympathy' and the 'propensity to truck, barter and exchange' are discussed, respectively, in the first chapter of *A Theory of Moral Sentiments,* and the second chapter of *The Wealth of Nations.*

13. BELL, A. (1832). *Mutual Tuition and Moral Discipline.* Edinburgh: Olver & Boyd, p. 15.

14. BELL, A. (1832). *Complete Works.* Edinburgh: Oliver & Boyd. The original pagination of the constituent pamphlets seems to have been retained.

15. BELL, A. (1797). *Report of the Military Male Asylum at Madras,* p. 20 (capitalization in original).

16. BELL, A. *Brief Manual of Mutual Instruction and Moral Discipline,* 10th edition (n.d.) p. 71.

17. *Ibid.,* p. 74.

18. BELL, A. (1832). *Mutual Tuition and Moral Discipline,* pp. 51 and 50.

19. TRIMMER, S. (1973). *A Comparative View of the New Plan of Education Promulgated by Mr. J. Lancaster* (1805), quoted in KAESTLE, C. (Ed) *Joseph Lancaster and the Monitorial School Movement.* New York: Teachers College Press, p. 101.

20. The editors of the Glasgow Edition of *The Wealth of Nations* suggest that the 'first considered exposition' of the concept of the division of labour occurred in William Petty's *Political Arithmetick* (1690) (see CAMPBELL, R.H., SKINNER, A.S. and TODD, W.B. [Eds] (1976). *The Wealth of Nations.* Oxford: Clarendon Press, 1, p. 13, footnote).

21. It has been suggested that Lancaster took the idea of monitorial instruction from his own childhood attendance at a dissenting charity school (see SALMON, D. (1904). *Joseph Lancaster.* London: Longmans, p. 2). Elsewhere, a contemporary review recorded that 'the school that Mr. Lancaster himself attended was organised into a plan of divisions into classes each superintended by a monitor' (FOX, J. (1808). *A Comparative View of the Plan of Education as Detailed in the Publications of Dr. Bell and Mr. Lancaster,* quoted in McGarry, K.J. *Joseph Lancaster (1778–1838): a Bibliographic Account of his Life and System of Teaching* [thesis submitted for Fellowship of the Library

Association, 1966] p. 14).

22. It has been reported that in the 18th century dissenters set up a school in Southwark in 'direct opposition' to an earlier charity school established by the Jesuits (ARMYTAGE, W.H.G. (1964). *400 Years of English Education*. Cambridge: Cambridge University Press, p. 41).

23. De la Salle's impact on education is seldom noted in British histories of education. The only accounts that seem available are a chapter in ADAMSON, J.W. (1947). *Pioneers of Modern Education in the Seventeenth Century*. New York: Teachers College Press; and BATTERSBY, W.J. (1947). *De la Salle: a Pioneer of Modern Education*. London: Longman. Neither author discusses the spread of de la Salle's ideas to Britain. A better review of the precursors of the monitorial system can be found in TRONCHOT, R. *L'Enseignement Mutuel en France de 1815–1833* (thesis of the University of Paris [Nanterre], 1972). Tronchot draws out the similarities and differences between the *Conduite des Ecoles* and the Bell–Lancaster systems in Chapter 2, pp. 70–3.

24. BATTERSBY, W.J. *De la Salle*, p.79. See also, HAMILTON, D., and GIBBONS, M. 'Notes on the origins of the educational terms class and curriculum' paper presented at the Annual Convention of the American Educational Research Association (Boston, April 1980).

25. LANCASTER, J. (1806). *Improvements in Education*. Printed and sold by the author, London, p. 98.

26. MACKIE, J.D. (1954). *The University of Glasgow 1451–1951*. Glasgow: Jackson & Son, p. 63.

27. *Ibid.*, p. 76.

28. For details of the plan for reforming education in 16th–century Scotland, see CAMERON, J.K. (1972). *The First Book of Discipline*. Edinburgh: St. Andrew's Press.

29. A discussion of the different forms of charity schooling that emerged in the 17th and 18th centuries can be found in SIMON, J. (1968). 'Was there a charity school movement? In: SIMON, B. *Education in Leicestershire 1540–1940*. Leicester: Leicester University Press, pp. 55–100; and MASON, J. (1954). 'Scottish charity schools of the eighteenth century,' *Scottish Historical Review*, 33, pp. 1–13.

30. *Abstract of the Rules and Regulations by which Hutcheson's Hospital is Governed* (printed at the Courier Office, Glasgow 1800) Appendix 3.

31. MASON, J. 'Scottish charity schools of the eighteenth century', p.2.

32. See GREER, K. (1979). *More Like a Palace: the Foundation and Early Development of the Town's Hospital at Glasgow*. M.Ed. thesis, University of Glasgow.

33. See SIMON, J. 'Was there a charity school movementt?' and LIS, C. and JOLY, H. (1979). *Poverty and Capitalism in Pre–Industrial Europe*. Hassocks: Harvester Press, *passim*.

34. The conservative standpoint on the monitorial system is clearly revealed by Sarah Trimmer's comments on Lancaster's creation of an 'Order of merit' for his best pupils. In *Improvements in Education,* Lancaster argued that such 'distinction' was based on the concept of service which, in turn, was 'the original principle of true and hereditary nobility' (pp. 94–5). Trimmer found Lancaster's arguments seditious: 'When one considers the *humble rank* of the boys of which common *Day Schools and Charity Schools* are composed, one is naturally led to reflect whether there is any occasion to put notions concerning the "origins of nobility" into their heads . . . Boys, accustomed to consider themselves *nobles of a school* may in their future lives aspire to be *nobles of the land* and to take [the] place of the *hereditary nobility' (A Comparative View,* pp. 105–6).

35. BELL, A. *Brief Manual of Mutual Instruction and Moral Discipline,* p. 71, footnote.

36. Between 1740–1749 and 1790–1799 the proportion of matriculated students at Glasgow with fathers in 'industry and commerce' rose from 26 per cent to 50 per cent (see MATHEW, W.M. (1966). 'The origins and occupations of Glasgow Students, 1740–1839,' *Past and Present,* 33, p. 78.

37. The use of 'rank', 'distinction' and 'station' to describe the order to society occurs in *A Theory of Moral Sentiments,* pp. 51–2.

38. One of the first persons to use the word 'class' in its modern sense was John Millar – a former student of Adam Smith (see MORRIS, R.J. (1979). *Class and Class Consciousness in the Industrial Revolution 1780–1850.* London: Macmillan, p. 9.

39. SMITH, A. *The Wealth of Nations,* p. 28.

40. *Ibid.,* p. 40.

41. STOW, D. (1833). *Infant Training.* Glasgow: William Collins, p. 11.

42. See, for instance, FORBES, D. (1954). 'Scientific Whiggism: Adam Smith and John Millar,' *Cambridge Journal,* 7, pp. 643–70; and HOPFEL, H.M. (1978). 'From savage to Scotsman: conjectural history in the Scottish Enlightenment,' *Journal of British Studies,* 17, pp. 19–40.

43. See CAMPBELL, T.D. (1971). *Adam Smith's Science of Morals.* London: Allen and Unwin, *passim.* Smith's discussion of sympathy and emulation occurs in *A Theory of Moral Sentiments,* especially pp. 62–3.

44. For a discussion of the priority of Smith's notion of sympathy and its consonance with his ideas about self–interest, see LAMB, R.B. (1974). 'Adam Smith's system: sympathy not self–interest,' *Journal of the History of Ideas,* 5, pp. 671–82.

45. See *Collected Works of Erasmus.* Toronto: University of Toronto Press, 1978, 24, p. 682.

46. Locke's discussion of emulation and group teaching appears in *Some Thoughts Concerning Education* (1693) (National Society's

Depository, London 1882) pp. 138–44 (section 7). Bacon's viewpoint appears in *De Augmentis:* 'I am clearly in favour of a collegiate education for boys and young men . . . For in colleges there is greater emulation of the youth among themselves' (quoted in ARMYTAGE, W.H.G. *400 Years of English Education,* p. 13).

47. See, for instance, Malthus's critique of 'Systems of equality' in Book 3 of *An Essay on the Principle of Population* (1798). In a later edition, prepared in 1817, Malthus directed certain remarks against Robert Owen, 'A state of equality', he argued, was unsuitable to the 'production of those stimulants to exertion Which can alone overcome the natural indolence of man' (Everyman Edition, Dent, London n.d.) Vol. 2, p. 25.

48. STOW, D. *The Training System,* p. 17.

49. Robert Owen's ideas on emulation and sympathy are reported by his son (see OWEN, R.D. (1824). *An Outline of the System of Education at New Lanark,* reprinted in SIMON, B. (Ed) (1972). *The Radical Tradition in Education in Britain.* London: Lawrence and Wishart, p. 175). For an historical review of emulation see QUEYRAT, F. (1919). *L'Emulation et son Role dans l'Education.* Paris: Alcan.

50. For Adam Smith's general influence on nineteenth-century social thought see HALEVY, E. (1955). *The Growth of Philosophic Radicalism.* Boston: Beacon Press, pp. 4 and 13 ff. Many of Smith's ideas were, of course, also carried into educational thought and practice by the generations of schoolmasters who studied at Glasgow University during that period.

51. JARDINE, G. (1825). *Outlines of Philosophical Education Illustrated by the Method of Teaching the Logic Class in the University of Glasgow,* 2nd edition. Glasgow: University Press, p. 435.

52. Other early practitioners of vernacular teaching in Glasgow included the philosopher Francis Hutcheson (in the 1730s) and the chemist William Cullen (in the 1750s).

53. The educational impact of Jardine and the other 'Glasgow men' is discussed in DAVIE, G. (1964). *The Democratic Intellect.* Edinburgh: Edinburgh University Press, p. 9ff.

54. JARDINE, G. *Outlines,* p. 31.

55. *Ibid.,* p. 45.

56. *Ibid.,* p. 47.

57. *Ibid.,* p. 51.

58. Comenius's views on perception and attention are well summarized in Charles Hoole's preface to the first English language edition of the *Orbis Pictus* (1659): 'See here then a new help for schooles. *A picture and nomenclature of all the chief things in the world* . . . This same little book will serve *to stir up the attention, which is to be fastened upon things and ever to be sharpened more and more.'* Menstone: Scolar Press, 1970). Facsimile edition.

59. JARDINE, G. *Outlines,* p. 105. Adam Smith had expressed a

similar view: 'Men are more likely to discover easier and readier methods of attaining any object, when the whole attention of their minds is directed towards that single object, than when it is dissipated among a great variety of things', *The Wealth of Nations*, p. 20.

60. JARDINE, G. *Outlines*, p. viii.
61. *Ibid.*, p. 282.
62. *Ibid.*, p. 284.
63. *Ibid.*, p. 290.
64. *Ibid.*, p. 284.
65. *Ibid.*, p. 378.
66. *Ibid.*, p. 377.
67. *Ibid.*, p. 378.
68. *Ibid.*, p. 377.
69. Lancaster, indeed, used classes and divisions synonymously: 'each monitor of a class or division', *Improvements in Education*, p. 97.
70. JARDINE, G. *Outlines*, p. 464 (referring to the teaching of John Millar).
71. *Ibid.*, p. 426.
72. *Ibid.*, p. 425.
73. The distance between the Glasgow lecture and the elementary schoolroom is also diminished by the fact that Scottish students in the logic class were, according to Jardine, below the age of 'seventeen or eighteen' (*Outlines*, p. 426). Elsewhere, Jardine also refers to his students as 'pupils' (p. 284). English schoolmasters who were aware of Jardine's ideas included Henry Dunn, Secretary of the British and Foreign School Society (see *Principles of Teaching* [Sunday School Union, London n.d., possibly 1837] pp. 16–17), and James Butler (of Handsworth, Birmingham) whose *Outlines of Practical Education* (Hamilton, Adams & Co., London, 1818) may have been deliberately titled to emulate Jardine's *Outlines of Philosophical Education*.
74. OWEN, R. *A New View of Society (Third Essay)*. In: SIMON, B. (Ed) *The Radical Tradition in Education in Britain*, p. 70.
75. OWEN, R.D. *An Outline of the System of Education at New Lanark*, pp. 153 and 160.
76. BELL, A. *Brief Manual of Mutual Instruction and Moral Discipline*, p. 67.
77. OWEN, R. *A New View of Society*, pp. 75–6.
78. *Ibid.*, p. 75.
79. *Ibid.*, p. 67.
80. Besides Stow's *Training System*, Scotland also furnished intellectual schemes in the form of the 'explanatory' system (see WOOD, J. (1828)). *Account of the Edinburgh Sessional School*. Edinburgh: John Wardlaw; and the 'lesson system' whereby pupils were expected to use 'intellectual' means in the 'concoction' of their answers (see GALL, J. (c. 1830). *The Effects of the Lesson System of teaching on Criminals, General Society, and the Lowest Orders of*

the Human Intellect. Edinburgh: James Gall, p. 58).

81. Robert Owen's arguments against the monitorial system and in favour of higher teacher pupil ratios occur in the evidence of the *Select Committee on the Education of the Lower Orders in the Metropolis* (1816) p. 241. David Stow's views appear in *The Training System,* pp. 199–203. For a detailed analysis of the ideological debates surrounding the growth of state intervention in schooling, see JOHNSON, R. (1970). 'Educational policy and social control in early Victorian England,' *Past and Present,* 49, pp. 99–119.

82. MILLAR, J. (1806). *The Origins of the Distinction of Ranks.* Edinburgh: William Blackwood, pp. 1–2.

83. Some of the more visible aspects of the classroom system are discussed in HAMILTON, D., Classroom research and the evolution of the classroom system (1978) ERIC No. 168139, in mimeo.

84. Some of the European developments in 19th–century elementary schooling are described in POLLARD, H.M. (1956). *Pioneers of Popular Education 1760–1850.* London: John Murray.

85. The motivation for writing this paper stemmed from two sources: (*a*) curiosity about Adam Smith's and David Stow's homologous use of 'sympathy'; and (*b*) dissatisfaction with accounts of Adam Smith's influence on education which ignored *A Theory of Moral Sentiments* (for example SZRETER, R. (1976). 'Adam Smith on education: a bicentennial note,' *History of Education Society Bulletin,* 18 pp. 2–5; and HIGGINSON, J.H. (1978). 'Michael Sadler on Adam Smith'. *History of Education Society Bulletin,* 21, pp. 39–43). Overall, this paper may go some way to meeting Harold Silver's criticism that educational historians of the 19th century have ignored the 'relationship between educational and social ideas and ideologies' (SILVER, H. (1977). 'Aspects of neglect: The strange case of Victorian popular education'. *Oxford Review of Education,* 3, p. 61).

Defining 'Literacy' in North American Schools: Social and Historical Conditions and Consequences

Suzanne de Castell and Allan Luke

Being 'literate' has always referred to having mastery over the processes by means of which culturally significant information is coded. The criterion of significance has varied historically with changes in the kind of information from which power and authority could be derived. Educational attempts to redefine literacy, however, have not always faithfully reflected this fact. Studies of literacy in the more distant past (Havelock,[1] Hoggart[2] and Graff[3]), have emphasized relationships of literacy to evolving modes of social and political organization, yet contemporary educators and researchers have been reluctant to analyse literacy in terms of explicitly normative or ideological conditions. The redefinition of the processes of literacy instruction by educational psychologists in recent years has effectively concealed the necessity for addressing both the subjective and the social dimensions of literacy development. This encourages a view of literacy as a context–neutral, content–free, skill–specific competence which can be imparted to children with almost scientific precision. Literacy so seen bypasses controversial claims about what curriculum is worthwhile, what moral, social and personal principles should operate within the educational context. This, as we can see historically, has never been the case. And as we can come to see conceptually, it never will be the case.

Literacy instruction has always taken place within a substantive context of values.[4] In the European Protestant educational tradition on which the public schools of the New World were first based, commonality of religious belief was central to literacy instruction. The 'criss–cross row' – the first line of the earliest

17th-century English reader, the Horn Book – was a graphic representation of the Cross, invoked to speed and guide the beginner's progress through the text. The expansion of literacy in Europe was initially inseparable from the rise of Protestantism, and the erosion of the Church's monopoly over the printed word (Eisenstein[5] and Chaytor[6]). The intent of the 16th- and 17th-century educational reformers was that 'whosoever will' should have access to the word of God. It was believed that individual access to the word, even though it might involve uncomprehending repetition, would improve the soul of the reader *without* authoritative mediation by the cleric. This explains in part the importance ascribed in European schools to repetition and recitation of texts which children could not have been expected to 'comprehend' – a religious and pedagogical tradition inherited by North American education in its earliest days. Aspects of that same tradition carried over into 19th-century 3Rs and classical literacy instruction, which augmented religious texts with venerable children's tales and literature. During the period of progressive reform, from 1900 to just after the Second World War, literacy instruction attempted to address the 'practical' speech codes of everyday life. 'Child-centred' curricula usurped the classics, and the normative stress moved from moral and cultural edification to socialization and civic ethics. After a neo-classical revival in the 1950s, the technocratic paradigm emerged, with a bias towards 'functional skills' and the universal attainment of 'minimum competence'. As the touchstone of educational excellence moved from text to interaction to evaluation, what counted as literacy was systematically redefined (see Figure 1).

Classical and 3Rs instruction

Long before the public schools movement in the 1860s, North American children received '3Rs' (reading, writing and arithmetic) in private and community schools. For the 'common' child, literacy instruction took place in the home, at church, in the local shops, and in the few charity schools. Most communities had one–room schools where a teacher would provide the 3Rs, and moral and religious instruction to those children of various ages whose labour was not required by the family. In the élite private

Theory into practice	Classical	Progressive	Technocratic
Philosophy	Cultivation of the 'civilized' person with the 'instinct' of a gentleman	Education as 'growth' the natural 'unfolding' of the child	Education as effective performance, behaviour modification
Psychology	*Plato:* Faculty psychology- reason, will, emotion. Learning by imitation. Reason must subdue the passions	*Dewey:* The mind as unfolding organism, social theory of mind (organism/environment)	*Skinner:* The mind as mechanism, learning through reinforcement (behaviour modification) *Thorndike:* Empiricism, testing
Sociology	Aristocracy	Democracy	Individualism/pluralism
Conception of literacy	Literacy as literature, detailed analysis of exemplary texts, specification of precise rules, principles, explicit attention to rhetorical appropriateness	Literacy as self-expression, communication as social interaction	Functional literacy 'survival skills', minimum competence
Attitude to education	Intrinsic worth	Subjective/social significance	Instrumental value
Curriculum	Exemplary texts (1) the Bible, (2) the Classics, (3) the English literature 'greats' (4) North American 'classics', grammar texts, handwriting, spelling, pronunciation	'Adventure' stories, civics, self-generated text, idiom of 'ordinary language'	De-contextualized sub-skills of literate competence. Systematic programmed instruction guided by behavioural objectives

Pedagogy	Rote-learning:oral recitation, copying, imitation of 'correct speech and writing', direct instruction	Projects: 'experiential' education, teacher/pupil interaction, teacher as 'guide', 'discovery' method. Socialized instruction.	Streaming or 'mastery learning' of common set of objectives. Learning 'packages' with teacher as (preprogrammed)facilitator. Programmed instruction
Evaluation	Connoisseurship model; oration, oral reading, direct questioning	Local, classroom tests, written tests stressed over oration, products (of 'projects'), social skills stressed	Meeting behavioural objectives. Objective standardized testing (mass scale)
Outcome	Domestication	Socialization	Individuation/commoditization

Vocational education

Figure 1

and preparatory schools of the mid–19th century, like Boston's
Roxbury Latin School (founded in 1645), children of the wealthy
and influential studied 'Latin for six years, French for five,
German for four, and Greek for three'.[7] Despite this differential
provision of linguistic competence and cultural knowledge
according to class status and geographic location, the blend of
formal and informal schooling, family and religious education, and
apprenticeship was nevertheless largely successful in creating a
literate populus. In Upper Canada this loosely organized system
'produced a basic literacy for a majority of students'.[8] Of the
mid–century US, Bowles and Gintis note that 'It is particularly
difficult to make the case that the objective of early school reform
movements was mass literacy. In the U.S., literacy was already
high (about 90% of adult whites) prior to the "common school
revival"'.[9] Whether there was a pressing economic need for a
literate populus at the time is problematic. Graff notes that most
mid–19th century occupations required a minimal competence
with print; far from requiring universal literacy, communities
typically featured a division of literate labour.[3]

Whatever the concrete practical demands for literacy, the
popular association of illiteracy with crime, poverty and
immorality fuelled public enthusiasm for a universal free public
education system. Ontario educator Archibald McCallum's
comments reflected the popular conception of the consequences of
illiteracy:

> Over seven percent of New England's population over ten years
> of age can neither read nor write; yet 80 percent of the crime in
> these states was committed by this small minority; in other
> words, an uneducated person commits fifty–six times as many
> crimes as one with education.[10]

The debate over illiteracy in 19th-century North America, then,
was intimately connected with religious, ethical and ultimately
ideological questions. We find evidence of this in the theory and
practice of 3Rs and classical instruction largely borrowed from
existing European and British methods and texts. An overriding
instructional emphasis on mental and physical discipline
complemented perfectly mid-century educational goals: the
domestication of a 'barbarous' population, whose inclinations

towards 'materialism' and 'ignorance' threatened cultural continuity, political order and Protestant morality.

Universal free public school systems had been established in the majority of states and in Upper Canada by 1860. In the US over half of the nation's children were receiving formal education, and more students than ever before now had access to levels of schooling previously restricted to an élite few.[11] In Canada, under the direction of Egerton Ryerson, the Ontario Schools Act of 1841 had subsidized the existing common school system; by 1872 British Columbia had legislated a public school system modelled on that of Ontario.

Late 19th-century literacy instruction in Canada differed in one crucial respect from its American counterpart. For while Canadian schools imported curricula from England, teachers in America were provided with locally developed textbooks, in the tradition of the *McGuffey Readers*. Noah Webster's *American Spelling Book* (1873),[12] the most widely used textbook in US history, promoted not only American history, geography and morals, but was itself a model for an indigenous vocabulary and spelling. Textbooks and dictionaries of this period attempted to engender a national literacy and literature free, in Webster's words, of European 'folly, corruption and tyranny'. In Canada, by contrast, classrooms featured the icons of colonialism: British flags and pictures of royalty adorned the walls, younger students were initiated to print via the *Irish Readers,* and literature texts opened with Wordsworth's and Tennyson's panegyrics to the Crown. In Canada, the reduction of pauperism and crime associated with illiteracy was seen to require the preservation of British culture and a colonial sensibility; in the United States, 'custodians of culture'[13] sought to assure economic independence and political participation. The match between these differing societal and educational ideologies, and the 'civilizing' effects of traditional 3Rs and classical education was near perfect.

The model for this classical education was found in the philosophy, psychology and social theory of Plato's educational treatise *The Republic*. Platonic faculty psychology subdivided the mind into three faculties: reason, will and emotion. The child, a 'barbarian at the gates of civilization'[14] was regarded as a bundle of unruly impulses needing to be brought under the control of the faculty of 'right reason', that is, morally informed rational judgement. Paraphrasing a speech of Ryerson's, the *Journal of Education* declared in 1860 that 'a sensual man is a mere animal. Sensuality is the greatest enemy of all human progress' (in Prentice,[8] p. 29). To that end, rigid discipline and rigorous mental training characterized classical instruction.

Adopting Plato's stress on mimesis and imitation as the basis for the development of mind, classical pedagogy stressed rote-learning, repetition, drill, copying and memorization of lengthy passages of poetry and prose. Mental, moral and spiritual edification were to be had through exposure to, in the words of Matthew Arnold (1864), the 'best that has been thought and said in the world'. Accordingly, the intermediate and secondary grades adopted a 'great books' literacy curriculum which featured the Bible, Greek and Roman classics and, after some debate, acknowledged works of English and American literature; 'far more time [was] spent . . . on ancient history and dead languages than upon the affairs of the present or even recent past' (Joncich,[7] p. 48). In the US, public high schools retained a modified classical curriculum, *sans* Greek, as a 'uniform program'. This uniform implementation of a classical curriculum in secondary schools forced practical studies of law, book–keeping, and vocational skills outside the public system. In Canada, it was left to industry to initiate vocational education.[15]

Curricular material did not vary from grade to grade: the same literacy texts, particularly the Bible, were studied in greater and greater detail and depth; underlying 'truths' were explicated in terms of grammatical rules, rhetorical strategies, moral content and aesthetic worth. In the elementary grades, students copied passages for 'finger style' penmanship exercise, in preparation for advanced composition study. Thus, stylistic imitation and repetition, guided by explicit rules, dominated writing instruction; students at all levels undertook précis and recitation of exemplary texts.

Following the European model, reading took the form of oral performance to an audience. Individual reading time was limited and all students progressed at a fixed rate through the text. Both in graded and secondary schools, each student in turn would read passages aloud; those not reading were expected to listen attentively to the reader, since the intent of oral reading instruction was not merely to ascertain the reader's ability to decode the text, but to develop powers of effective public oration. Pronunciation, modulation and clarity of diction were stressed. In the 19th–century classroom, reading was neither a private nor reflective art, but a rule–bound public performance.

While texts were meticulously dissected and analysed, and block parsing was a daily routine, the emphasis was not on mere grammatical correctness. In theory, analysis and repetition subserved the development of sensitivity to the aesthetic and didactic features of the text. Thus, the student's encounter with the text, from fairy tales and Shakespeare, was to be both aesthetically pleasing and morally instructive – in accordance with the Horatian edict that literature should be *dulce et utile*.

In the same way, vocabulary study subserved the ends of moral and literary education. Spelling lists often featured poetic language, Biblical and literary terminology. Precision of meaning and rhetorical effectiveness were to be achieved through the apt selection of words from this cultural lexicon: the range of vocabulary legitimated by 'literati' as appropriate for each generic form of literate expression. The overriding sense of conformity and decorum was reflected in the rules which constrained classroom discourse and behaviour. Corresponding to each literate act was a correct bodily 'habitus',[16] reading, writing and speaking were performed in prescribed physical postures. Moreover, 'provincial' speech codes were frowned upon as evidence of rudeness or ignorance; textbooks of this period advised students to cultivate the friendship of children of higher station, so that they might assimilate more cultured and aristocratic speech habits.

At the secondary and college levels, unreflective and mechanical imitation was despised as the mark of an ill-bred social climber. Oration was the epitome of classical literate expression, for in the performance all of the diverse rules governing textual analysis and production could be organically unified. The truly successful high school student displayed not only a knowledge of rule-following, but of skilled and effective rule-breaking, which may have been, in the final analysis, what elevated performance from mere technique to the level of art. Implicit was an 18th-century ideal of 'wit', following Addison (1714), that 'there is sometimes a greater judgement shown in deviating from the rules of art than in adhering to them'.

But if technical correctness was not a sufficient criterion of educational success beyond the grade school level, how could the attainment of classical literacy be evaluated? Evaluation in the 3Rs and classical classroom was carried out on a 'connoisseurship' model. Under the oratorical model of formal examination, the examiner embodied, however tacitly, standards of cultural and disciplinary excellence and applied these unstated criteria to laud or correct the performance, often undertaken in the presence of trustees, clergy and parents. This system of assessment vested total control over evaluative criteria and procedures with the teacher or examiners, who retained the authoritative and final 'word' in literacy instruction.

This view of knowledge was encouraged by an historically and critically specific ontology: the idealist conviction that knowledge was immutable, that forms of beauty, truth and morality were embodied, so far as they could be realized in the phenomenal world at all, in those authoritative texts passed down by each generation of élite literati. The experience of becoming literate was to be an initiation into a continuing cultural conversation with exemplary texts and human models.

The principle intent of 19th-century literacy instruction, then, was inextricably bound to the transmission of a national ideology and culture. In practice, this translated into a regimen of 'benumbing'[17] drill, repetition and physical constraint. This mode of literacy instruction meant to provide a universal sense of physical, legal and moral discipline for a growing, diverse, and increasingly mobile populus while simultaneously ensuring that neo-British 'high culture' would be preserved in North America well into the next century. For late 19th- and early 20th-century students – even those 80 to 90% who left school by age 13 – it would have been impossible to conceive of reading and writing as entities, or 'skills', distinct from codes of conduct, social values and cultural knowledge.

Socializing the recitation

Between 1900 and 1914, the number of public high schools in America doubled, and the student population increased by 150 per cent. With increasing immigration and regional migration to urban centres, the provision and enforcement of compulsory education expanded; educational costs spiralled and per capita expenditure in the US rose from $24 in 1910 to $90 in 1930.[18] With the largest part of these costs shouldered by local taxpayers, the fact that in the early 1900s only about 15 per cent of students continued beyond elementary school led to public complaints that schools were élitist, authoritarian, outmoded and inefficient. E.P. Cubberley, Stanford University's advocate of modern management, noted in 1913 that Portland schools had become a 'rigidly' prescribed mechanical system, poorly adapted to the needs of the children of the community.[19]

Like their private school predecessors, late 19th- and early 20th-century public high schools continued to exclude those students unwilling or unable to demonstrate excellence at the 'civilizing' activities of recitation and literary study. And what *use* were these competencies anyway? The legitimation potential of classical literacy in a developing industrial democracy was rapidly eroded as the public was nurtured on scientific ideals and evolutionary theory by intellectuals of the day, and on scientific management and cost-accounting by its leading businessmen. And although these two influential groups expressed divergent views about what should be done, they were united in opposition to 3Rs and classical instruction.

The material stimulus for reform came from the application of business methods to schools. Educational administrators were called upon to produce results consistent in the public mind with the increasing tax burdens they were compelled to shoulder. The stage was set by the application of F.W. Taylor's.[20] and later J.F. Bobbitt's[21] work on 'cost-efficient scientific management' to school administration, curriculum, and instruction. Accordingly, measures of costs per minute of instruction in each subject area were used to adjudicate educational value. Finding that 5·0 recitations in Greek were equivalent to 23·8 recitations in French, F. Spalding (1913) declared:

> Greater wisdom in these assignments will come, not by reference to any supposedly fixed and inherent values in these subjects, but from a study of local conditions and needs. I know of nothing about the absolute value of a recitation in Greek . . . the price must go down, or we shall invest in something else,[18]

Extensive building programmes were initiated, curricula were standardized, class size was increased, teaching hours were extended; testing of teacher, pupil and administrator was introduced, and records and documents were collected to evaluate everything and anything pertaining to schools. With a supply-and-demand mentality, and a cost-benefit analysis, schools were seen as 'factories in which raw materials are to be shaped and fashioned into products to meet the various demands of life' (Cubberley in Callahan[18]).

But the fact that it was traditional pupil recitations that 'educational experts' were quantifying illustrates the impoverishment of their ideas on instructional reform. Beyond the belief that schools were maintained by and for business and public interests, administrative efficiency experts had little of substance to offer teachers. With the failure of platoon schools in the later 1920s, unmanageably large classes, and organized teacher resistance to 'industrialization', the stage was set for a new educational philosophy, one which would accommodate both scientific management and democratic individualism.

What Plato was for the classicists, John Dewey was for the progressives. Dewey articulated a philosophy of education which drew from experimental science, child psychology, evolutionary theory, and the moral aspects of American pragmatism. Adopting William James's[22] critique of innatism, and his call for early training in an optimal environment, Dewey saw educational reform as the principal means for American social evolution. Deweyan progressivism, therefore, originated as a self-conscious attempt to make schooling socially responsive: oriented towards a social future rather than a cultural past. Its goal was to provide the skills, knowledge, and social attitudes required for urbanized commercial and industrial society.

Progressives derived their definition of literacy from the social psychology of James and G.H. Mead.[22, 23] Language, for Mead, was created and sustained by the pragmatics of intersubject communication – communicative 'acts' involving 'symbolic interaction' with a 'generalized social other'. Within the pragmatists' expanded theory of communication, linguistic development and socialization were deemed inseparable. Hence, the classroom was to be a microcosm of the ideal social community, one which fostered the development of equality and social exchange, rather than authority and imitation. Teachers of the 1920s and 1930s were trained to view their classrooms as 'learning environments'; within these democratic communities, children could 'act out' the skills required for social and vocational life. Said Dewey:

> The key to the present educational situation lies in the gradual reconstruction of school materials and methods so as to utilize various forms of occupation typifying social callings, and to bring out their intellectual and moral content. This reconstruction must relegate purely literary methods – including textbooks – and dialectical methods to the position of necessary auxiliary tools in cumulative activities.[24]

The 'integrated curriculum', 'learning by discovery', and the 'project method' were to enable the natural unfolding of the child in accordance with his/her developing interests.

Rote recitation of literature was replaced in this reconstructed environment. Dewey noted that conventional reading instruction 'may develop book worms, children who read omnivorously, but at the expense of development of social and executive abilities and skills'.[25] Thus, whereas classical literacy was grounded in the exemplary text, progressives focussed on questions of instructional method and social use.

Nonetheless, the progressive mandate that education be socially useful, that training 'transfer' across contexts,[26] made the content of literacy texts a crucial matter, albeit secondary to instructional concerns. Beginning in the 1910s and 1920s, American-prescribed and authorized readers, also used in Canada, reflected the dominant values and popular culture of commercial and industrial life. Stories of 'adventure' and 'friendship' featured vignettes of family life, work and play, and encouraged community service and individual achievement. Dick and Jane usurped Arthurian heroes; by the 1930s discussions of the latest 'moving pictures' and radio programmes coexisted in secondary classrooms with the study of Shakespeare. Literacy texts portrayed a vision of a harmonious American social community, blessed with the gifts of technological advancement and material prosperity.

Progressive speaking and writing instruction placed an emphasis on practicality and expressiveness, rather than propriety. Students were encouraged to talk about their daily 'experiences', to discuss emotional and contentious matters; colloquialism and regional dialects were more readily accepted, and practical 'plain speaking' encouraged. In 'creative writing' instruction students were expected to express their own ideas and experiences, rather than to reproduce literary style. Courses in 'Business English' and journalism were introduced and grammar study became 'functional' rather than 'formal'. Students learned library techniques and book reviewing, how to record the minutes of a meeting, and how to write laboratory reports.

This stress on the cultivation of practical linguistic expression was matched by a virtual reinvention of reading. Dewey's call for a more scientific method of instruction was answered by the developments in educational psychology. Influential studies by E.B. Huey, [27] E.L. Thorndike,[28] and W.S. Gray[29] indicated that oral reading instruction was inefficient and counterproductive. Thorndike proposed that:

> In school practice it appears likely that exercises in silent reading to find answers to given questions, or to give a summary of the matter read, or to list the questions which it answers, should in large measure replace oral reading (p. 324).

Reading then, was a form of 'reasoning'; the psychologists convincingly argued that oral decoding and memorization did not engender an understanding or 'comprehension' of textual meaning.

Accordingly, classroom reading instruction was reformulated; students read silently and responded to 'objective' comprehension questions. Within this new system, the teacher would be freer to attend to individual remediation, small-group projects, grading and classroom management, while each student progressed through the text at an 'individualized' rate. However, many teachers were burdened with far larger classes as pedagogical reforms remained subservient to industrial reorganization. A 'child-centred' instruction which attended to 'individual differences' was more often a theoretical rationale than practical reality.

Throughout North America, school and public libraries flourished under both government and corporate financing; as a result, the classical school master's monopoly over the selection and use of the text was diminished. Students were encouraged to undertake popular and technical works 'outside of what is conventionally termed good reading matter' (Dewey,[25] p. 549): 'dime-store' novels, magazines and newspapers, 'how-to' books, and biographies of contemporary sports and political heroes. The curricular provision for 'recreational' and 'work reading' instruction was a sign of the attempt to integrate schooled literacy with all aspects of home and work life.

Oral examinations of reading were replaced with standardized and, hence, allegedly equitable, instruments of student assessment and teacher accountability. Standardized tests, like the *Thorndike-McCall Silent Reading Test,* were efficient and time-saving pedagogical devices and, moreover, provided valuable data which could be used to determine instructional efficiency and individual progress. It is significant that these first psychometric measures of literacy, early reading and language achievement tests, were welcomed by educators as objective and neutral devices which would end the nepotistic and arbitrary evaluative criteria of the connoisseurship model.[30]

Spelling instruction, as well, was modernized. Systematized pre- and post-test spelling instruction, for which students maintained their own progress charts, superseded the traditional 'spelling bee'. The lexicon of school literacy instruction changed noticeably; literary and religious terms were replaced by the language of democratic social life, names of institutions and occupations, and the terminology of business transactions and the industrial work-place.

Thus, evolutionary social reform and industrial development was the value framework pervading early and mid 20th-century literacy instruction. Literacy was seen as a vehicle for expression, social communication and vocational competence, rather than for the improvement of the soul. But its moral imperatives were no less strongly instilled. It was not until well after the Second World War that the neutrality of scientific pedagogy came to be seen as absolving teachers of their traditional moral and spiritual leadership roles. For the progressives, scientific intervention meant only the more equitable and efficient realization of stated normative and political goals, not their elimination from the educational field. In Dewey's words, education was both an art and a science; science enabled the optimal development of the art of education.

But the attempt to reconcile apparent contradictions and conflicts within social praxis, to totalize personal, social and empirical natures – Dewey's intellectual inheritance from Hegel – was, finally, the undoing of progressivism. For it was the very ambiguity of progressive rhetoric and sloganism in its attempt to dialectically resolve contradictions (between self and society, individual and institution, science and art, education and socialization) that led to the transformation of progressive ideals into industrial practices. The popular rhetoric of 'individualization' of instruction, for example, was employed by both progressives and industrialists, but to very different ends. Throughout the progressive era, apparently harmonious, but actually divergent goals and practices caused education in general, and literacy instruction in particular, to vacillate between the extremes of a socialized education and an industrial socialization.

The technology of literacy instruction

By the end of the Second World War, social and political conditions were set for a major shift in literacy instruction. Assessing the post-War era, historian H. Covell explained:

> The shocking discovery that many of the young men in military service could not read adequately, and the impetus given the study of science by the discovery of nuclear energy and the space race have combined to result in a greater emphasis on the need for continuing instruction . . . of the specific skills needed in reading.[31]

The term 'functional literacy' was coined by the US Army to indicate 'the capability to understand instructions necessary for conducting basic military functions and tasks . . . fifth grade reading level'.[32] While our inheritance from the Army testing of the First World War was the concept of 'IQ' as a measure of ability,[33] the educational legacy of the Second World War may have been 'functional literacy' as a measure of vocational and social competence. Throughout the 30–year development of the technocratic model, functional literacy remained a goal of North American schools, leading ultimately to the competency-based education movement of the 1970s.

After the Second World War, progressive education was besieged by public and media criticism. In his nefarious search for Communist influences, US Senator Joseph McCarthy singled out progressivism as overly permissive and anti-American. Scientists and industrialists indicted American schools for failing to keep pace with the Russians in the production of technical expertise. In *So Little for the Mind,* classicist educator Hilda Neatby argued that the 'amorality' of progressive education had spawned 'an age without standards'.[34] Out of the by then unruly weave of 'child-centred' instruction and industrial management, a 'neutral' and efficient system of instruction emerged: the technocratic model was a refinement of the scientific strand of progressivism.

To educators of the 'Atomic Age', then, it must have seemed eminently reasonable that schooling, along with other institutions, should become more scientific in order to promote universal literacy. Educational science would provide both the means and ends of education: a body of universally applicable skills of reading and writing, transferable to a variety of social and vocational contexts. The psychological research which had fitted so neatly with the industrial reforms of the progressive era, now established the direction of technological literacy instruction. Throughout the 1950s and 1960s, evaluation-oriented reading research stipulated to an ever-greater extent the instructional form and curricular content of North American literacy instruction. Following Thorndike, literacy was conceived of according to a behaviourist stimulus/response model. The linguistic and ideational features of the text, the stimulus, could be structured and manipulated to evoke the desired skill-related responses, ranging from rudimentary 'decoding' to more advanced skills of 'comprehension'. Student response could then be measured to determine the student's level of language development.

Literacy was thus scientifically dissected into individually teachable and testable subskill units. Educational publishers and, later, multinationals developed total packaged reading 'systems', based as much on exacting marketing research, as on the insights of reading psychology. Beginning in the 1950s, teachers were introduced to the first in a series of 'foolproof' methods for developing the 'skills' of literacy (SRA, and later DISTAR, CRP). Among the inbuilt incentives of packaged programmes were promises of decreased planning and grading time, diagnostic tests, glossy audiovisual aids, precise directions for effective 'teacher behaviour', and the assurance of scientific exactitude and modernity.

One widely used reading series, *Ginn 720*, a XEROX product revised for different countries to enable international distribution, defines its approach to literacy instruction:

> By using a management system the teacher can select specific objectives to be taught, monitor pupil's learning progress continuously, and diagnose the source of individual learning problems, prescribe additional instruction and meet pupils' needs and make sure the pupils have achieved proficiency in skill objectives (p. ii).

As a 'professional', the technocratic teacher is encouraged to see the educational process in medical and managerial metaphors. Students are diagnosed, prescribed for, treated and checked before proceeding to the next level of instruction, which corresponds to a theoretical level of advanced literate competence. The *Ginn 720* student, for instance, is processed through 14 such skill levels from ages six to 14.

A strong selling point of these programmes is their capacity to 'individualize' instruction, based on the students' needs as assessed by accompanying diagnostic tests. Students with the same 'needs' are grouped, and each reading group is assigned a basal reader, with adjunct worksheets and exercise books. Then, instructional 'treatment' begins. Typically, teachers will monitor oral reading, review stories and conduct discussions with one group, while other groups work at their desks, completing worksheets of 'fill in the blanks' and multiple-choice formats. Composition and literature study are not undertaken intensively until the secondary grades, when it is assumed that the student will have acquired the basic 'skills' of literacy.

Because the dominant view since the Second World War has been to equate functional literacy with basic *reading* skills, it is only recently that a correlative systematization of writing instruction has begun. Elementary writing instruction remains a highly variable blend of progressive 'creative writing' and 'language experience' with skill-based exercises; most secondary writing instruction is undertaken in the context of literature study. This is partially the result of the continuing influence of university English literature departments on conventional approaches to writing and criticism. However, in light of increasing complaints about high school graduates' inability to write both essay and business formats, writing instruction is likely to follow a similar 'research-and-development' process towards increased standardization.

How are speaking and listening skills defined within technocratic literacy instruction? The progressive acceptance of the child's own dialect and speech has carried over into today's schools, having been sustained by the progressive revival of the later 1960s. But relatively little attention is paid to oral language instruction in intermediate and secondary classrooms, apart from discussions of highly variable quality. As for listening skills, 'management instructions' and 'comprehension questions' delimit teachers' verbal behaviour. Student listening becomes first and foremost listening to instructions and questions, rather than to substantive explanations of curricular content.

Every attempt is made within technocratic literacy instruction to specify its 'behavioural objectives' in value–neutral terminology. Consequently, explicit ideological content is absent, overriden by the instructional format and skills orientation of the literacy text. The 'skills' to be taught are thus ideologically neutralized; lessons aim to improve students' ability to grasp 'word meaning', 'context clues', and 'decoding skills'. In the teacher's overview chart of the Ginn programme, literature study – the focal point of moral and social instruction in previous eras – is reduced to a body of neutral skills (for example 'note the poet's use of animal symbolism', 'use alliteration'). These guidelines clearly indicate to teachers that they need not consider literacy instruction a matter of moral or social edification, but should simply 'facilitate' the programme as professionally as possible.

But such goals and practices are not value neutral. How is it possible to 'infer character motivation', for instance, without calling into play personal and social values? Similarly, we must ask how a student can determine 'structures of cause and effect' in a textual narrative without invoking normative rules of social context and action? As Wittgenstein[35] observed, every question and statement embodies a normative assumption; skills and concepts are not learned in isolation, but in the context of judgements.

The kind of research which focusses on the manner in which school readers inculcate social attitudes through the portrayal of particular roles, personality structures, and orientations to action, [36, 37, 38] yields little beyond a surface level of understanding of the cumulative effects of technocratic texts. Instructional systems – however non-sexist, non-racist and non-secular in *content* – communicate not only a synthetic world-view, but a particular attitude towards literacy; literacy is conceived of as a set of neutral behaviours within an attendant fabricated world-view, in which little of cultural or social significance ever occurs. What is conveyed to the teacher, correspondingly, is a reductive view of literacy instruction as the scientific management of skills transmission.

This claim to 'neutrality' and cross-contextual validity places literacy instruction in line with the dominant belief that North American schools should assume no particular moral or political bias; there is an explicit avoidance of any story content or language that might appear to discriminate against, or exclude, any subcultural viewpoint. The result is an inherent blandness, superficiality and conservatism in the texts children read. What standardized readers communicate to children is 'endlessly repeated words passed off as stories'.[39] In order to capture the multinational market, publishers and editors must create a product which will pass as culturally significant knowledge in diverse social contexts, without offending the sensibilities of local parents, teachers, special-interest groups, politicians, and, of course, administrators who decide purchases. The result is a 'watering down' of the content for marketing purposes. As Williams suggests, the larger the audience of a communications medium, the more homogenous becomes the message and the experience for its consumers.[40] Technocratic literacy systems posit an imaginary 'every-student' much as television networks seek to identify and communicate with 'the average viewer'.

Ironically, by attempting to address everyone, such literacy texts succeed in communications with no one. As a result, this literacy model actively militates against the development of full communicative competence. In the attempt to design behaviourally infallible instructional systems, curriculum developers exclude all but the most trivial levels of individual and cultural difference. As a result, the dramaturgical aspect of teaching, the moral convictions and cultural experience of students and teachers – key to both progressive and classical instruction – become 'variables' which potentially interfere with the smooth operation of systematized pedagogy.

In secondary schools, the linear information processing model of technocratic instruction (stimulus/response, input/output), has led to an increase in 'functional' exercises, such as reading classified advertisements, filling out job and credit applications, and so on. To enable ease and consistency of assessment, however, such tasks often encourage the learning of linear modes of functioning which exclude contextual factors. Several studies have questioned the validity of functional literacy assessment and the success of instruction in producing vocational competence.[41, 42] Often, the pursuit of an explicitly 'functional' literacy presents as legitimate educational knowledge information which is artificially simplified, linear, mechanistic and essentially powerless.

Classicism was condemned for imposing a colonized aristocratic world view on every student. Progressivism was criticized for its subversive and 'left-wing' ideology. But technocratic education imposes only the surface features, the 'skills', of a world-view, and a predominantly 'middle class' one at that. We argue that where technocratic instruction dominates in classrooms and in teacher training institutions, the literacy of students will remain culturally and intellectually insignificant. And, given the informational content and cognitive simplicity of the texts and methods used, and the mechanistic character of the interactions prescribed, we have good reason for concern about the students who *succeed* in the programmes.

Literacy instruction: derived or imposed?

By way of conclusion, we have little to offer beyond the observation that cries of falling standards and widespread 'illiteracy' among today's graduates appear vacuous given the non-comparability of 'literacy' as defined by the public education system since its inception. What we wish to consider in closing, however, are certain implications of this analysis for contemporary problems of pedagogy and research.

As the number and variety of students in public schools has increased, literacy curriculum, instruction and evaluation have become more and more standardized. With the relinquishing of family and community control over education to centralized government agencies came the expectation of universal mechanisms of accountability. The rise of standardized testing culminated in the recent move throughout North America towards universal functional literacy testing. The popular ethic of functional literacy, however, begs crucial questions: Functional at what? In what context? To what ends? And is it in the interests of the literate individual to become 'functional' within any and every economic and political circumstance?

In liberal-democratic societies, participation in the political process implies not only the ability to operate effectively within existing social and economic systems, but also to make rational and informed judgements about the desirability of those systems themselves. Where the citizen has rights and duties with respect to political, social and economic orders, the literate exercise of such rights necessarily presupposes competences above and beyond those required to carry out limited interpersonal and occupational responsibilities. The glory of technocratic education – its neutralization of personal, social and political sanctions, indeed its independence from any substantive context and, therefore, content – produces students who follow instructions simply because they are there: the designated and assessed conditions of proceeding to the next level of instruction. In disregarding the social and ethical dimensions of communicative competence, technocratic education nurtures the literal, the superficial, the uncommitted, but 'functionally' literate.

The tendency among both national and international development agencies has been to assume that increasing the percentage of a populus that can read and write – as measured by years of schooling or standardized texts – is essential to furthering a nation's political interests and social participation. The rush to modernize schooling in devloping countries serves to increase the appeal of cost-efficient and scientifically based 'state-of-the-art' literacy programmes.

Yet models of literacy instruction have always been derived from concrete historical circumstances. Each has aimed to create a particular kind of individual, in a particular social order. In the US, the substance of literacy instruction was derived from distinctively American language, culture and economic life. In Canada, on the other hand, each era involved the importation of a model of literacy instruction, first from Britain, and subsequently from the US. School children recited 'power should make from land to land, the name of Britain trebly great' (Tennyson 1883), evoking *en masse* God's salvation of their majesties in morning song, and learning to read and write, in the end, 'for Queen and country'. The question 'Whose country?' was never asked. Later, in residential schools, Indian children were beaten for speaking their native tongue, and were taught to read 'See, Jane, see! Jane helps mother in the kitchen'. In effect, an imposed literacy model was reimposed to eradicate an indigenous native culture. As A. Wilden notes, the colonized sensibility is often convinced of the inauthenticity of its own cultural messages.[43] What are the social, cultural and political consequences of a national literacy which is based on imposed, rather than derived, culturally significant information?

Today, locally adapted literacy curricula are purchased from US-based multinational publishers. These corporations are able to absorb research and marketing costs, taking what are called 'loss leaders' in the certainty of dominating the international educational market. Crucial in the success of this enterprise are two beliefs: first, that there is no necessary relationship between the processes of literacy acquisition and the literate product; and second, that it is possible to transmit literacy *per se*, as a value-free, context-neutral set of communicational skills. Both beliefs are false. Unless the instructional process itself is educational, the product cannot be an educated individual. The context within which we acquire language significantly mediates meaning and understanding in any subsequent content of use. Our analysis has indicated that the processes and materials of literacy instruction have been based historically on the ideological codes and material constraints of the society from which they are derived. We argue that the wholescale importation of a literacy model, imposed and not locally derived, into both developed and developing 'colonies' counts as cultural imperialism. We cannot look at reading and writing *per se*. We have to ask instead what kind of child will take readily to and profit from a given model? What is the nature of motive formation that an instructional model depends on and develops? And, most importantly, what form of individual and social identity will the programme engender?

It is within this set of questions that educators have defined 'what will count' as literacy in a given era. A literacy curriculum which is imposed, whether on individuals or entire cultures, cannot serve the same ends as one that is derived. We confront today two practical problems: solution of the alleged 'literacy crisis' in developed countries, and the advancement of mass literacy in developing nations. The intention of this historical reconstruction has been to refocus debate on these questions, and to broaden the context of that debate beyond the disciplinary constraints of educational psychology and commerce, within which it has been largely confined for the last 30 years.

Acknowledgements

The authors would like to thank Kieran Egan, Carmen Luke, Linda Ruedrich and David Maclennan for their criticism and suggestions. An earlier version of this paper was read at the Xth World Congress of Sociology, Mexico City (August 1982).

References

1. HAVELOCK, ERIC (1976). *Origins of Western Literacy*. Toronto: OISE Press.
2. HOGGART, RICHARD (1958). *The Uses of Literacy*. Harmondsworth: Pelican.
3. GRAFF, HARVEY. (1979). *The Literacy Myth: Literacy and Social Structure in the Nineteenth Century City*. New York: Academic Press.
4. GRAFF, HARVEY (1982). 'The legacies of literacy', *Journal of Communications*, 32, 1, pp. 12–26.
5. EISENSTEIN, ELIZABETH (1979). *The Printing Press as an Agent of Change: Communications and Cultural Transformations in Early Modern Europe* (2 vols). Cambridge: Cambridge University Press, p. 431.

6. CHAYTOR, H.J. (1966). *From Script to Print: An Introduction to Modern Vernacular Literature* (2nd edn). London: Sidgwick and Jackson.
7. JONCICH, GERALDINE (1968). *The Same Positivist: A Biography of Edward L. Thorndike.* Middletown, Conn.: Wesleyan University Press, p. 48.
8. PRENTICE, ALISON (1977). *The School Promoters: Education and Social Class in Mid-Nineteenth Century Upper Canada.* Toronto: McClelland and Stewart, p. 17.
9. BOWLES, SAMUEL and GINTIS, HERBERT (1977). 'Capitalism and education in the United States'. In: YOUNG, M.F.D. and WHITTY, G. (eds.). *Society State and Schooling.* Brighton: Falmer Press, pp. 192–227.
10. MacCALLUM, ARCHIBALD (1975). 'Compulsory education'. In: PRENTICE, A. and HOUSTON, S. (eds.) *Family, School and Society in Nineteenth Century Canada.* Oxford University Press, pp. 176–7.
11. CREMIN, LAWRENCE (1961). *The Transformation of the School.* New York: Random House, p. 16.
12. WEBSTER, NOAH (1873/1962) *American Spelling Book.* New York: Teachers College.
13. MAY, HENRY F. (1959). *The End of American Innocence.* New York: A. Knopf, p.30.
14. PETERS, RICHARD S. 'Education as Initiation'. In ARCHAMBAULT, R.D. (ed.) *Philosophical Analysis and Education.* London: Routledge and Kegan Paul, p. 197.
15. JOHNSON, HENRY (1964). *A History of Public Education in British Columbia.* Vancouver: University of British Columbia Publications Centre, p. 65.
16. BOURDIEU, PIERRE (1977). 'The economics of linguistic exchange,' *Social Science Information,* 6, pp. 645–68.
17. PUTMAN, JOHN and WEIR, GEORGE M. (1925). *Survey of the Schools.* Victoria: King's Printer.
18. CALLAHAN, RAYMOND E. (1962). *Education and the Cult of Efficiency.* Chicago: University of Chicago Press.
19. TYACK, DAVID (1967). 'Bureaucracy and the common school: the example of Portland, Oregon, 1851–1913,' *The American Quarterly,* 19, 3, pp. 475–98.
20. TAYLOR, FREDERICK W. (1911). *Principles of Scientific Management.* New York: Harper and Bros.
21. BOBBITT, JOHN F. (1918). *The Curriculum.* Boston: Houghton Mifflin.
22. JAMES, WILLIAM (1899). *Talks to Teachers on Psychology.* New York: Henry Holt and Co.
23. MEAD, GEORGE H. (1934). *Mind, Self and Society from the Standpoint of a Social Behaviourist.* Chicago: University of Chicago Press.
24. DEWEY, JOHN (1915). *Democracy and Education.* New York:

Macmillan Co., p. 315.
25. DEWEY, JOHN (1929). *The Sources of a Science of Education.* New York: Liveright Co.
26. THORNDIKE, EDWARD L. (1906). *Principles of Teaching.* New York: A.G. Seiler.
27. HUEY, EDMUND B. (1909). *Psychology and Pedagogy of Reading.* New York: Macmillan.
28. THORNDYKE, EDWARD L. (1917). 'Reading as reasoning: a study of mistakes in paragraph reading,' *Journal of Educational Psychology,* 8, pp. 323–32.
29. GRAY, W.S. (1952). *The Twenty–fourth Yearbook of the National Society for the Study of Education.* Bloomington, Indiana: Public School Publishing Co.
30. GOODENOUGH, FLORENCE (1949). *Mental Testing: Its History, Principles, and Applications.* New York: Rinehart.
31. COVELL, HAROLD M. (1961). 'The past in reading: Prologue to the future,' *Journal of the Faculty of Education of the University of British Columbia,* 1, 6, pp. 13–18.
32. SHARON, AMIEL T. (1973). 'What do adults read?' *Reading Research Quarterly,* 3, pp. 148–69.
33. GOULD, STEPHEN J. (1981). *The Mismeasure of Man.* New York: Norton.
34. NEATBY, HILDA (1953). *So Little for the Mind.* Toronto: Clark, Irwin.
35. WITTGENSTEIN, LUDWIG (1953). *Philosophical Investigations,* G.E.M. Anscomb, trans. Oxford: Blackwell and Mott.
36. PRATT, DAVID (1975). 'The social role of school textbooks in Canada.' In: PIKE, R. and ZUREIK, E. (eds.) *Socialization and Values in Canadian Society* (Vol. 2). Toronto: McClelland and Stewart, pp. 100–26.
37. REPO, SATU (1974). 'From Pilgrim's Progress to Sesame Street: 125 years of Colonial Readers'. In: MARTELL, G. (ed.), *The Politics of the Canadian Public School.* Toronto: James Lewis and Samuel, pp. 118–33.
38. FITZGERALD, FRANCES (1980). *America Revised: Schoolbooks in the Twentieth Century.* New York: Vintage.
39. BETTELHEIM, BRUNO and ZELAN, KAREN (1981). 'Why children don't like to read,' *Atlantic Monthly,* 248, 5, pp. 25–31.
40. WILLIAMS, RAYMOND (1976). *Communications.* London: Oxford University Press.
41. KIRSCH, IRWIN and GUTHRIE, JOHN (1977). 'The concept and measurement of functional literacy,' *Reading Research Quarterly,* 4, pp. 487–567.
42. DE CASTELL, SUZANNE, LUKE, ALLAN and MACLENNAN, DAVID (1981). 'On defining literacy,' *Canadian Journal of Education* 6, 3, pp. 7–18.
43. WILDEN, ANTONY (1981). *The Imaginary Canadian.* Vancouver: Pulp Press.

Bibliography

BRYCE HEATH, SHIRLEY (1980). 'The functions and uses of literacy,' *Journal of Communications,* 30, 1, pp. 123–33.
GOODY, JACK (1977). *The Domestication of the Savage Mind.* Cambridge: Cambridge University Press.
HABERMAS, JURGEN (1974). *Communication and the Evolution of Society.* Boston: Beacon.
LOCKRIDGE, KENNETH A. (1974). *Literacy in Colonial New England.* New York: Norton.
McGUFFEY, WILLIAM H. (1879/1962). *McGuffey's Fifth Eclectic Reader.* New York: New American Library.
OLSON, DAVID R. (1977). 'From utterance to text: the bias of language in speech and writing,' *Harvard Educational Review,* 47, 3, pp. 257–86.
OLSON, DAVID R. (1980). 'On the language and authority of textbooks,' *Journal of Communications,* 30, 1, pp. 186–96.
STUBBS, MICHAEL (1980). *Language and Literacy: The Sociolinguistics of Reading and Writing.* London: Routledge and Kegan Paul.
TAXEL, JOEL (1981). 'The outsiders of the American revolution: the selective tradition in children's fiction,' *Interchange,* 12, 3, pp. 206–28.
Tell Me How the Sun Rose. New York: Ginn and Co., 1980.

Part Three

Subjects of the Curriculum

For many educationists the core curriculum question is 'What subjects shall we teach?' With this question settled the issue then becomes 'To whom shall the subject be taught and how much time shall be devoted to them?' Much less attention is paid to the nature of the messages that the subjects may convey or to the assumption underlying them. Rather subjects are taken at face value: it is good to teach mathematics, science, history, geography and art. The substantive experience which they afford is the focus of attention.

In the three articles to follow, the focus is on the nature of the subjects: what they are and might become. McEwan's short paper argues for a Geography which will adopt:

– a phenomenological model of man with the concept of the active pupil, the questioning of taken-for-granted assumptions about the curriculum, the recognition of the socially constructed nature of knowledge, the rejection of objectivist epistemologies . . .

In fact Geography would be a vehicle for the development of a questioning stance toward man in his environment.

Portal takes up where McEwan ends, though he does not embrace phenomenology, at least not directly. He argues that empathy is a skill in the affective domain and is derived mainly from the literature of psychotherapy. Empathy is seen as 'a condition of interaction and mutual understanding'. In fact an imaginative transposition of 'self' and 'other' which should, Portal urges, be a part of historical learning. Just how such an end is to be achieved is uncertain; perhaps via dramatization in History teaching which reference to the hermeneutic literature would support or then again, perhaps by using the personal experience of pupils. Each of these possibilities is carefully examined by Portal in an open and critical manner.

Such an approach also characterizes the style of Harris and Taylor's article. Here the focus is on the pedagogy of the subject which both McEwan and Portal see as just as important as a subject's content. In their article Harris and Taylor systematically examine whether there can be learning by discovery in science education, an approach so strongly commended by curriculum designers in recent years. Their examination of discovery learning though salutary is in the end positive and helpful.

Further Reading

ARMBRUSTER, B.B. and ANDERSON, T.H. (1984). 'Structure of explanation in history textbooks,' *Journal of Curriculum Studies*, 16, 3, 173–9.

CRISMORE, A. (1984). 'The rhetoric of textbooks: metadiscourse,' *Journal of Curriculum Studies*, 16, 3, 279–96.

DAMEROW, P. and WESTBURY, I. (1985). 'Mathematics for all – problems and implications'. *Journal of Curriculum Studies*, 17, 2, 175–84.

HARLEN, W. and DAHAR, R.W. (1981). 'A scientific approach to the improvement of science teaching', *Journal of Curriculum Studies*, 13, 2, 113–20.

JONES, J. (1981). 'Curriculum process in school and university physics', *Journal of Curriculum Studies*, 13, 4, 349–59.

ROBITAILLE, D.F. (1980). 'Intention, implementation, realisation: the impact of curriculum reform in mathematics,' *Journal of Curriculum Studies*, 12, 4, 299–306.

Empathy as an Aim for Curriculum: Lessons from History

Christopher Portal

Faced with the materialism and determinism which he finds implicit in the 'new' geography, McEwan has proposed an alternative paradigm deriving from Husserl's phenemology.[1] The focus, as I understand it, for approaching a geographical problem is, for McEwan, to be the way in which an individual involved in the situation would structure its meaning. Central to this is the *purpose* or *intention* of such an individual, which rests upon the ability to share meanings with others and on the power of 'everyday' language and practical knowledge to establish mutual understanding. The outcome of geographical study would thus shift from analysis of social relationships in terms of 'facts' and figures to an increase of the sensitivity of the geographer to the attitudes, beliefs and values that social relationships must involve.

Such a phenomenological geography would involve a change of syllabus, and possibly of teaching method, in favour of topics and activities best suited to the exploration of social relationships. However, the problems of standards (what is to count as adequate sensitivity) and of pedagogy (by what steps or stages such insight is to be established) would appear sufficient to prevent any significant alteration of schools' practice. For geography, as for other school subjects where positivism is now dominant, some form of accommodation between the abstract and the personal is likely to be a more practical proposition. Such interaction and mutual illumination might even succeed in developing curricula which were humane without becoming undisciplined or partisan. To this purpose, we should need to explore more systematically the phenomenological aspects of various school subjects and to build bridges between these aspects and the cognitive objectives now so generally accepted as guides for syllabus building.

The resort to phenomenology is only one possible refuge of curriculum planners from the scepticism about *what* we know implicit in the 'sociology of knowledge'. More widespread has been the shift to objectives defined in terms of *how* we know: the familiar constellations of skills and concepts arranged in 'stages', 'taxonomies' and 'structures'. The claim that such process objectives are universal in terms of development, or learning or of thought carries obvious advantages in relation to unstable societies with unknown futures (whether Utopian or cataclysmic); advantages that are expressed in terms of transferability or learning how to learn.

So far, the 'skills' or process approach to the curriculum has made most headway in relation to positivist knowledge – explanatory use of evidence and abstract generalization. Bloom's cognitive 'domain' has now been established for many school subjects,[2] often supported by the development of behavioural objectives which reinforce the materialism, reductionism and implicit determinism which embody McEwan's objection to positivism. It is true that Bloom and his collaborators have shown some awareness that cognitive skills do not comprise the whole curriculum,[3] although the labels 'affective' and 'psycho-motor' tend to obscure any relation of the remaining skills to the acquisition of knowledge. The same reservation arises regarding Eisner's 'expressive' objectives,[4] which may also be equated with self-expression rather than with specific powers of understanding or standards of truth.

The tactical withdrawal of positivism from propositional knowledge to the forms or processes by which it is attained may seem to make little difference to its stranglehold on the academic curriculum, but this is to underrate the importance for alternative modes of knowledge of admitting the legitimacy of knowing how in relation to cognition. It should now be possible to develop the sketchy suggestions of Bloom and Eisner (among others) that educational processes other than cognitive skills may constitute routes to knowledge of comparable importance. With this educational development in mind, I now turn to the nature of empathy as a learning-related skill.

Empathy as a skill

Theorists of the history curriculum have been particularly active in developing a framework of skill-based objectives, perhaps as a means of liberating the subject from culture-specific interpretations such as nationalism or Marxism.[5] It is within such a framework that the somewhat shadowy skill of empathy has gained an established place. One recent contribution defined empathy as 'the capacity to understand another person's behaviour on the basis of one's own experience and behaviour and on the basis of information about the other's situation',[6] which raises interesting comparisons with McEwan's conception of a phenomenological approach to geography. Coltham and Fines placed empathy in the 'affective domain',[7] but Lee has called attention, rightly I think, to the contribution factual and rational knowledge may make to it, as well as to other aspects of imagination.[8] However, the current assertion that empathy includes both 'cognitive and affective skills'[9] gives little help to the establishing of its relationship with other objectives or to the justification for its pursuit.

The classification of empathy as a discrete skill derives mainly from the literature of psychotherapy and the application of a broadly positivist approach to the curriculum of moral education.[10] Moral judgement is here regarded as the interaction of recognizable and mainly cognitive abilities of which one (EMP) involves understanding the viewpoints of others. It was in this connection that Natale published *An Experiment in Empathy*[11], which seems to have established the concept in educational usage.

In psychotherapy, as in moral behaviour, one is concerned with the interaction of individuals having different purposes and different points of view. A condition of interaction and mutual understanding is for one or both of the participants to transpose themselves imaginatively 'into the thinking, feelings and actions of another and so structure the world as he does'.[12] Such counselling aims at the *convergence* of ideas and feelings, as opposed to the pre-established *congruence* implied by sympathy. Presumably, the adjustment to achieve convergence will come mainly from the client, the ability required from the counsellor being the understanding of the client's viewpoint and the expression of this understanding in terms that will make sense to the client. Empathy is contrasted with diagnostic understanding of a client derived from general principles; scales have been constructed by which it may be measured and different forms of training have been assessed. Experimental work generally supports the development of empathy as a recognizable skill, subject to successful training through some combination of instruction, imitation and practice. However, Natale's own experiment, involving the development of empathy for characters in literature, showed empathy responding not to direct training but to a programme of 'critical thinking,'[13] of a mainly cognitive kind.[14] Again, the classification as a skill appears to be justified, but its components and its development remain elusive or obscure.

Empathy in historiography

Interest in empathy as an important aspect of historical understanding dates from the mid 19th-century German Enlightenment. Then, as now, historiography was threatened by the imperialism of the social sciences. In self-defence, historians laid stress on the particular and the unique, and first became aware of what now would be called the phenomenological complications of a study with intentions, meanings and feelings as part of its subject-matter. Wilhelm Dilthey (1833–1911) was a foremost exponent of the distinctiveness of historical study.[15] Broadly, Dilthey distinguished two contrasting ways of thinking: 'we explain nature but we understand mental life';[16] both were involved in the study of history, but it was the second, the understanding of persons, that distinguished history from the sciences. For this Dilthey employed the term *Verstehen* (understanding) in a general sense and *Einfühlung* (empathy) for the 'projection of self' that understanding of other people required.[17] Dilthey's aims for historiography were ambitious and universal, related to Hegel's attempts to plumb the destiny of mankind, and I think this pursuit of the unattainable has obscured, in his work, the fundamental importance of this distinction between explanation and understanding. Despite the dialectical interaction of these two processes in all historiography, they serve different purposes and involve distinct and even contrasting modes of thought.

Explanation, as in natural science, is concerned to understand causation, and subserves the general purposes of political education. It is in relation to explanations of social developments at various levels that we may learn to be more effective as citizens, to make sense of world politics and to be better able to adjust to economic and social changes – these are the aims to which much history teaching is quite properly directed; from them most works of regional or national history, and nearly all school textbooks, obtain their justification. It has provided the paradigm for the most influential studies of historical thought and for the development of the 'New History' in schools. Unfortunately, it seriously misrepresents the nature of historical study in adopting uncritically an outdated model of scientific method. There is, on the other hand, the possibility of vicarious experience directed to the development of the inquirer's own standards of judgement. Here the historian (or more properly the biographer) is able to explore aspects of life, social relationships and intellectual positions that could never be open to him within the limits of his own milieu. Dilthey, although an atheist, was able to experience religion in a new dimension after exploring empathetically the beliefs of Luther.[18] Obviously, a significant account of Luther's religious life would require much knowledge of the politics and culture of the 16th century, but such knowledge would not, of itself, entail the insight that Dilthey describes; for this, we seem to respond directly as persons in the sense that we respond to other persons in life. Dilthey compares this kind of understanding to the response we make in the arts, such as drama, literature, painting etc. We attend here to the work of art which incorporates the meanings of its creator, but our aesthetic experience transcends rational knowledge, involving feelings and attitudes that may only be indirectly expressed in words. So in understanding the sources of personal history, our first need is the sensitivity to bring it into contact with our own world of purposes and values.

Dilthey at first suggested that we learn about other people by observing our own states of mind and comparing them with those of historical subjects, but he later adopted the view, now generally held, that introspection of this kind is unreliable. There is, however, an important point behind this: the idea that the way 'to develop a sense of the situation and life of the other [is] not first of all by making it our own but by identifying what we feel and experience with the other'.[19] From this initial step of the imagination we can proceed to further and better approximations in the light of information arising as we explore 'the other' systematically.[20] Thus propositional knowledge, conscious hypotheses and inference are in no way excluded from the knowledge we can gain of other people; what is proposed in that intuitive, empathetic insight is both our point of departure and the link by which we can use such knowledge to modify our own experience and expectations.

Empathy in historical learning

The interactive relationship that exists between explanation and empathetic understanding may seem to support the view that formal teaching comes first and that imagination can only come into play when the facts are fairly well established. This is no doubt very true in relation to explanatory imagination, but I have maintained that empathy pursues general aims different from those of explanation and that it is likely to depend upon a range of experiences and skills different from, and even in conflict with, the conventional range of logical operations. Such preliminary steps will need to be identified and given adequate exercise for empathy to operate effectively.

First, to follow Dilthey, stands the relation to the source material. This needs to be presented in a direct relationship with a specific person and to have about it sufficient 'atmosphere' to invoke its creator or user. Visual or tactile qualities are likely to appeal more directly than verbal meaning, even for competent readers, and aesthetic power may be directly relevant. Beyond this, sources can make a direct appeal if they present a problem for the empathetic subject to which the outcome is unknown or not yet revealed. The interactive nature of empathy now requires an offering from the student's own frame of reference, to which the experience of the historical subject may be mentally connected and extended. Analogy with contemporary situations and expectations would be highly appropriate here, but answering the question 'how would I have acted in his situation?' may reveal great differences from the actual course of events. Empathy is anticipatory, and will involve gradual modification of anachronistic preconceptions until the actual responses of the subject are foreseen, as well as the ways in which these might have been justified. The choice of a subject for whom sympathy is possible (i.e. similarity of outlook) would be one way of engaging the feelings of the student and thus preparing the way for empathy, but empathy should not be confined to sympathetic subjects. Contrary to the suggestion of Lee,[21] it would be possible to develop empathy even for a person we abhor, or within a society very different in values and culture from anything we may have experienced. Indeed, on the grounds presented here, the value should be greater according to the differences from our own ways of living and thinking.

The training of empathy as part of historical learning will thus require a range of experience and appropriate instruction, comparable to that already formulated for developing cognitive skills. Perhaps the most clearly empathetic prescription of this kind is the approach to dramatization of history advocated by Fines and Verrier.[22] Improvization permits initial projection of the self into historical circumstances, while adopting the role of spectator or minor participant minimizes the gulf in experience between schoolchildren and historical figures. Although the lessons described are largely colloquial and informal, encouraging the pupils to react and contribute directly from personal experience, considerable emphasis is laid also upon didactic instruction about the limiting conditions of the action, while the dramatization itself gives rise to formal analysis and discussion.

Dilthey emphasized the importance of 'expressive' sources as a stimulus for empathy, where the purposes and problems of individuals are clearly embodied. For relatively unsophisticated pupils the tendency, already common among history teachers, to use visual materials (objects and pictures), to present verbal sources by tape-recording wherever possible and to make full use of films and direct observation of local evidence would go some way to meet this need; it may, however, need stressing that these approaches would be of equal importance to all pupils, not merely the 'less able', if empathy is to be accepted as a major objective. Availability of such sources is not something that can be taken for granted and the obligation to provide them could be one of the most influential factors in the choice of syllabus content. Apart from the qualities of vividness and immediacy in the source material, topics suitable for empathetic treatment will require opportunities for study in depth of issues affecting individuals, while the choice of narrative form for presentation allows the incorporation of personal viewpoints. (Narrative forms would include, for example, dramatic enactment, tape–recording, strip-cartoons, as well as formal essays.)

A significant attempt to provide for the development of empathy through choice of subject-matter and source material can be found in the series of vivid films upon which *Man: a Course of Study (MACOS)* is built. The aesthetic quality of some of these, particularly those portraying the Eskimo section of the course, is claimed by Bruner as important in evoking a receptive response, and this accords with Dilthey's conviction that the empathetic response was related closely to the aesthetic.[23] This film material on the Canadian Eskimos also raises the question how far absolute authenticity is a requisite of classroom sources. It is not only with films that a serious attempt at reconstruction may be easier to work with or, indeed, the only way of presenting the sources in question to school pupils. By following the reconstructed films, by comparisons and further information about the actual and more prosaic circumstances of the Eskimos today, *MACOS* seems to have gained an empathetic entry from which more generalized ideas may be developed using factual and accurate information.

The other pole of the empathetic contact is the contribution made by the historian in terms of feelings and personal experience. In seeking this among pupils, a teacher will have a good deal of guidance from the literature of 'open' education.[24] In brief, a warm, accepting style, cooperation rather than competition, opportunity for pupil to pupil discussion, and questioning tactics that employ plenty of 'open' questions will be among the features of such lessons. By such means the experience of pupils can be elicited and then developed or applied in directions that offer connections with historical situations; it would be entirely appropriate to introduce the experiences pupils may have of institutional authority and disorder in school as a frame for the study of the French Revolution, despite the strictures of Partington[25] who sees this suggestion merely in terms of the concept of revolution. One other background condition is important here; one that applies to every possible intellectual objective. This is the importance of the teacher's own attitudes and behaviour as a model of the qualities he is trying to induce. History teachers are often, perhaps as a result of their own training, unduly modest about their powers of imagination. It is hardly surprising if pupils dismiss as marginal frills the responses that teachers seldom employ orally or demonstrate to the class.

Provision for the teaching of empathy in 'History 13–16'

In seeking to specify instructional sequences and assignments appropriate for the teaching of empathy, we are fortunate to have available the work of the Schools Council project *History 13–16*. Its aims include specific reference to empathy, and the published materials fulfil many of the criteria suggested above for its encouragement. There is much documentary material, some of it vivid and first–hand, pictures are used as sources and pupils are encouraged to think rather than just to remember; however, the treatment of individuals seems to me inadequate. The introductory section, 'What is history?' directs attention mainly to the placing of people in time, and to aspects of motivation and achievement that might be summarized as the way people may act as the causes of historical events. This over-emphasis upon the place of people in causative chains is repeated in the otherwise illuminating discussion, in the evaluation, about individual contributions to events.[26] It is not, therefore, surprising that:

> Some pupils encounter further difficulties when they are asked to imagine that they were 'there at the time' . . . to ask pupils to put aside their own feelings and concerns . . . defeats some. After a night's sentry duty on Hadrian's Wall pupils can comment on the cold and boredom but often they cannot reconstruct the wider perspective. When they look over the wall they see Scotland, not world's end, they cannot feel a long way from Rome – the centre of their world.[27]

A number of assignments used by teachers to evoke empathy are printed here,[28] together with selected responses from pupils, and we see the kind of exercise that proved difficult about Hadrian's Wall: 'Reconstruct the daily life of a soldier stationed on the wall'. Guidelines were given, such as the advice to include topics like 'equipment' and 'a training session', but this almost invites a rehash of essentially factual information under appropriate headings. In another example pupils are asked to make a decision as a 19th-century pauper whether or not to accept a place in an almshouse. Much realistic detail was supplied and the assignment was presented in the form of a personal dilemma;[29] here the response shows considerably more empathy. Conflict situations, such as those involving American settlers and Indians, have potential for defining personal standpoints and feelings. From the examples quoted[30] it seems more fruitful to give a biased point of view or description and seek for its refutation from pupils, than it would be to require expression of more than one point of view in the same exercise. Perhaps the latter involves a more developed sense of empathy than would normally be found among 16+ public examination candidates. The attempt at a radio interview with a cowboy[31] seems to fail mainly from the restrictiveness of the structuring questions (for less able pupils). One might expect a more vivid reconstruction if pupils were inventing as well as answering the questions. In this form the idea would seem admirably suited as an activity to stimulate empathetic ways of thinking, though perhaps less so as a formal assignment.

The setting of examination questions that are specifically empathetic may, in view of what has been said above, seem less valuable than inviting empathetic exploration of more general questions and allowing for this in the mark allocation. Certainly the types of 'empathetic questions' listed in 'Explorations'[32] do not meet the conditions likely to be necessary for empathetic insight, and the invitation to 'Explain the point of view of . . . ' or even to 'Write . . . as if you were . . . ' could be answered quite satisfactorily from an analytical or diagnostic knowledge of the person concerned.

Conclusion

The problem of providing in the curriculum for the imaginative, aesthetic and intuitive aspects of understanding is a general one, not merely the concern of arts subjects, where the inadequacy of behavioural criteria is most evident. However, the most fruitful attempts to integrate such provision with precise cognitive objectives may be made in 'humanities' subjects such as history and geography, where concern for personal values and vicarious experience has always rubbed shoulders with attempts to be more scientific. Such integration requires prior recognition of the distinct kinds of knowledge to which intellectual skills may give access. Here, in particular, we have considered the explanation of social developments in terms of causation as essentially different from the historian's extension of his repertoire of meanings and values. As with the dialectical relationship Piaget has envisioned between assimilation and accommodation, we have argued that empathy will require adequate support from positivist knowledge but, where people are concerned, will determine the categories available to us for elucidating their intentions.

The acceptance of empathy as a phenomenological dimension of all the 'humanities', and of its dialectical relationship with deductive reasoning, would involve considerable change of emphasis from current models of curriculum planning. We should first need to recognize steps or stages on the road to empathetic understanding – whether, for example, sympathy is a primitive form of empathy or an alternative to it. Some work of this kind is reported by Natale in the field of psychotherapy,[32] but the distinctions are not readily applicable to academic material. Given such a guide to direction, we need to know much more about teaching methods both to foster empathetic development and to establish effective interaction with explanatory skills. In assessment, we have urgent need for assignments more specifically demanding than retelling a story in the first-person singular. In general it should provide a valuable antidote lest the tyranny of skills should merely replace the tyranny of facts.

References and notes

1. McEWAN, N. (1980). 'Phenomenology and the curriculum: the case of secondary-school geography', *Journal of Curriculum Studies*, 12, pp. 323–30.
2. COLTHAM, J.B. and FINES, J. (1971). *Educational Objectives for the Study of History*. London: Historical Association.
3. KRATHWOHL, D.R., BLOOM, B.S. and MASIA, B.B. (1964). *Taxonomy of Educational Objectives. Vol. 2: The Affective Domain*. London: Longman.

4. EISNER, E.W. (1969). 'Instructional and expressive objectives.' In: POPHAM, W.G. *et al. Instructional Objectives.* AERA I. Chicago: Rand McNally.
5. ROGERS, P.J. (1978). *The New History.* London: Historical Association.
6. SCHOOLS COUNCIL (1976). *Place, Time and Society 8–13.* London: Collins, p. 119.
7. *Op. cit.,* pp. 7–8.
8. LEE, P.J. (1978). 'Explanation and understanding in history'. In: DICKENSON, A.K. and LEE, P.J. (eds.) *History Teaching and Historical Understanding.* London: Heinemann, p. 74.
9. BODDINGTON, A.J. (1980). 'Empathy and the teaching of history', *British Journal of Educational Studies,* 28, p. 13.
10. WILSON, J.B., WILLIAMS, N. and SUGARMAN, B. (1967). *An Introduction to Moral Education.* Harmondsworth: Penguin.
11. NATALE, S. (1972). *An Experiment in Empathy.* Windsor: NFER.
12. *Ibid.,* p. 16.
13. RATHS, LOUIS E. *et al.* (1967). *Teaching for Thinking.* Columbus: Merrill.
14. NATALE, S., *op. cit.,* p. 68.
15. Throughout this section I am much indebted to PLANTINGA, T. (1980). *Historical Understanding in the Thought of Wilhelm Dilthey.* University of Toronto Press.
16. *Ibid.,* p. 33.
17. *Ibid.,* p. 95 n.
18. DILTHEY, W. (1976). *Selected Writings.* Cambridge: Cambridge University Press, p. 227–8.
19. PLANTINGA, T., *op. cit.,* p. 47.
20. *Ibid.,* pp. 113–14. The discussion here is of understanding an historical age, but I conclude that Dilthey would invoke the same procedure for understanding an individual.
21. LEE, P.J., *loc. cit.,* p. 88.
22. FINES, J. and VERRIER, R. (1974). *The Drama of History.* London: New University Education.
23. PLANTINGA, T., *op. cit.,* p. 61.
24. PORTAL, C. (1976). 'The place of open learning in secondary school history,' *Journal of Curriculum Studies,* 8, pp. 35–43.
25. PARTINGTON, G. (1980). *The Idea of an Historical Education.* Windsor: NFER, p. 201.
26. SHEMILT, D. (1980). *'History 13–16 Evaluation Study.* Edinburgh: Holmes McDougall, pp. 22 and 32–3.
27. SCHOOLS COUNCIL (1980). *Explorations.* (SREB, Avondale House, 33 Carlton Crescent, Southampton), p. 108.

Ibid., p. 209.
Ibid., pp. 215–19.
Ibid., pp. 234–37.
Ibid., p. 239.
Ibid., p. 278.
NATALE, S., *op. cit.*, p. 35.

Phenomenology and the Curriculum: the Case of Secondary–School Geography

Neil McEwen

Since *Knowledge and Control*[1] was published in 1971, sociologists of education and subject-orientated academics have reappraised the assumptions which underpin the school curriculum and the methodology and content of particular subjects within that curriculum. Young's work is now well known: it has been analysed and criticized and indeed the author has substantially altered his views. However, the concepts which Young introduced have much to offer as they challenge the academic and the teacher to adopt a phenomenological 'model of man', to question their taken-for-granted curricular assumptions, to accept knowledge as a social construct, to reject objectivist epistemologies and to call into question the philosophy of positivism. For the academic or teacher who takes up this challenge, the ramifications for subject teaching within the secondary school are far-reaching and immense.

Nowhere is this more true than in the case of geography, a subject which in the 1950s and 1960s, was under attack for its lack of theory, its failure to be an art or a science, its failure to contribute to knowledge and its lack of a philosophical underpinning. The reaction of geographers to these criticisms was an unconscious[2] but Messianic espousal of the tenets of positivism, following Park's precept to 'Reduce all social relations to relations of space and it would be possible to apply to human relations the fundamental logic of the physical sciences.'[3] The paradigm which has resulted, in both academic and school geography, demonstrates the overwhelming acceptance of, and commitment to, the tenets of positivism. Many significant articles and texts, for example, Bunge,[4] Burton,[5] Haggett,[6] Harvey,[7] and Davies,[8] have put forward methodological and philosophical arguments to demonstrate the relationship between positivism (described by Haggett as 'a philosophical approach which holds that our sensory experiences are the exclusive source of valid information about the world'[9]) and geography, on which the paradigm is based. The paradigm itself is one which is 'committed to material phenomena, explicit reductionism and implicit determinism, and analysis which separates fact from value',[10] so that values become submerged and thus implicit. It is dedicated to the scientific method, to high–order measurement, to hypothesis testing of theory and general laws and it assumes that an objective truth can be ascertained from the examination of a consensually accepted geographical reality.[11]

However, many geographers have been concerned over the strength of positivism in current geographical thinking, and the view expressed by Mercer and Powell that 'the major thrust of positivism in the 1960s added essential rigour to geographical analysis, but there is a growing fear that it has left the subject with too many technicians and a dearth of scholars'[12] is one which has been echoed in many quarters. The drift away from positivism which these fears prompted has taken several paths. Firstly, behavioural geography can be seen as a reaction to positivism in that it attempted to build a geography orientated around man rather than laws or systems. However, behavioural geography is still essentially positivist in that it is a mechanistic conception which is premised on the natural science view of man and thus is fundamentally rooted in the logic of positivism. In the behaviourist model man is regarded as a decision–maker but his behaviour is restricted by determining conditions and his role in the world is essentially passive since, in Lockean terms, 'The unifying principle [of behaviourism] is a balance of exchanges and the ordering principle of value is adjustment to external conditions.'[13] Secondly, in answer to the question which Chisholm posed of what should follow the quantitative revolution,[14] there has been a move toward a more 'relevant' geography. New subject matter for 'a relevant and useful' geography was promulgated at the 1971 conference of the Association of American Geographers, and Smith[15] listed a whole series of areas, such as racial segregation, poverty, drug addiction, social deprivation, which should come under scrutiny by 'radical' geographers in their quest for humanizing social change.

The 'radical geography' of the 1970s can be seen to have two major strands. One group, of whom Bunge and Harvey may be seen as representative, has adopted a structural view – Harvey for example regards Marx as an operational structuralist[16] and argues that since inequalities are enhanced by certain structures, then the substitution of other structures should correct injustice and guarantee equality. Thus, while condemning positivism and positivist geography for its encouragement of the social, economic and political *status quo* Harvey adopts the same set of parameters and puts them within a Marxist perspective in order to encourage structural change. Implicit in this structural view is the concept of a 'passive' man and it is this concept which separates the two strands in radical geography. The other group looks upon man as both 'active' and 'intentional'. In their view geography should focus on 'the actor in the social world whose doing and feeling lies at the bottom of the whole system'.[17] In order to do this geography must be related to philosophical parameters which concentrate on an understanding of the human being in the world, which throw off the positivist straitjacket and which 'view problems, not only from our own perception, but from the actor's frame of reference'.[18] Such philosophical parameters are available within the transcendental phenomenology of Edmund Husserl.[19]

Husserl's phenomenology

Edmund Husserl opposed the objectifying reductionism of positivism through the project of phenomenology which he described as the description of the phenomenal – that which is given or indubitable in the perception or consciousness of the conscious individual, precisely as it appears in the consciousness. Such consciousness may be viewed as the relationship between a subject and an object, or more clearly, the relationship of being between man and the world which was expressed by Heidegger thus 'Wenn kein Dasein existiert, ist kein Welt da'[20] and which Husserl denotes as intentionality.

Intentionality is a key concept of phenomenology because its central assumption is that man is the source of acts of intention and thus the creator of meaning and action. Thus the concept of an active man is posited, such a man not being held powerless within the structural constraints inherent in positivism. Further, the relationship between subject and object embodied in intentionality represents the de-reification of consciousness from the Cartesian Dualism of *res extensa* and *res cogitans* accepted in positivism. The world towards which the intentional consciousness is directed is a group-centred world of events, relations and places infused with meaning which Husserl in his later writings characterized as the 'life world'. This life world is 'intersubjective' in that the experience of an individual will have areas in common with other individuals and therefore different actors will act in similar ways in similar circumstances. The concept of intersubjectivity points to the inherent sociality of consciousness and together with 'life world' and 'intentionality' forms the basic props of phenomenological thinking.

There are two other terms essential to an understanding of phenomenology which must now be considered. Firstly, 'the natural attitude', a term which stands at the interface between phenomenological philosophy and sociology, and simply means the mundane practical reasoning of everyday life; and secondly the 'phenomenological reduction', the intuitive method by which all prejudgements are abandoned so that nothing is taken for granted. The actor thus suspends all judgements which are made within the natural attitude so that what is left is pure consciousness.

Husserl's work and ideas point to a paradigm which posits an intentional and therefore active man creating meaning and action, which focusses on the taken-for-granted realm of everyday experience and which embraces both subject and object, fact and value, and restores to these dualisms the unity they carry in the everyday world. Such a paradigm has much to offer in opposition to what Lichtman describes as the 'Banal perversity of Logical Positivism'.[21]

Phenomenology and geography

The fusion which has taken place between geography and phenomenology has sought to emphasize, in opposition to positivism, the subjective nature of human experience and the importance of values, in order to emphasize the problem of relevance. Mercer and Powell, for example, note that:

> the apparently rapidly growing contemporary emphasis on
> relevance in the social and natural sciences has much of its
> philosophical grounding in phenomenology; for what is
> relevance if not the fusing of the worlds of fact and value for so
> long artificially divided? Are not the increasingly severe
> environmental and social problems with which we are
> confronted due almost entirely to a world view which sees the
> environment 'out there' as an object which is acted upon?[22]

In their article Mercer and Powell are pointing to an
'intentional' geography, where fact and value are inseparable,
where problems should be viewed from the actor's angle and in
which there are no right and wrong solutions to social questions,
only certain attitudes, values and beliefs relating to these
problems.

The arguments put forward by Mercer and Powell have been
expanded by Buttimer in what is perhaps the clearest statement of
the relationship between phenomenology and geography. For
Buttimer 'Phenomenology invites us to shift our focus away from
spatial systems to man's experience, its meaning and
intentionality'.[23] Her arguments revolve around the notion of the
geographer as an intentional being, for if geographers are
recognized as intentional beings then that which they teach should
be imbued with intentionality. In other words, the content of
geography should be recognized as value-oriented and
subjective and should revolve around what she terms the
'conscientious engagement of social problems'.

However, Buttimer extends her phenomenological view beyond
a change in geographical content to look at the methods by which
that content may be taught. She correctly points out that such a
conscientious engagement of social problems requires that certain
concepts and relationships be redefined in the light of the fact that
a phenomenologist cannot impose normative judgements on
courses of societal action. (The phenomenological reduction.)
Thus, in her view, the relationship between academic and student,
teacher and student, in respect of social issues and problems,
should be resolved in the following way:

Intersubjective dialogue with another person or context should elicit a strict growth of consciousness on both sides, . . . we may not emerge with any specific plans for the resolution of our problems as our disciplinary models define them, but we may witness an awakening of consciousness among those people who could guarantee their long term resolution.[24]

Buttimer, through her concept of an 'intentional' geographer teaching 'intentional' geography, has postulated a geography of social action which is taught by geographers sympathetic to radical social change. However, while it is Buttimer's stated wish to promote radical social change, and while she would probably agree with Blaut's comment that 'Geography works for the oppressor, not the oppressed. It destroys communities, perpetuates poverty and lies to little children,'[25] her radicalism is intellectual rather than political and based on ideas, rather than ideologies, which she regards as closed systems of thought. Thus in her desire to remain intellectually free she is emphasizing the anti-structural and anti-positivist nature of the phenomenological view.

Towards a phenomenologically based school geography

The alternative paradigm which Mercer and Powell, Buttimer, Ley, Relph and others have proposed, uses the phenomenological concepts of intentionality, intersubjectivity and natural attitude in order to produce a geography which concentrates on values, subjective experience and the everyday world. It is a geography which seeks to explicate social problems and issues and which has been dubbed by Graves[26] and others 'humanistic geography'.

The question must now be posed as to whether it is possible to translate this type of geography into the context of the school so as to provide a new paradigm for secondary-school geography. The contention of this article is that the process is possible and the paradigm is desirable. However, if the geography teacher is to teach a humanistic geography which is opposed to the prevailing positivist view, then he or she must reject all positions which regard man as a passive agent who tacitly accepts received truths. Further, the geography which is taught should be seen as a means towards improving the human condition and therefore the teacher should be in agreement with the re-evaluation of the subject matter of geography given by Smith[27] and the comments in the recent HMI paper that geography should have 'a much greater concern for social issues and problems, for example those of the inner areas of larger cities, and the siting of activities which may create disturbance, environmental pollution and social conflict'.[28]

When teaching this alternative paradigm the geography teacher should not merely engage social problems but should be aiming in Buttimer's terminology, at 'a conscientious engagement of social problems'. The key word is conscientious, for the phenomenological view looks towards the stimulation of the individual's consciousness, in relation to social issues, rather than the imposition of an alien system of relevances. In a truly humanistic geography, social issues, values and relevance are vital, not because the teacher is seeking to prescribe reactions to observed facticities, but because the key notion of intentionality dereifies the dualism inherent in positivism between subject and object, fact and value. That is, there will be a relationship of being between man and the world which refutes the notion that man can be isolated from the world as if it were external to him.

The geographic relationship of 'man in the world'[29] must be viewed in the same way so that geographic experience and learning can be seen to emanate from the values, feelings and relevances which make up the everyday world of students. It is also essential that this everyday world is regarded as not only subjective but 'intersubjective' in that many students, through the shared realities of the local environment and the common experience of school, will have similar definitions of the everyday world. Thus acceptance into the conceptual apparatus of geography of the concepts of intentionality, intersubjectivity and natural attitude with their emphasis on the lived experience, values and attitudes, both individual and shared, of the students provides a framework around which to hang a new paradigm of humanistic geography.

Turning from the framework of the paradigm to the fabric of its construction, the first task of the phenomenologically inclined geography teacher should be to highlight the subjective experience of students through making problematic that which is taken for granted within the natural attitude so as to raise their levels of consciousness and understanding in relation to the problems as defined. Thus the starting point for secondary school geography should be those areas of the man-environment relationship which are most taken for granted by the students – their perception of the local environment, their aesthetic and functional appreciation of that environment and the ways in which the environment impinges on the conduct of their everyday activities. From a student-orientated view there should be consideration of the way in which their daily lives are organized, the socioeconomic forces that affect their lives and futures and the human decisions which affect the environment in which they live and act.

Inevitably in such a scheme, intentional students learning intentional geography will define social problems and issues, whether they emanate from personal experience or perceived altruism. Thus for example; the need to alleviate the anomie of the post-industrial metropolis, to reinstate meaning to the land through 'the protection of public buildings, preservation of neighbourhoods, opposition to demolition for motorways and public works, and asserting the sanctity of open space'[30] ought to be part of the geography syllabus. Further, the concern relating to pollution and nuclear power, the sanity or otherwise of continually demanding increased industrial production in a world of finite resources; the whole area of planning and public policy and the burgeoning problems of the inner city; the relations between the developed and underdeveloped worlds are all problems and issues which should be tackled in a geographical paradigm in which fact and value are inseparable and in which intersubjective dialogue between teacher and student, aimed at raising levels of consciousness relating to these problems, is the order of the day.

While the taken-for-granted world should be the starting point for a phenomenologically based geography, it is important that students progress beyond this realm of taken-for-granted experience if the teacher is to claim to have truly raised their levels of understanding. The basic content of geography must remain related to issues, values and relevance but a dynamic epistemology is necessary in order to take account of the students' increasing intellectual maturity and their growing ability to transcend the active present. Such a dynamic epistemology has been presented by Bruner, whose ideas are related to those of Schutz and Mead.[31] Bruner stated that 'the heart of the educational process consists of providing aids and dialogues for translating experience into more powerful systems of notation and ordering'.[32] He suggested that there are three levels of consciousness operating within an epistemology, which he termed enactive, iconic and symbolic. The enactive 'texture' or mode denotes action, the iconic mode relates to direct experience and the symbolic mode assumes the ability to think beyond direct experience, this mode being comparable with Piaget's stage of formal operations. In Bruner's view, even though students may have ways of viewing experience which do not include the symbolic mode, this should not debar them from working within areas which state propositions in highly abstract terms. In order to facilitate this view Bruner proposed what is commonly termed the spiral curriculum whereby the same areas of content can be presented in gradually increasing degrees of difficulty, so as to raise levels of consciousness in the pupils. Clearly, by adopting this epistemology it is possible to start from the base of taken-for-granted experience, to explicate this realm and to use the students' commonsense knowledge to transcend the level of direct experience so as to arrive at symbolic modes of consciousness, without becoming separated from the roots of that symbolic consciousness.

Finally, it is not possible to establish changes in the geographical curriculum without stressing the interrelationship between curriculum and pedagogy. Any change in curriculum should be accompanied by changes in pedagogy. In a philosophical stance which regards the students' experience and view of the world as central, the onus should be put on geography teachers to present their subject in a manner which is consonant with that view of the world. Therefore methods of didactic transmission may be inappropriate and due consideration should be given towards harnessing the students' intentionality and intersubjectivity through group work, heuristic activity and the like.

Conclusion

This article has sought to demonstrate that the precepts introduced by Young (1971) can be transposed into a new paradigm of secondary school geography. The adoption of a phenomenological 'model of man' with its concept of the active pupil, the questioning of taken-for-granted assumptions about the curriculum, the recognition of the socially constructed nature of knowledge, the rejection of objectivist epistemologies and the calling into question of the philosophy of positivism has led to the proposition of a paradigm of school geography which stands opposed to the prevailing positivist paradigm. The basis for the new paradigm is the transcendental phenomenology of Edmund Husserl and in particular his concepts of intentionality and intersubjectivity. The humanistic geography which has resulted takes as its starting point the taken-for-granted experience of children and develops that experience through Bruner's epistemological model of learning and pedagogic processes which recognize the active nature of the student in the classroom. The paradigm presents a practical, intellectually radical geography which attacks issues, recognizes subjective values, restores unity to the man-environment relationship and seeks to expand students' consciousness through subject matter which is relevant to their daily lives and activities. Such consciousness-raising, without the imposition of ideological parameters, will be regarded by some as an impossible task, but if the geography teacher is aware of the implicit and explicit ideological forms which come into his or her explanations then it should be possible to expose pupils to the range of issues involved in the solution of a particular problem without imposing normative judgements on them.

References and notes

1. YOUNG, M.F.D. (Ed) (1971). *Knowledge and Control. New Directions for the Sociology of Education*. London: Collier-Macmillan.
2. GREGORY, D. (1978). *Ideology, Science and Human Geography*. London: Hutchinson University Library, p. 47.
3. PARK, R.E. Quoted in LEY, D. (1977). 'Social geography and the taken-for-granted world,' *Transactions of the Institute of British Geographers*, 2, 4, pp. 498–512.
4. BUNGE, W. (1962). *Theoretical Geography*. Lund Studies in Geography, Series C. General and Mathematical Geography. Sweden: Lund University.
5. BURTON, I. (1963). 'The quantitative revolution and theoretical geography,' *Canadian Geographer*, 7, pp. 151–62.
6. HAGGETT, P. (1965). *Locational Analysis in Human Geography*. London: Edward Arnold.

7.   HARVEY, D. (1969). *Explanation in Geography*. London: Edward Arnold.
8.   DAVIES, W.K.D. (Ed) (1972). *The Conceptual Revolution in Geography*. London: University of London Press.
9.   HAGGETT, P., CLIFF, A. and FREY, A. (1977). *Locational Models*. London: Edward Arnold, p. 23.
10. LEY, D., *op. cit.*, (see Note 3).
11. For a useful summary of the relationship between geography and positivism, see GUELKE, L. Chapter 2 in HERBERT, D.J. and JOHNSON, R.J. (Eds) (1978). *Geography and the Urban Environment*, Vol. 1. New York: Wiley, pp. 35–63.
12. MERCER, D. and POWELL, J. (1972). *Phenomenology and other Non-Positivist Approaches to the Social Sciences*. Geography Department, Monash University.
13. BUTTIMER, A. (1974). *Values in Geography*. Association of American Geographers Commission on College Geography, Resource Paper No. 24.
14. CHISHOLM, M. (1971). *Geography and the Question of Relevance*. Area. 3, pp. 65–8.
15. SMITH, D.M. (1971). *Radical Geography: the Next Revolution*. Area 3, pp. 153–7.
16. HARVEY, D. (1973). *Social Justice and the City*. London: Edward Arnold, p. 129.
17. SCHUTZ, A. Quoted by LEY, D., *op. cit.* (see Note 3).
18. MERCER, D. and POWELL, J., *op. cit.* (see Note 12).
19. HUSSERL, E. (1970). *The Crisis of European Sciences and Transcendental Phenomenology. An Introduction to Phenomenological Philosophy*. Evanston, Illinois: Northwestern University Press.
20. Quoted by RELPH, E. 'An enquiry into the relations between phenomenology and geography,' *Canadian Geographer*, 41, pp. 193–201.
21. LICHTMAN, R. (1970). 'Symbolic interaction and social reality: some Marxist queries,' *Berkeley Journal of Sociology*, 15, pp. 75–95.
22. MERCER, D. and POWELL, J., *op. cit.* (see Note 12).
23. BUTTIMER, A., *op. cit.* (see Note 13).
24. *Ibid.*
25. BLAUT, J. (1974). *Commentary on Values in Geography*. Association of American Geographers Commission on College Geography, Resource Paper No. 24.
26. GRAVES, N.J. (1979). 'Contrasts and contradictions in geographical education,' *Geography*, 64, 4 (November) pp. 259–68.
27. SMITH, D.M. (see Note 15).
28. H.M. Inspectorate. (1978). *Matters for Discussion. 5. The Teaching of Ideas in Geography*. London: HMSO, p. 1.
29. See TUAN, YI–FU (1971). 'Geography, phenomenology and the study of human nature,' *Canadian Geographer*, 15, pp. 181–92.

30. LEY, D., *op. cit.* (see Note 3).
31. MEAD, G.H. and SCHUTZ, A. Respectively the chief proponents of symbolic interactionism and social phenomenology.
32. BRUNER, J. (1967). *Toward a Theory of Instruction.* Cambridge, Massachusetts: Belknap Press, p. 21.

Discovery Learning in School Science: the Myth and the Reality

David Harris

and Michael Taylor

Introduction: the problem

Discovery learning in school science continues to be beset by a number of deep-seated confusions and contradictions. There is considerable literature (Dearden, 1973; Herron, 1970 and Swartz, 1974), which is highly critical of discovery learning in the school curriculum. Dearden suggests that behind discovery learning is abstractionism[1] – the view that concepts can be learnt by drawing them out of objects or apparatus in which they are embedded. Herron attacks discovery learning in the Physical Science Study Committee (PSSC) curriculum which is based 'on a universe governed throughout by fixed and unchanging laws which it is the difficult business of physics to uncover'.[2] Swartz is critical of 'inductive empirical methods'.[3] He argues that children are being encouraged to look for confirming instances which will make them 'dogmatic and closed-minded'.[4]

In spite of these and other criticisms, however, discovery learning has attained the status of near orthodoxy among some science educators. In the two science curricula, PSSC and Nuffield Physics, which we propose to examine later in this article, discovery learning has at times almost a prescriptive flavour, the implication being that discovery learning is indispensable if science teaching is to succeed. To say this is not to attack indiscriminately the imaginative new science curricula of the early 1960s. Some science teachers may be resistant to criticism and reluctant to change practice, but they are at least entitled to ask science educators what discovery learning could mean in school classrooms and laboratories. Are children expected to play the role of research scientists? Are they expected to hit upon the concept of acceleration from their observations of trolleys being tugged along benches? Or is discovery in the context of school science much closer to a more prosaic view of the child re-creating for himself the discoveries of Newton or Boyle under the covert stage-management of the science teacher? Is science waiting locked up in nature to be peered at and dug out by schoolchildren?

It could be that individual science teachers have their own specific answers to these questions on the basis of their own hard-won experience of school laboratories. They may have a view of the philosophy of scientific discovery which comfortably fits their own set of operational strategies when confronted by children struggling to make sense of the natural world. On the other hand, they may feel, as we do, a sense of unease about the obvious disparity between views of an influential contemporary philosopher like Popper and the picture of science which emerges from certain science curricula. A glance at a recent *Nuffield Teachers' Guide,* for example, could give the impression that to discover is to play freely. There is advice to the teacher such as 'Our essential aim, almost the sole aim now, is for pupils to enjoy their experimenting. For what they need are simple general instructions, where to look but not what to look for.'[5] But what are the hidden agendas here? Is it meant that children will naturally discover what to look for by a process of induction and equipped only with general instructions? Or is it meant that children will somehow discover what to look for by interacting with nature at random? Such questions may be unfair to the designers of the Nuffield physics course, but the instructions do suggest a line of inductive thinking which could be open to serious objections.

In this article we propose to look at a number of assumptions and claims concerning discovery learning and to offer tentative suggestions as to what they could mean in the context of school science. At the outset, it needs to be explained that this article is not intended to report any empirical study of the views of science teachers or curriculum designers. We wish, therefore, to draw a sharp distinction between the psychology of discovery learning and its logic. We accept the distinction of Popper[6] (*pace* Kuhn[7]) between the psychology of 'conceiving of a new idea' which is an empirical task, and the logic of various competing claims for discovery learning in school science. At a psychological level, it may be that the act of discovery involves elements of intuition, inspiration, chance – and possibly the irrational – which rule out systematic investigation. It may be, as Einstein put it (quoted by Popper), that 'there is no logical path leading . . . to these laws. They can only be reached by intuition based on something like intellectual love of the objects of experience.'[8] Our concern, however, is not with the psychology of discovery learning, but with the relation between what curriculum designers and science teachers assume about discovery learning and what might be possible in the school laboratory.

Philosophical perspectives

The problem of induction is clearly at the centre of any discussion about discovery learning. This is not the place to rehearse the philosophical arguments in detail. However, ever since Hume displayed the problem, no teacher with any trace of philosophical awareness can fail to wonder at the connection between particular experiments in a school laboratory and the universal propositions of science. As Hume says:

> As to past *experience,* it can be allowed to give direct and certain information of those precise objects only, and that precise period of time which fell under its cognizance: but why this experience should be extended to future times and to other objects which, for aught we know, may only be in appearance similar, this is the main question on which I would insist.[9]

Hume's example is that of eating bread. We always identify bread by colour and consistency. But on another occasion, when we meet another object of similar colour and consistency, we cannot from this observation alone infer that it is edible. We need the additional premise that all such objects of this colour and consistency are edible. Similarly, in science education, there would be no problem with discovery learning if there were a watertight chain of inference from sensory input to universal proposition – from the rolling of trolleys on a bench to Newton's Second Law of Motion. However, the account of discovery learning which starts with observation and progresses to ever-increasing generalizations is utterly at variance with the views of most 20th-century philosophers of science. It is not just that Popper rejects the inductive account of science completely: all his successors, however much they may argue about the difficulties of his falsificationist account of science, are in substantial agreement that, not induction, but hypothesis and then deduction is the method of science.

Nevertheless, the tradition of induction from Bacon and Locke to Mill continues to exercise a persistent influence on science education. For Mill, 'all we know of objects is the sensations which they give us and the order of occurrence of these sensations'.[10] Discovery, according to him, consists firstly in observing, which means receiving particular sensations; and, secondly, in making inferences from these sensations. From these sensations are assembled ideas of objects and then there is a process of generalization to more and more universal theories. 'Laws of Nature . . . ' and ' . . . nothing but the uniformities which exist among natural phenomena . . . when reduced to their simplest expressions.'[11] A teacher's enthusiasm for discovery learning might be further increased by reading that, 'Many of the uniformities existing among natural phenomena are so constant, and so open to observation, as to force themselves upon involuntary recognition'.[12] The objections to these views are well known. In the context of the school laboratory we may point out that a concept such as 'molecule' cannot be assembled out of such sensations as are offered by the moving points of light in the Brownian motion experiment. Nor is it obvious that $F=ma$ is some kind of summary of the experience of children playing with trolleys or similar mechanical apparatus.

Popper's view of science is contrasted with Mill's, but he too makes difficulties for discovery learning and offers no simple non-inductive alternative on which we could base curricula. Popper's criterion for propositions to be scientific is not just that they should be empirically testable but that it should be possible to falsify them. At first sight Popper's position seems fairly simple. If proposition t representing some theory implies an empirically testable proposition e, then the truth of t does not follow from the truth of e (to say so is the fallacy of affirming the consequent) but if e is false then t is also false.[13]

Popper's philosophy of science, however, is not as simple as propositional logic would suggest. While he rejects the inductivist view that observations can 'prove' a theory, he does not, as at first it might seem, replace this view with the alternative one that observations can refute a theory. In fact he denies the possibility of theory–free observations. Even the sentence 'Here is a glass of water' involves the universal terms 'glass' and 'water' and a universal cannot be correlated with a specific sense of experience.[14] Thus Popper is not only denying that a child in school might theorize from simple observation alone: he is denying that there are any such simple observations.

According to Popper it is only 'basic statements' which can refute a theory. These are neither statements of pure sensation nor of observation. A basic statement must be able to falsify a universal statement of the theory, and is thus a singular existential statement.[15] For example, if Newton's First Law of Motion is written as 'All objects with zero force on them are objects moving at constant velocity', then this implies (in this case is logically equivalent to) the statement 'There is no object with zero force and not with a constant velocity'. The negation of this would be a basic statement and a potential falsifier, *viz.* 'There exists an object with zero force which is not moving at constant velocity'. Such an object would be a trolley (such as that used in the PSSC course of Nuffield physics) which accelerated away across the bench by itself. The basic statement in this example is not a simple observation statement: only if the student could apply the concept of 'constant velocity' could he observe that here was a trolley 'disobeying' Newton's First Law of Motion. We hope this perverse example makes clear how difficult it would be to implement a new form of 'discovery learning' on strictly Popperian lines. (Though Swartz has recommended this.[16]) There are also many other difficulties in any curricular use of Popper's account of science. As Duhem originally pointed out, what is offered for refutation is not one proposition *t*, but a whole conjunction of propostions including ones that say 'other things being equal' – that there is no hidden motor in the trolley or that the bearings are rusty.[17] A child in school might be as likely to refute the proposition, 'The apparatus is in good working order and I understand its function', as to refutre a theory of his own. Furthermore, as we have seen when Popper quotes Einstein, he offers no simple recipe as to how a child might in the first place produce theories for testing. Popper offers no replacement for Mill's methods, however much we may disagree with them. In such a curriculum as (Harvard) Project Physics there is a consistently Popperian perspective. For example the text invites the student to examine various possibilities as to how Galileo reasoned about falling bodies. The student is advised:

. . . ask yourself whether Galileo is
— presenting a definition
— stating as assumption (or hypothesis)
— deducing predictions from his hypothesis
— experimentally testing the prediction.[18]

Clearly, the student is being offered these alternatives within the hypothetico-deductive framework.

Pedagogical perspectives

By contrast, in the two curricula which we are about to look at, it may be that the strength of the hypothetico-deductive case is recognized, but the practicalities of the classroom demand a set of procedures based on very different assumptions. The reasons for this are difficult to disentangle but we will suggest that there are perhaps two major factors favouring inductive procedures in the school laboratory. The first is their apparent simplicity. The route suggested by Popper from tentative conjecture via falsification to new hypothesis is difficult enough for scientists (whether or not they are self-conscious of the philosophical niceties of their actions). For children with limited background knowledge, the procedure would seem to be unworkable. Induction, on the other hand, does seem to offer a degree of comforting certainty. The second reason is the apparent scientific credibility the methods of induction have lent pedagogical methods of discovery. When Rousseau said of nature 'all that comes from her will be true' he set in train an inductivist philosophy of education which today is broadly classified as 'child centred' or 'progressive'.[19] Its adherents have included Pestalozzi, Montessori, and in certain respects contemporary psychologists, among them Gagné, Bruner and

Piaget. For example, Montessori appealed to the 'free natural manifestations of the child' as the reason for her advice that the teacher should stand back and observe rather than interfere.[20] It is the child's environment which educates, rather than the teacher. She says, 'In the intellectual life simplicity consists in divesting one's mind of every conception and this leads to the discovery of new things . . . If we study the history of discoveries we will find that they have come from real objective observation and from logical thought.'[21] She provided children with objects of discovery: hollow cylinders that would or would not 'nest'.[22] Thus, not only did she follow Locke in requiring an empty mind to be filled with knowledge, but also, as Dearden points out, she accepts that from things themselves (toys) concepts may be abstracted.[23] Other child-centred educators employ similar 'scientific' terms, such as experiment, observation and investigation; they use a language which stresses the role of the critical, self-motivated, disciplined investigator who rejects not only custom and tradition, but also the teacher as the dominant conveyor of knowledge. The extent to which this inductive view of science and the progressive child-centred approach of discovery learning give one another mutual support in the two curricula under review is one of our concerns.

Two curricula

We would like to look at two recent secondary science curricula to see how they use 'discovery learning'. We saw that, though some kind of rationale for discovery learning could be found in the work of a philosopher like Mill, none such could be found in the works of philosophers of science in this century. However, we cannot rule out the possibility that in recent curricula there are new and convincing ways in which Mill's philosophy has been rehabilitated. We do not undertake the immense task of reviewing whole curricula. We concentrate on two only: PSSC and Nuffield Physics, and we look only at the way in which they prescribe the teaching of 'atoms and molecules' and Newton's Second Law of Motion. The topic, 'atoms and molecules' illustrates the problem of 'discovering' what there is, and Newton's second law has as much claim as any to be a 'law' of science. We keep in mind the questions already raised. What view of science is assumed? In terms of this, how is it possible for children to learn? How may they give reasons to support their new knowledge?

Atoms and molecules: PSSC

The PSSC course introduces atoms as objects as real as 'bricks and chairs'.

> Twentieth century developments of new instruments and new measuring methods have provided us with many independent and fairly direct measurements of atomic dimensions – all of them agreeing so well that there is no longer any doubt about the reality of atoms as building blocks of matter. They are as real as bricks and chairs; they are as much a part of our scientific thought as are rocks and stars – and they are often much easier to manipulate.[24]

There is no suggestion at this stage of atoms and molecules as constructs occurring in models. Thus we might expect that they could be 'discovered', if not by the senses, then with the help of instruments. This is indeed the approach of the PSSC course. There are displays in the students' text of regular structures at varying magnifications, including the 'cannon ball' pattern of a crystal of viruses. There is, however, the caution, 'It is true, of course, that before we use such instruments intelligently we must learn how to interpret what we see'.[25]

There is a long account of Dalton's work. The student is invited to make calculations from data, and the text says that the Law of Multiple Proportions, which the student can see is satisfied by the data, is 'strong evidence for the existence of atoms'. Reference is made to the decay of polonium. It seems that the volume associated with each atom of helium produced is very much larger than the volume of the polonium atom from which it came. The text says, 'These common observations indicate that gases may consist of many particles which take up only a small part of the space occupied by the gas as a whole'.[26] Now these volumes are *not* 'common observations'. They are indirectly inferred. If we pause to imagine how the experiment could be carried out, it becomes evident that the PSSC text must simplify the details, as indeed it does. So far, it looks as if the PSSC text is forcing its story about atoms and molecules to fit a 'look-then-think' account.

However, the student is then told that the intention is to construct a model of a gas. He is told that models are tested to see what properties the physical system that they represent should have so that these properties can be sought in the laboratory. The text goes on to describe the usual kinetic model of gases and shows how it explains their properties.

We now seem to have departed from the inductive approach which has been criticized by Elkana[27] and Herron.[28] Molecules not only appear as objects in the world, but as constructs in the model. In an account of how kinetic theory explains Boyle's Law, there appears to be a mixing of the model and the experiment which it interprets. For example we read, 'By closing the valve we can keep the gas compressed in that volume which now contains more molecules than before'.[29]

In the context, the *valve,* a piece of laboratory hardware, and the *molecules,* constructs in the kinetic model, are in quite different categories. Before criticizing the PSSC course for lack of clarity, it is worth remembering that this mixing of observable objects and postulated entities is just what scientists do all the time without hesitation. Most scientists are realists, and part of learning science is to learn to use the accepted concepts almost as if they were in the same category as objects. The designers of PSSC were academic physicists, not schoolteachers, and the text reflects this. Brownian motion comes at the *end* of the section of kinetic theory. There are no experiments (in contrast, as we shall see, to Nuffield Physics), and the student is just told that, 'the chaos of the molecules can be seen in a fascinating group of experiments. The botanist Robert Brown . . . .'[30]

The PSSC course seems to use two, at first sight contradictory, approaches to atoms and molecules. At first they are taken as real objects and it is implied that the student could discover them for himself if he had the apparatus to do so. This is what Elkana and Herron have criticized. But then the course mixes construct and object in the way that working scientists do.

Atoms and molecules: Nuffield Physics

Nuffield physics has a long, and for the teacher, complicated, treatment of atoms and molecules and we only indicate the overall approach. The introduction to the *Year 1 Teacher's Guide* says, 'we shall treat atoms as familiar things from the beginning and encourage children to learn more about them; but we shall maintain a warning flag by asking again and again in the early years: How do you know there are atoms? How . . . .'[31] The *Guide* also advises:

> Start the year by letting pupils look at a variety of materials: looking, feeling, smelling, weighing them by hand and so on . . . Science is rooted in observation, so our physics course may well start with a gathering together and extension of children's experience. We can raise questions from these observations, which may direct the work in various ways.[32]

And yet when the children handle crystals the *Guide* says, 'Both teachers and pupils should ask questions about crystals and we should encourage the suggestion that some things must be arranged in a regular array inside crystals, things too small to see – "atoms"'.[33]

These three quotations seem almost inconsistent. In the first one children are to take atoms for granted, even if they are to worry as to how they know about them. In the second quotation their knowledge is to be an extension of experience. In the third one the teacher is to encourage the children to say that there 'must' be things too small to see, as if this was implied by the regular shape of crystals. We suggest that an enthusiasm for letting children be 'scientists for the day' has distorted this advice to teachers. Later on, it is made quite clear where the idea of atoms comes from: 'when we [sic] have given the children the idea of small particles or bits of which everything is composed . . . '.[34]

We saw that in the PSSC course Brownian motion is used in a confirmatory way *after* the introduction of kinetic theory. In Nuffield Physics, the experiment is used to *introduce* kinetic theory and is done by the children themselves *three* times during the course. The teacher's guide says, 'This is one of the most crucial experiments in the whole course and should not be sacrificed or rushed. Pupils need a considerable time to look into a microscope and decide what they are seeing.'[35] The teacher is to say, 'Watch the tiny specks and you will see them dancing about. You cannot see the air molecules but you can see that something is jostling these much bigger specks.'[36] Not only are the children told that they 'can see that something is jostling these bigger specks', but they are shown mechanical models – steel-balls being knocked about, and marbles rolling on a tray. It would now be more correct to say that they are being told what to make of the experiment rather than being left 'to decide what they are seeing'. Though the *Teacher's Guide* says that children should be given time to do the experiment themselves, nothing would be lost by a demonstration. There is only one thing to see – how the specks of light move. The experiment is not open-ended in the sense that different outcomes are possible. The difficulties of persuading the smoke to stay in the cell and of adjusting the microscopes are distractions rather than valuable experience. In short, this is *not* discovery learning, however much it may be dressed up as such in the quotations which we have seen from the *Teacher's Guide*.

There is no space here to describe the long sequence of demonstrations and reasoning about molecules related to observation of diffusion of bromine.[37] This continues with hints and leading questions from the teacher. Perhaps more surprises (as when the bromine almost instantly fills the evacuated tube, which children could be led *not* to expect) would help children to generate their own questions, rather than follow the questions of the teacher. It is difficult to summarize the Nuffield Physics treatment of atoms and molecules. The apparent inconsistencies seem to be related to an ideology of discovery learning which it is difficult to implement.

Newton's Second Law: PSSC

We now move from 'atoms and molecules' to see how Newton's Second Law of Motion is introduced by the same two curricula.

The PSSC *Teacher's Resource Book* says, 'Newton's law of motion is based on a wide range of experiments and observations, which are described in this and succeeding chapters'.[38] And goes on to say that, 'The quantitative relationship between force and motion is formulated directly from simple experiments'.[39] The experiments involve accelerating a puck with one, or two, or three rubber loops and calculating the corresponding acceleration from measurements of marks on the paper-tape. The students are asked to find how the change in velocity depends on the force ($\Delta v \alpha F$), and how the change in velocity depends on the time ($\Delta v \alpha t$), so that $F \Delta t \alpha \Delta v$. The test says, 'Further experiments show that this result is general'.[40] Inertial mass is introduced as the constant of proportionality and so, with choice of absolute units, $F=mv/\Delta t$.

The text discusses other experiments which the student cannot do, and refers to Einstein's work saying, 'This modification does not overthrow Newton's law: it includes and extends it'.[41] Kuhn would not agree.[42] We see here what Herron means when he says that PSSC has a 'logic of conclusions' in which there is only one truth about the universe to be approached.[43]

Newton's Second Law: Nuffield Physics

The Nuffield Physics course devotes a lot of time to the teaching of Newton's mechanics and provides extensive advice for teachers of which we can only indicate the outlines relevant to Newton's Second Law of Motion.

There is a version of Galileo's experiment with 'diluted gravity' using a trolley on a slope. The *Teacher's Guide* says,

Then each pupil should make his own chart and look at it carefully. The teacher should not suggest what the result should be or what the actual result means: this should be an interesting discovery for pupils even though they do not know quite how to describe the result that they see. Some pupils will see clearly that they have 'constant acceleration', in the sense that the speed increases by the same amount from each time interval to the next. To others, the straight line of the tops of strips will merely mean that there is something interesting about the motion – and for them we should leave it like that.[44]

The 'interesting discovery' could be, as the text says, that the tops of the strips of paper-tape form a slanting line. But this could more correctly be called an 'interesting observation'. It is quite another matter for the pupils to infer from this that the speed increases by a constant amount in a constant time interval. Even with help from the teacher, the pupils would have to understand that the length of each tape is proportional to the speed and then that the 'extra length' will be proportional to the increase in speed during the time interval in which the tape was made.

In Year IV of the course, the work of Year III is repeated in a spiral curriculum and then extended to Newton's Second Law of Motion. The guide says about Newton's laws, 'The laws are great guiding summaries, consistent with the behaviour of things in our world'. And 'we do not regard them as simple experimental laws: to us they are a mixture of experimental knowledge and definitions which we assume to organise our science'.[45] It is consistent with this view that the *Teacher's Guide* advises, 'In Year IV we should give pupils a good opportunity to explore Newton's Laws of Motion by their own experimenting – not to discover those laws, but to make measurements that illustrate them'. And 'Our object is not so much to provide a convincing demonstration of Newton's Second Law as to give pupils a personal feeling for forces and masses and their connection with motion – through their own experimenting'.[46]

In spite of the consistency of these quotations, there remains a curious submission to the idea of discovery learning. After the pupils have pulled a trolley with one, two or three units of force, the *Guide* recommends that:

> Pupils should be left on their own to draw conclusions from their graphs. It is much less valuable, though much quicker for the teacher to impose a well-taught conclusion. What the pupils find out for themselves from the slopes of these graphs (without ever being told to look at the slopes) will remain in their minds as one of their discoveries in physics – particularly if we can tell them that they are finding out part of the story of Newton's great Laws of Motion.[47]

We may ask what it is that the pupils 'find out for themselves' from the graphs. They *may* be able to spot that the gradients of the graphs are in the ratio 1 : 2 : 3, but it is a big step to say that the acceleration is proportional to the applied force. It is only *after* experiments that acceleration is formally given as 'gain in speed/time taken for the gain'.[48]

Trolleys are used again in experiments to lead directly to Newton's Second Law of Motion. The *Teacher's Guide* says that when they have finished the experiment, pupils should have seen for themselves that:

(1) a constant force makes the trolley accelerate, with a constant acceleration.

(2) doubling the force doubles the acceleration, and so on . . .

(3a) the force needed for a chosen acceleration is proportional to the mass;

(3b) when a chosen force acts upon different masses the accelerations are inversely proportional to the masses.[49]

The pupils will have pulled trolleys, seen dots on tape, used rulers on the tape to measure the distances between dots on the tape and so on. But only with a lot of help from the teacher could they have 'seen for themselves' the conclusions listed here. Of course it could be that they have already been taught so well by previous work in the spiral curriculum that they could reach these conclusions, but we suggest that if that were the case, if they understood enough about force, mass and acceleration, then they would already, before doing these experiments, have reached these conclusions.

Progressive pedagogy and inductive science

In the above brief survey of 'atoms and molecules' and Newton's Second Law of Motion in the two curricula, we have made no attempt to infer a single coherent philosophy of science implicit in either of them. However, we would like to use these two curricula to illustrate further our theme that an inductivist view of science has become fused with a 'progressive' view of education.

In the following quotation from the PSSC *Laboratory Guide*, we see an inductivist view spelled out first as experiment preceding theory, secondly as a pedagogical philosophy suggesting that the teacher should respect the feelings of personal participation of the student interacting with nature, and thirdly as a didactic method by which ideas, in some sense already existing, can be drawn out by leading questions:

> Most of the experiments in this guide are so presented as to
> pave the way for reading the text. Thus, students can
> investigate physical phenomenon rather than just verifying
> known conclusions. When a student performs experiments, the
> results of which are not known to him in advance, he gains a
> feeling of personal participation in the discoveries of science;
> both science and the role of the scientist becomes more
> meaningful to him. For this reason detailed instructions have
> been limited to purely technical aspects of the experiments; and
> the necessary guidance on the physical ideas is supplied in short
> introductions and by asking leading questions.[50]

In the next quotation from Nuffield Physics, we find a
parallel view of an inductivist philosophy of science mixed in with
a progressive child-centred philosophy of education. Emphasis
here is on the autonomy of the child, the authenticity of his
laboratory experience, and his emotional involvement in 'being a
detective'.

> A very strong influence in young people's understanding of
> science and scientific work is their own experimental work.
> Professional scientists devise their own experiments, meeting
> difficulties as well as successes, trying things out with a watchful
> eye and a critical mind, more often making short notes than
> writing a long formal report. Our pupils can do the same, with
> both understanding and delight, if we give them opportunity
> and plenty of time. They need this personal experience of
> science. For that, they need time and encouragement; but not
> too much detailed instructions, because they need to feel that it
> is their own experiment and to learn by their mistakes as well as
> their successes. Then they can acquire the feeling of doing
> science, of being a scientist – 'a scientist for the day'. They feel
> the thrill of being a detective – not only finding the clues, but
> doing their own reasoning from them and even assessing their
> reliability.[51]

Conclusion

It might by way of a conclusion be tempting to ignore the philosophical inconsistencies which we have noted and simply resort to a thorough-going pragmatic approach. If there are no clear-cut philosophical guidelines and if there are no direct deductive or inductive connections between, for example, the observation of trolleys rolling on a bench and Newton's Second Law of Motion, then why not resort to what works best in practice? There are two main objections to this. Firstly, successful practice is not in itself any guarantee that the child has learnt from discovery learning. For example, we are sceptical that any method of learning could ever allow children to acquire an understanding of Newton's Second Law of Motion from the unbiased observation of rolling trolleys. Hume's objections, to which we have referred, are fatal to such a conception of discovery learning. If a teacher believes that children are learning in such a way, then we suggest that he is deceiving himself and the children. Secondly, successful practice is also dependent upon value judgements. Unless a science is some unproblematic catalogue of agreed facts, a teacher is forced to endorse a particular view of science. This again is not an empirical matter. Even if a teacher held that science was a rehearsal of agreed facts, that in itself would be a judgement about the nature of science.

If we try to use the pragmatic maxim – 'Do what works', we would need to know in any particular context the criterion for 'what works'. A good example is the 'Copper problem' of Nuffield Chemistry to which Selley has drawn attention.[52] Children see a black coat appear on copper as it is heated and from this are expected to 'deduce' that it has taken something (oxygen) from the air. The *Teacher's Guide* says:

> the idea is to lead the pupils to find out that air is needed for copper to gain weight when heated and thus that the copper has 'taken' something from the air. Once again the pupils are learning to make deductions strictly from the evidence that they see before them and to plan experiments to test those deductions.[53]

Selley correctly points out that it is 'induction' not 'deduction' that is being asked for. We would further add that this experiment might well 'work' for a teacher who had accepted the particular inductive view of science implicit here. If it does work, it is only, however, in the context of a tightly circumscribed (not to say dogmatic) conception of science. In this case there is a surreptitious value judgement within the concept 'works' as to how science ought to proceed, *viz.* inductively. It could be claimed that the experiment 'works' for children. Children may, for example, derive from it some understanding of oxidation. We might ask a child how he knew that the copper had combined with oxygen and how this explained the change in mass. What could he reply? The experiment would have 'worked' for him if he said, 'I discovered that the copper had got heavier'. But if he goes on to say that he 'discovered' that the copper took something from the air, he is not, of course, misinformed, but he is utterly mistaken if he believes that he has discovered this from the experiment alone.

A curriculum-designer, too, might claim that the experiment 'works'. He might, for example, test children's understanding of the experiment but this test would only give him 'feedback' in a form predetermined by the concept of inductive science within which he was operating.

If a child is being educated rather than just trained or indoctrinated, he must have at least some grounds for his belief. The problem with an inductive view of science which suggests that there is an immutable chain of inferences from initial observation to final conclusion is that it rules out the possibility of alternative explanations. The complaint then would be that science teaching is indoctrination. Alternatively, it could be argued that a genuine science education is a practical impossibility for most children and the most that we can hope for is a form of training. The critical difference between indoctrination and training is that while indoctrination always involves a closed system of teaching and learning, training leaves open the possibility of eventual critical reassessment. Perhaps, for most children, training in getting apparatus to work, using it for a simple purpose, and carrying out simple calculations is the most that we can hope for. For some children we may have the additional hope that they can give some kind of justification for their beliefs in a critical way. It is more likely that these educationally desirable objectives will be picked up as an integral part of good non-dogmatic science teaching rather than formal lessons in the philosophy of science. Paradoxically, it is the education of science teachers rather than the education of children where the philosophy of science matters. We would like to encourage teachers to be more critical of the assumptions on which many science curricula are based. We suggest that science teachers be encouraged to take an interest in the controversies in the philosophy of science. It is our hope that they may approach their task with a greater appreciation of the intentions of curriculum-designers and be less likely to accept naïve approaches to discovery learning – less likely to waste the time of children with undirected experimenting, and less likely to deceive them with oversimple justifications.

References

1. DEARDEN, R.F. (1973) 'Instruction and learning by discovery.' In: PETERS, R.S. (ed.) *The Concept of Education.* London: Routledge & Kegan Paul, p. 144.
2. HERRON, M.D. (1970). 'The nature of scientific inquiry,' *School Review*, 79, p. 199.
3. SWARTZ, R. (1974). 'Induction as an obstacle for the improvement of human knowledge,' *Proc. Phil. Educ.*, p 376.
4. *Ibid.*, p. 375.
5. *Revised Nuffield Physics Teachers' Guide, Year 3.* London: Longman, p. 8.
6. POPPER, K.R. (1972). *The Logic of Scientific Discovery.* London: Hutchinson, p. 31.
7. KUHN, T.S. (1972). *The Structure of Scientific Revolutions*, 2nd edn. University of Chicago Press, p. 9.
8. POPPER, *op. cit.*, p. 32.
9. HUME, DAVID (1962). 'An inquiry concerning human understanding.' In: FLEW, A. (ed.) *On Human Nature and the Understanding.* London: Collier-Macmillan, p. 53.
10. MILL, J.S. (1925). *A System of Logic*, 8th edn. London: Longman, p. 38.
11. *Ibid.*, p. 208.
12. *Loc. cit.*
13. POPPER, *op. cit.*, p. 76.
14. *Ibid.*, p. 94.
15. *Ibid.*, p. 102.
16. SWARTZ, *op. cit.*, p. 382.
17. DUHEM, P. (1977). *The Aim and Structure of Physical Theory.* New York: Atheneum, p. 187.

18. *Project Physics Text* (1970). New York: Holt, Rinehart and Winston, Unit 1, p. 47.
19. ROUSSEAU, J.J. 'The origins of inequality.' In: *The Social Contract and Other Discourses.* Everyman Translation, Dent and Sons, London, p. 176.
20. MONTESSORI, M. (1912). *The Montessori Method.* London: Heinemann, p. 15.
21. *Ibid.,* p. 253.
22. *Ibid.,* p. 338.
23. DEARDEN, R.F. (1967). 'Instruction and learning by discovery.' In: PETERS R.S. (ed.) *The Concept of Education.* London: Routledge & Kegan Paul, p. 145.
24. PHYSICAL SCIENCE STUDY COMMITTEE (1965). *Physics,* 2nd edn. Boston: Heath, p. 125.
25. *Ibid.,* p. 126.
26. *Ibid.,* p. 137.
27. ELKANA, Y. (1970). 'Science, philosophy of science and science teaching,' *Educational Philosophy and Theory,* 2, p. 22.
28. HERRON, *op. cit.,* p. 199.
29. PHYSICAL SCIENCES STUDY COMMITTEE, *op. cit.,* p. 165.
30. *Ibid.,* p. 171.
31. *Nuffield Physics Teachers' Guide, Year 1* (1966). London: Longman, p. 11.
32. *Ibid.,* p. 114.
33. *Ibid.,* p. 123.
34. *Loc. cit.*
35. *Ibid.,* p. 253.
36. *Ibid.,* p. 228.
37. *Nuffield Physics Teachers' Guide, Year 4* (1966). London: Longman, p. 210.
38. PHYSICAL SCIENCES STUDY COMMITTEE (1966). *Teacher's Resource Book and Guide,* Part III. 2nd edn. Boston: Heath, p. 19.
39. *Loc. cit.*
40. PHYSICAL SCIENCES STUDY COMMITTEE, *Physics, op. cit.,* p. 325.
41. *Ibid.,* p. 329.
42. KUHN, *op. cit.,* p. 101.
43. HERRON, *op. cit.*
44. *Nuffield Physics Teachers' Guide, Year 3* (1966). London: Longman, p. 245.
45. *Nuffield Physics Teachers' Guide, Year 4* (1966). London: Longman, p. 8.
46. *Ibid.,* p. 3.
47. *Ibid.,* p. 37.
48. *Ibid.,* p. 39.
49. *Ibid.,* p. 45.
50. PHYSICAL SCIENCES STUDY COMMITTEE (1967). *Laboratory Guide,* 2nd edn. Boston: Heath, p. iv.

51. *Nuffield Physics Teachers' Guide, Year 1, op. cit.*, p. 3.
52. SELLEY, N.J. Models, theories, and Nuffield Chemistry. Submitted to *Education in Chemistry.*
53. *Revised Nuffield Chemistry Teachers' Guide I* (1975). London: Longman, p. 73.

Part Four

Curriculum, School and Teacher

It would be trite but true to say that the school is the context for the transaction of the curriculum and that its transaction is the prime justification of the teacher's role. Without something to teach, teachers would be other than they are and without courses of study schools would have little meaning. As it is, they are central to the process of education as the first two papers in this section fully recognize.

Linblad's paper examines the role of the school as an agent of curriculum innovation. He asks:

Where does the initiative for an innovation originate?
Who participates in the innovation and why?
Who communicates the experience of the innovation?
Who are the receivers of the information about the innovation and how highly do they rate it?

He employs empirical data to answer these questions and concludes by answering a more fundamental question. Does school-centred innovation work?

Popkewitz's canvas is broader, though he is also interested in studying change and development. He uses as his 'case' a curriculum development project, that of Individually Guided Education (IGE), rather than the school as Lindblad did. In order to see how development worked in six exemplary elementary schools which had adopted IGE, he postulates three contexts: a pedagogic context, the occupational context of teaching and a social-cultural context, each of which he explains in detail; characterizing each as a mirror *to hold up to the sample schools and from the* reflections *discern how each of the schools and its teachers in their particular milieu respond to the innovation. By this means Popkewitz seeks to make reliable generalizations about the configurations of schooling – the balance between its contexts – which make for differing responses to change.*

Lampert's paper belongs to a different genre *for seeking to understand an aspect of the curriculum in transactions. She recounts how teachers (and others) talk about teaching thinking and from these accounts attempts an analysis of how teachers think about teaching. In using anecdotal material to effect, Lampert shows how valuable insights may be gained into the way in which teachers think about dealing with the commonplaces of the curriculum – subject matter, the student, the context and the teacher himself, in the business of teaching – which the use of a rational scientific research paradigm would not have revealed in anything but a limited and dessicated fashion.*

Further reading

ANDERSON, L.W. (1981). 'Instruction and time, on lax,' *Journal of Curriculum Studies* 13, 4, 305–12.

CORNBLETH, C. (1984). 'Beyond the hidden curriculum,' *Journal of Curriculum Studies,* 16, 1, 29–36.

GRIFFITHS, J. (1984). 'Eggy bread and Paddy's bacon: instances in the traffic in knowledge in a classroom of children with severe learning difficulties,' *Journal of Curriculum Studies,* 16, 1, 67–74.

SCHMIDT, W.H. (1983). 'High school course-taking: a study of variation *and* High school course-taking: its relationship to achievement,' *Journal of Curriculum Studies,* 15, 2, 167–82 and 15, 3, 311–32.

STODOLSKY, S.S., FERGUSON, T.L. and WIMPELBERG, K. (1981). 'The recitation persists, but what does it look like?,' *Journal of Curriculum Studies* 13, 2, 121–30.

The Practice of School-Centred Innovation: A Swedish Case

Sverker Lindblad

Introduction

Times have changed – and so have strategies for achieving and maintaining innovations in education. Such changes in the UK and USA are described by House.[1] Roughly the same pattern of change has occurred in Sweden.[2] One main feature of these changes will be in focus here, namely that of decentralizing innovative work.

Reasons for such a decentralization are manifold. I will mention two of them. First, criticism of centralized innovative efforts has been intense, particularly with reference to the R & D model.[3,4] This criticism has focussed on many aspects – ideological as well as that of actual impact.[5] Second, in Sweden at least, there have been structural changes in the educational system towards more decentralization in administration and decision-making, as well as in curriculum activities.

At the same time as centralized innovative work has been criticized, more decentralized variants have been proposed.[3,6] In a recent article Hargreaves has questioned the promises of current decentralized attempts to deal with innovation in education – which he labels 'school-centred innovation' (SCI):

> In effect, although the heady rhetoric of SCI persists, promising everything from an effective method of managing innovation in schools, to the realization of staff democracy, fraternity and liberty, its practical success in actual instances of local changes is, judged by the very limited amount of research available to date, precariously balanced on a knife edge of uncertainty.[7]

In the present study I will deal with some features of an early example of decentralized innovative work in Sweden. The question in focus is 'Who is doing what?' The reason behind this question is as follows. Decentralization and democratization are concepts often linked to each other in various ways. Sometimes these concepts are held to be synonymous, but it is also possible to treat them as independent – decentralization can occur without democratization. Since the school system – even at the local level – is a formal as well as an informal hierarchy, it seems realistic to assume that this hierarchy will influence decentralized innovative work. This means that those in higher formal and informal positions will exert greater influence on such work. It is this assumptions that will be tested here.

The case and its context

The context of the case is the Swedish educational system in the 1970s. This system has long been centralized to a high degree – parliament decides on the curriculum and organization of both primary and secondary education; there are very few private schools.

In 1962, primary and lower secondary schools were integrated to form a single compulsory school – the comprehensive school reform. This reform to a very large extent was based on political consensus, but was carried through in the face of resistance from large groups of teachers and teacher educators.[8] The comprehensive and integrative reform of the compulsory school had implications for the non-compulsory school. This resulted in an integrated upper secondary school in 1972. Although there have been further curricular reforms since then, in 1972 the main feature of Swedish primary and secondary education today were established.

Parallel to these school reforms a significant change in the organization of Swedish society occurred. In 1950 there were about 2500 municipal councils, these being the local education authorities; this number was reduced by 90 per cent 20 years later. The argument for such centralization at the local level was that it would increase the capacity of local authorities to meet their obligations in the welfare state. As a consequence the administrative apparatus at the local level expanded considerably.

That the main features of the school reforms were established, and centralization at the local level achieved, can be regarded as two premises for a decentralization of school administration, planning, etc., at least from the central authority's point of view. Taking into consideration demands for cuts in public expenditure and the political instability of the government in the 1970s, an increased decentralization has to date been carried out in various ways – in administration, curriculum and finance for example.

Corresponding to these changes in the educational system, a decentralization of innovative work also occurred. This had been preceded by increasing demands for such innovative work since the early 1970s. These demands can to some extent be regarded as a reaction against an earlier predominant model of educational innovation. The strength of this reaction increased as the situation in the educational system changed as described above.

From the early 1960s there had been organized attempts to carry out decentralized innovative work in the form of 'local multi-project development schemes'. Such a scheme is based on the following premises:

(a) A scheme is located in a municipal district for five years, during which time it is financed on an equal-shares basis by the state and the local authority. After that period the support of the state is discontinued, with the expectation that innovative work will continue in the district and serve as 'a mechanism of self-renewal'.

(b) About one scheme a year is started. The central authority determines where it should be set up after consulting with a number of municipal councils (mostly large or medium-sized). The central authority determines the general theme of the scheme in question. Under this theme a large number of innovative projects can be carried out.

(c) One aim of the schemes is to involve as many teachers as possible in innovative work. Attention is not focussed on transferable solutions to school problems, but on solving problems of a situation-specific character and producing a climate more conducive to innovation in the schools concerned.

(d) To support the various project groups there is a project guidance team consisting of two to four people, who advise and give assistance with evaluations, reporting, etc. The guidance team also reports back to the decision-making committee responsible for the scheme.

The multi-project schemes lived a life of obscurity until the early 1970s when other decentralization tendencies grew stronger. They then came into focus, and were analysed and evaluated from different points of view.

In the present study I will describe and analyse some features of the schemes – a reanalysis of findings published earlier.[9] In my analysis I will concentrate on one scheme in order to support my arguments.

Method

The following analyses are based on information obtained by two main methods: documents such as minutes, agendas and reports; and a postal survey of the school staff in the municipality concerned. The survey was directed to all participants in the development scheme and to a random sample of non-participants. A major principle was to cross-validate findings achieved in one way with those achieved in another way. Since other schemes have been studied in similar ways it is possible to relate the findings to these other cases. However, this will only be done in my concluding discussion.

The postal survey was designed to obtain information about two populations – voluntary participants in the innovative work of the local multi–project development schemes ($N = 176$) and members of school staffs who did not take part ($N = 1580$). For the first population, the sample was identical with the population; for the other, a simple random sample of every fourth individual was made.

The final response level was 91 per cent of the participators and 84 per cent of the sample of non-participators. Since there was some ambiguity about a few responses, the replies available for the analyses presented here was reduced to 82 per cent of participators ($N = 152$) and 82 per cent of non-participators ($N = 332$).

In order to define different categories in the sample, the

following distinctions were made:

Formal position:	High:	Headteachers (principals), heads of department.
	Low:	class teachers, primary level.
Informal position:	Higher:	more than 10 years' work in school.
	Lower:	less than 10 years' work in school.

These distinctions are based on conventional assumptions about the schools' formal and informal hierarchies. The distinction concerning formal position excludes a number of persons in the sample – this was necessary in order to simplify the presentation and discussion of results.

Results

The questions asked will be answered one by one and then considered as a whole in the final section.

Where does the initiative for innovative projects originate?

It is usually argued that the initiative for projects of this kind is taken by the grassroots – by ordinary teachers. In the present case the picture emerging from an analysis of the documents available is quite different. In fact, 18 out of 28 projects were set up by the Swedish National Board of Education, eight by the local education department and two by teachers. Thus, initiatives originated to a very limited extent in schools themselves.

The same conclusion could be drawn when studying other multi-project schemes. In one case this manifested itself in a slightly different way. The local education department turned to the local conference of principals for suggestions on innovative projects. Having been given such suggestions, it then turned to the National Board of Education and asked what to do. These manoeuvres resulted in a cluster of projects perceived as coming from the schools but in fact initiated by the National Board of

Education.

From the description above it could be concluded that the direction of the innovative work undertaken as part of the local development schemes would be of very great interest to the National Board of Education. However, analyses of the operations of the Board showed that the direction of such work seemed to be of minor interest.

Who participates in the innovative work and why?

Participation in projects was a question for each individual to decide upon – with the claimed ambition that as many members of school staff as possible would be engaged in the innovative work. In the present case we found that just over 10 per cent were actually participating. One way of determining why they participated is to analyse how they became members of the project group. From Table 1 we can see that their own initiative played a minor role. The fact that so few of the participants were 'self-recruited' can be put down to the way the scheme was implemented via established communication channels from the local centre to the periphery.

What kinds of people, then, participate? According to the criteria of positions – formal and informal – it is possible to conclude from Table 2 that a high formal position is related to eased entry to the development work, perhaps to a greater extent than a high formal position.

Table 1:   Recruitment of project members

Recruited by	Percentage
Education department/headteachers (principals)	42
Other teachers	32
Own initiative	20
Other ways	6

To conclude: participators in innovative work occupy to a fairly great extent a high formal position in the hierarchy of the local

Table 2. Formal and informal positions among participators and non-participators in the local development scheme

Position	Participators		Non-participators	
	N	%	*N*	%
High formal position	62	41	64	20
Low formal position	44	29	139	43
Intermediate formal position	46	30	119	37
Σ	152	100	322	100
Higher informal position	106	70	172	53
Lower informal position	46	30	150	47
Σ	152	100	322	100

school system. They participate mostly – according to their own statements – because they have been asked to participate.

Who communicates experiences from innovative work?

Experiences from such activities as innovative work as part of the local development schemes can be communicated in various ways. There are informal channels, such as discussions among colleagues on the school staff – channels which more than half the participants stated that they had used.

As for more formal ways of communicating experience, we find the following in order of frequency: written reports, teachers' one-day seminars, departmental staff meetings, prepared materials, meetings of heads of department, courses etc. Almost half of the group participants spent time writing reports and about one-third presented their work at one-day seminars and department staff meetings. In all, nearly 75 per cent of the participants used these more formal means of communication.

What kind of people, then, communicate their experiences? We can study this in Table 3. From the results shown in Table 3 we can conclude that position in the school staff hierarchy is closely related to the actual use of different kinds of communication channel, even in this very selected group. A high formal or informal position seems to be accompanied by easier access to information channels.

Table 3: The use of different kinds of communication channels in relation to formal and informal position

Position	Number of channels used			Total
	0	*1*	*2-5*	
High formal position	18	29	53	100
Low formal position	43	18	39	100
Higher informal position	10	31	59	100
Lower informal position	83	15	2	100

Who are the receivers of information and how highly do they rate this information?

A total of 1625 copies of reports (51 titles), relating to the local development scheme in question were sent out. About half of these were distributed within the local school system and a quarter to political/administrative bodies (the National Board of Education, other local education departments). Very few reports were sent to people involved in other multi-project developments, schemes (three per cent) or to university departments of educational research (0 per cent).

It is not possible to analyse the total impact of communication from the present local development scheme. I will restrict myself here to the target of the local school system. The sample of the school staff were asked to say whether they had come into contact with the local development scheme via various channels of communication – a total of eight different options (reports, personal communications, seminars, etc.) that turned out to be used in practice. Table 4 shows how different positions are related to quantitative access to channels. We can see that position – formal and informal – is related to access to information about the lessons learnt by the local development scheme. But access to information is not the same thing as access to subjectively valuable information. Thus, in Table 5, it is shown to what extent the different categories valued the information they received via the different information channels. Those who had no contact with the local development scheme are not included in the table. So those who fall under the heading 'O' are the percentage of the population which had contact with the scheme, but considered it to be of no value. From Table 5 we can conclude that the access of staff to information of value for their own work is related to their position in the local school system: those holding higher positions tend to find the information of more value than those in lower positions.

Table 4: Number of communication channels by which non–participating school staff came into contact with the local development scheme

Position	Number of channels				Σ
	0	1–2	3–4	5+	
High formal position	7	12	38	43	100
Low formal position	18	27	32	14	100
Higher informal position	7	22	31	39	100
Lower informal position	20	28	39	9	100

Table 5. Number of information channels considered to be of value by those coming into contact with the local development scheme in relation to position

Position	Number of valued information channels				
	0	1-2	3-4	5+	Σ
High formal position	37	26	30	7	100
Low formal position	59	22	11	7	100
Higher informal position	45	29	17	9	100
Lower informal position	61	19	15	5	100

Discussion

The results give us a picture of a form of decentralized innovative work adjusted to the hierarchy of the school. The work is initiated from above. It is performed to a great extent by individuals holding higher positions in the local school system's hierarchy. To a still greater extent, individuals belonging to these categories are those who communicate their experiences to others and receivers of this information are to a great extent individuals in a similar position. Such individuals hold the information received to be of more value than do individuals in lower positions. In sum: decentralized innovative work is – in the present case – run by and for the establishment of the school system.

Is this a unique pattern – or is it possible to generalize it to include other instances of decentralized innovative work? First, it can be stated that similar tendencies predominated in other local multi-project development schemes in Sweden.[9] The most immediate explanation, then, is that the features are consequences of the organizational framework within the given historical context. From this conclusion, it is perhaps possible to generalize to decentralized innovative work in other contexts, but with a similar organizational structure. Such a generalization depends on how the context is dealt with.

Second, it might be argued that the features presented can be predicted as manifestations of certain characteristics of educational phenomena. The potential for generalization is dependent on the theoretical meaning of the pattern presented. Such an attempt to generalize might be fruitful in the long run, since it provides opportunities to link the question of innovative work in education to more general concepts concerning schooling.

From this point of view, the fact that decentralized innovative work is under the control of the school establishment can be regarded as an expression of the reproduction of power and legitimacy within the school system – subsumed under the reproductive function of the school in society. From this general theoretical point of view the results seem fully intelligible.

If one considers the potential impact of innovative work, two outcomes are possible. First, we might assume that the impact is forceful. In order to maintain the *status quo* or to strengthen its own position, the establishment has either to control the products of the work (including implementation and adaptation) or the process (via initiation, direction and regulation or via reliable actors). The last alternative seems to tie in rather well with the picture presented earlier of the current case. However, it can easily be shown that there was little or no overt conflict over the direction of and participation in the innovative work concerned here. This goes against the first theoretical outcome – at least to some extent.

Let us turn to the other theoretical outcome, where it is assumed that the impact is of little importance. In this case the control of products or the process is rather unnecessary. If one looks at the present results, such an outcome seems to tally fairly poorly. There is selective recruitment, etc. On the other hand, the impact actually seems far from forceful – a feature this work has in common with many other attempts in the history of educational innovation – when one considers the assessments made by those informed of the experiences. How does the impact fit in with the nature of recruitment? This question might be answered as follows: innovative work of the present kind has less to do with the struggle for change than with the maintenance of the *status quo* and the promise of improvement within current frames. Innovative work of this kind implies loyalty to the establishment. Such loyalty is most easily found among higher positions in the school system. The work performed is an act of loyalty or a fulfilment of obligations.

However, it does not follow from this that all decentralized innovative work is of the present kind. Thus, in a more politicized context, where the implications of different alternatives stand out more clearly, the struggle for change versus the preservation of the *status quo* will perhaps become more clearly visible.

References

1. HOUSE, E. (1979). 'Technology versus craft: a ten year perspective on innovation,' *Journal of Curriculum Studies*, 11, 1.
2. LINDBLAD, S. (1980). 'Om decentraliseringen av det svenska 'skolväsendet och det pedagogiska utveck-lingsarbetet,' *Arbetsrapporter från Pedagogiska institutionen, Uppsala universitet*, 29. (On the decentralization of the Swedish school system and the educational development work.)
3. HOUSE, E. (1974). *Politics of Educational Innovation*. Berkeley: McCutchan.
4. TRAVERS, R. (1973). 'Educational technology and related research viewed as a political force.' In: TRAVERS, R. (ed.) *Second Handbook of Research on Teaching*. New York: Rand McNally.
5. PAPAGIANNIS, G., KLEES, S. and BICKEL, R. (1982). 'Toward a political economy of educational innovation.' *Review of Educational Research*, 52, 2, pp. 245-90.
6. LORTIE, D. (1976). *School Teacher: A Sociological Study*.

Chicago: The University of Chicago Press.
7. HARGREAVES, A. (1982). 'The rhetoric of school–centred innovation,' *Journal of Curriculum Studies,* 14, pp. 251-66.
8. KALLÓS, D. and LUNDGREN, U.P. (1979). *Curriculum as a Pedagogical Problem.* Gleerup, Lund: CWK.
9. LINDBLAD, S. (1982). 'Pedagogiska utvecklingsblock. Studier i en form av lokalt pedagogiskt utveck-lingsarbete,' *Pedagogisk Forskning i Uppsala,* 31. (Local multi-project development schemes. Studies in a form of decentralized educational development work.)

The Social Contexts of Schooling, Change and Educational Research

T.S. Popkewitz

Introduction

'Educational research', 'development' and 'evaluation' are social activities with a related set of ideologies which create perspectives within which classroom practices are viewed. These perspectives are significant, not only because they define the range and nature of the relationships considered in research, but also because they determine the way in which the task of school change and reform is articulated, perceived and realized. Much behavioural and ethnographic research on schooling, for example, tends to treat 'teaching' only as interaction in the specific settings in which teachers and children work. Research within the sociology of educational knowledge, on the other hand, has sought to broaden accounts of 'teaching' and 'classroom life' by focussing on the interplay among classroom practices, professional ideologies and social and cultural interests. Teacher behaviours, classroom patterns, standards of pupil achievement and competence are seen, in this perspective, within the larger historical and social conditions which make specific school practices appear reasonable and credible. In the former perspective, the problem of change is often seen as technical and administrative, in the latter, as political and ideological.

This essay explores some of the ideas suggested by a broad perspective on teaching and learning by considering how a particular reform programme, *Individually-Guided Education* (IGE), is filtered through, and transformed by, the social conditions in which it is realized.[1] By integrating an analysis of a particular programme with other literature that deals with the institutional character of schooling, the potency of an institutional context not only for channelling thought and action, but also for reinforcing and legitimating social values about authority and control can be illuminated.

Individually-Guided Education is an approach to elementary school reform widely used in the United States. Developed at the Wisconsin Research and Development Center to overcome the seeming conservatism of existing institutional patterns, the programme uses mastery-learning techniques (behavioural objectives, criterion–referenced measures) and 'instructional systems' approaches to school organization. It has been adopted by over 3000 elementary schools in the US. Our investigation into the use of the programme in six exemplary IGE schools revealed very different social configurations within the schools that gave coherence to and sustained the practices of schooling we saw. Each school used the reform technologies in a different way, one which responded to its unique social situation. The schools did not merely adapt the programme, making modifications to reach the same goal. Rather, they *revised* both the technology and its espoused goals. These revisions helped to conserve the different institutional conditions in which the IGE technologies were used. In each of the schools, different styles of work, conceptions of knowledge, and professional ideologies were maintained, and each condition of schooling was related to the particular social values and interests found in its larger social/cultural community.

To explore this relation and interaction among the patterns of schooling and their external dimensions we can consider schooling as containing three contexts: *(a)* a *pedagogical context; (b)* the *occupational context of teaching;* and *(c)* a *social/cultural context.* The pedagogical context includes the daily practices and discourse of classroom life and the patterns of this activity which produce conceptions of school work and knowledge. The occupational context of teaching refers to the teaching occupation as a social community which maintains ideologies and mechanisms of legitimacy. The social/cultural context refers to the community in which schools are located; discussions of this context treat the manner in which a community's social/cultural and economic orientations, sensibilities and awarenesses affect school practices. Needless to say, specific teaching behaviours and achievement outcomes, or changes in the nature, quality and effects of schools cannot be considered in isolation from these contexts.

Pedagogical context

We can think of schooling as a socially-chartered institution with a mandate to perform certain agreed-upon functions.[2] These functions generally centre on the forms of socialization in which children are to grow into adulthood. Schooling as an institution constructs and legitimates social categories of competence, defines public classifications of people and knowledge, and provides credentials by which people gain access to valued positions in society. Schooling also has, of course, a mandate to educate, but that mandate is ambiguous and is open to many interpretations. To 'prepare children for a democratic society', for example, can mean (a) to develop individual intellectual capacity so one can engage in rational discourse; (b) to develop an appreciation of and loyalty to given social and political institutions and practices; (c) to learn functional skills so one can be a productive member of a workforce. A general slogan obscures these differences and the possible social values that can be reflected in the practices of schooling.

Because of different, and possibly contradictory, interpretations of the school mandate, the actual purposes or social values created in school experience cannot be taken for granted. We need to recognize that as students participate in the world of a school, they participate in a particular social world which maintains particular lines of reasoning, values and rules. The patterns of schoolwork, for example, teach children to modify and enlarge the possibilities of their human conditions. In doing a reading assignment, manipulating objects for an art lesson, or answering questions on a test, students and teachers alter and improve their world, produce social relations, and intervene in and realize human conditions. But schooling can also be viewed as containing patterns of communication maintaining conceptions of knowledge. As participants in classroom interactions, children develop particular vocabularies, styles of reasoning, myths and commonsense ideas about what is normal, reasonable and permissible in their social encounters. The organization of social studies, for example, provides students with definitions of which social problems are important, with criteria for judging the truth and validity of social statements, and with assumptions about what the elements of a social world are.

In other words, the socially-constructed character of schooling compels us to consider what is learned in school as more than mere subject matter. The dispositions which guide individuals as they act in their world are an essential component of schooling. The form and content of schooling contain assumptions and presuppositions by which students orient themselves to situations and make sense of their activities. Children in school must not only learn the academic subject matter but also the appropriate form in which to cast their academic knowledge.[3] Research about schooling and reform must consider the rules and procedures underlying work and knowledge in pedagogical settings.

The *institutionalized* world of schooling, however, has at least two different layers. First, schooling is a universal moral category. Everyone is expected to go to school. its social arrangements establish categories of knowledge and experts as 'sacred' within society. School provides evaluations of individual competence and achievement that are used not only within school processes but also for providing access to positions of status and privilege in the adult society. The knowledge selection and processes of evaluation seem objective: all are to learn mathematics, science and social studies; all are to believe that they have been dealt with fairly and equitably, in a context in which success and failure are due to personal rather than institutional attributes. But while the rituals and ceremonies of schooling establish the legitimacy of its moral order, the actual social interactions and patterns confronted in the daily life of schooling introduce the second layer of the *curriculum*. Rather than one common school there are different forms of schooling, each with different curricula: ways of dealing with ideas, social values, principles of legitimacy and forms of control. Social science, science and mathematics for example, are not the same for all students. Some are taught that mathematics involves a personal playfulness with numbers, or that science has a tentativeness and scepticism towards the phenomena of the world. For others, mathematics is a maze of facts, and science is a body of predefined tasks and facts. These different forms tend to be obscured by the rituals and ceremonies which make schooling seem common to all.

Schooling as styles of work and conceptions of knowledge

The particular assumptions, rules and procedures that underlie school practices are different from the forms of reasoning and thinking in the larger social world. While public rhetoric uses commonsense labels like 'science', 'social science', 'research', 'literature' or 'poetry' to convey the organization of school activities, it is clear from investigations of schooling that actual classroom practices have little, if any, relation to the occupational communities from which their labels are drawn. How many poets would sit at a desk for six hours a day, following directives of a person who assigns 'creative writing' through notes on a blackboard? Or how many social scientists would check their understanding through essay or multiple-choice items, or gain knowledge about a culture's history, myths and aspirations by reading chapters in a textbook? While the adult community would not accept these activities as worth their effort, the assumptions and models of socialization of schooling form a background in which these curriculum practices are seen as plausible.

Moreover the language that children encounter in schooling is fundamentally different from that which children encounter in their home communities. Comparing interactions in a school and community of working-class black students, Brice-Heath (research in progress) observed that teacher questions were often about things. They asked for labels, attributes and discrete features of objects and events in isolation from the context. Someone always had an answer for the school question, typically the teacher or brightest children in the class, and the answer could usually be given in one word. The interactional tasks of classroom life called for particular types of responses that related to the rituals and routines, the information and skills acquired in the classroom. By contrast, in community interactions 'people asked questions about whole events or objects and their uses, causes, and effects'. The questions in the community generally had no 'right' answer. Instead, the response would involve telling a story, describing a situation, or making comparisons between events or objects. People in the community asked questions that called for analogies, asking 'what is that like'? In those instances in which teachers adopted the question strategies of the community, the movement of ideas was two-way and lessened the dichotomy between us and them. But this was not common.

Classroom interactions typically require that children adopt peculiar ways of reasoning and working, and peculiar notions of competence that relate to the institutional demands of schooling.[4] In doing this, a child's commonsense experiences are reshaped. MacKay explored the dialogue of a reading lesson in which children listened to the story of 'Chicken Little'.[5] In one part, the teacher asked, 'What did it say in the story about Chicken Little, ah, where the nut fell on Chicken Little?' A child responded to the question by saying 'at the tree'. The response was a reasonable answer to the question. However, the teacher treated the child's answer as incorrect and imposed his own scheme of interpretation, without any explanation. 'Um hum what part of his body did it hit or did it say?' The assumption of this, and other teachers' responses is that children have no competence in reasoning and that the purpose of schooling is to impart particular modes of thought and reasoning different from those found in the home or community.

The peculiar forms of reasoning learned in school can be illustrated by the distinction between *work* and *play*. Work is what the teacher gives directions for children to do.[6] Children perceived colouring, drawing, waiting in line, cleaning up or singing as *work* because these were the activities they were told to do. The definitions of work had no intrinsic relation to the specific activities being performed. Classroom work was related to certain social relations in classroom life. All work activities were compulsory and done in unison. Identical products were sought to produce the same ends. Classroom work was arbitrarily defined and given meaning by the teachers. *Play* was those activities which were permitted only if time allowed and only when children had finished their assigned work.

We have considered the social patterns of schooling as maintaining forms of consciousness different from those of larger adult communities. *However, these styles of thinking and forms of schoolwork must not be seen as unidimensional or universal.* There is no archetypical school. Rather, different types of schooling emphasize different linguistic, intellectual and social competencies. Different institutional structures provide children with various ways of engaging in social relations, comprehending the world, and defining possibilities for enlarging social and cultural conditions. Thus Keddie, in a study of three social studies streams in an English high school, argues that, while teaching the same material, the teachers adjusted educational goals, rewarded and punished different behaviours, and emphasized different criteria for social science inquiry according to their perceptions of the children's competence.[7] The analysis found that the expectations and responses teachers maintained for the different tracks of students were based upon latent social-class criteria. The differences between the 'A' (high ability) and 'C' (low ability) students responded not so much to the qualities of the groups but rather to willingness of the 'A' students to accept the teachers' categories and definitions, which conformed to certain middle-class expectations. The 'C'-track students were thought to need 'non-intellectual' materials and were instructed in ways that reinforced the teachers' perception of the students' ascribed status as workers in adult life. Keddie concludes that ability is an organizing notion deriving largely from *social* judgements; the patterns of schooling reflect, in their turn, this organizing notion of differential ability.

Curriculum and pedagogy in IGE schooling: technical, constructive and illusory

The IGE evaluation, like Keddie's study, found different conditions of schooling.[8] In the six schools studied, significant differences in discourse and practice were observed. Three schools maintained overriding styles of work and conditions of knowledge which we labelled *technical;* one school we labelled *constructive* and two *illusory*. These different conditions can be described as follows.

In technical schooling, the focus of curricular thought and teaching practice was a search for the most efficient ways of processing people. The curriculum was organized into systems of hierarchically-ordered objectives, and record-keeping procedures were developed to control children's progress. Responsibility on the part of teachers meant ordering objectives, keeping proper records, and insuring orderly movement of children. Responsibility on the part of children meant learning and obeying the rules of the classroom, listening to authority, and striving to master the predetermined objectives.

This emphasis on procedures and efficiency introduced a particular style of work and conception of knowledge. Knowledge was standardized; all important ideas and skills were measurable and expressed in a discrete, sequenced form. This emphasis on planning and measurement eliminated the serendipitous, the accidental or the problematic. In fundamental ways, technologies and procedures rose to the status of values. Technique became an independent moral domain; it was the criterion for choosing curriculum, instructional processes and evaluation.

The technical emphasis created a division between the conception and the execution of work. Work can be viewed as the interplay of practical skills, situational factors and conceptual thought to shape and fashion objects of the physical world. Technical schooling separates the conception and execution of work; this results in fragmented, over-simplified human activities. Work is dehumanized as the self-organized and self-motivated community is destroyed.

Constructive schooling, in contrast, reflects a belief in the relativity of knowledge. This form of schooling emphasizes multiple ways by which children can come to know about the world – drama, music, and art, as well as social studies, science or reading. The pedagogy stresses how knowledge is created and variation in *ways* of knowing. Students are offered a range of viewpoints for understanding social situations and are expected to consider different ways of attaining various kinds of knowledge. Knowledge is treated as permeable and provisional, ideas as tentative and often ambiguous. These pedagogical assumptions increase students' responsibilities and rights: personalized knowledge is emphasized; children are encouraged to develop facility with language, and responsiveness to the subtleties of interpersonal relations can be established. The emphasis on communicative skills, however, devalues any constructive knowledge related to physical labour such as the craft-skills of a carpenter or a car mechanic; and the emphasis on children's attitudes and dispositions in teaching and evaluation produces subtle forms of social control.

Illusory schooling presents a different configuration of schoolwork and knowledge. Children engage in the traditional patterns of schoolwork: they have classes in reading and arithmetic; they go to the gymnasium or have an art period. Much of the behaviour creates an image of schooling. When scrutinized, however, the behaviours of schooling are contradicted by the actual practices. There is little content in the teaching: children and teachers engage in the rituals and ceremonies of reading, writing and arithmetic, but in practice the lessons contain many instances in which the substance of the teaching is not carried through. What occurs is an emphasis on the form *as* substance. The social processes convey emphasis upon how a moral person is to *act*. The discourse of schooling emphasizes cooperation, hard work, respect for property, and delay of gratification – qualities that teachers in illusory schools believe are not taught at home and have to be built into the school before any 'real academic' learning can take place. This hidden curriculum is the only curriculum. Illusory schooling, then, provides a third institutional configuration, different from technical and constructive schooling. Its forms of work and knowledge establish a moral basis by which children could be 'socialized', and this moral basis stands in juxtaposition to the perceived pathologies of the children's community life. School is, in a fundamental sense, a missionary effort to convert the children for their own good.

It was within these differential contexts that the technologies of Individually-Guided Education were realized and given meaning. Our investigations of pedagogy and change, therefore, had to identify what patterns of social conduct existed in a school, how they were maintained, and how they influenced the practice of schooling. Further, teachers' definitions of pedagogy and their perceptions of the social/cultural backgrounds of the children who came to school had to be related to the expectations for student achievement these teachers held, and to the forms and content of reasoning expressed in their schooling.

Beliefs, ideologies and practices of teaching as an occupational community

To understand pedagogical contexts, we must also link teaching activities to aspects of their occupational context. Occupational groups use the label 'professional' to emphasize the specialized knowledge of a particular sector of the public. Acceptance of the label is based on the belief that a highly-trained, competent and dedicated group can serve the public trust most effectively and efficiently. The term professional, though, has another aspect as well. It is more than a declaration of public trust. It is a social category that implies status and privilege. For teachers, the label signifies not only technical knowledge and service but also the power to bestow social identity on clients (students), supported by the school's ability to provide occupational credentials.[9] In order to *help* its clients, however, the teaching profession is faced with the necessity of identifying a class of needy or deficient persons to serve. A contradiction thus exists between helping the deficient and maintaining a pool of deficient subjects to help. Further, as the occupational group grows, it develops ideologies to preserve and expand its social position as well as accomplish its socially-mandated tasks. Some of the ideologies and the practices that result may have consequences of their own for pedagogy. While one can point to the 'helping' services and the heroic deeds of people within the 'helping' occupations, my intention here is to make that world-view problematic. I will consider how the inherent contradictions of *possibility* and *pathology* in the occupational ideology of the teaching profession give direction to schooling.

To understand the contradictions in the occupational community of teaching, we need to view this social group in relation to larger social and institutional transformations. The past century has witnessed a change in the nature of authority and the manner by which it is legitimated.[10] In particular, intellectuals as a social group have changed from sacerdotal personages to secular experts, independent of the patronage of church and aristocracy but dependent upon the state or the bourgeoisie. The secular expert's 'currency' is the production of knowledge whose validity is based upon rules of logic and reference to the empirical, rather than on the social status of the speaker or the authority of God.

Yet despite this transformation of the intellectual's social status, the knowledge of secular experts continues to be treated as transcendent. The style of discourse in the social sciences and education makes knowledge *seem* neutral, objective and independent of social context or biography. This practice, however, is in conflict with the historical nature of social knowledge, which is never separate from social location and cultural circumstances. It reflects the values, hopes and desires of the people who practice social and educational inquiry, and is not immune to human values and interests.[11]

Thus the knowledge of social science is the knowledge of a particular social group.† To argue that rational styles of analysis and problem-solving are needed to deal with the complexity of industrial society is also to argue that we need the skills and sensibilities of the experts who maintain and develop those styles of analysis. While other possibilities exist – one could argue that folk knowledge or aesthetic forms, as well as scientific thought, can provide a vantage point for understanding and challenging the world – the reduction of knowledge to a particular style of discourse, the scientific mode, makes that single form of knowledge ideological. It legitimates a particular social group as the arbiter of human knowledge, awareness and responsibility.

---

†The problematic nature of the role of the intellectual has been noted throughout history. Marx and Bakunin debated the role of the intellectual and the vanguard. Gramsci pointed to the contradiction in the position of the intellectual in society: intellectuals' status outside social movements, their tendencies toward reform, and their membership in a new educated class pose possible conflict as the intellectual seeks to postulate what would be good for others in society.[12] The intellectual has also served to mediate or transform the relationship of the rulers and ruled into a single dynamic entity. The mediating role, Gramsci argues, is not through coercion or force but through persuasion and consent. This occurs as a specialized group assumes responsibility for defining conceptual and philosophical notions that are to give organization to social life. The intellectual becomes the expert in legitimation, influencing moral conduct and direction of will by controlling the communications through which a society establishes purpose and describes and evaluates its institutional conditions. The differing possible roles of an occupational community makes the particular role of the intellectual as educator problematic.

The role of the intellectual takes on a particular historical form with the rise of the professional. The languages and practices of an occupational community begin to draw upon science not as transcendent language but as political language. The discourse of science is not simply an instrument for describing events but is itself a part of the event, helping to create beliefs about the nature, causes, consequences and remedies of educational policies.[13] In such discourse, the image of science as a self-reflective, logical, neutral descriptor of social conditions must be challenged. Rather than a formal language, it must be viewed as the public language, used by an occupational group, which encourages sensitivity to particular social patterns and interactions and validates the beliefs and strengths of the authority structure in which it is used.

Definitions of self, of society, and their interplay are created, legitimated and ministered through the technological claims of the expert. These claims, however, are not necessarily based upon the technological superiority of scientific knowledge over commonsense knowledge but may rest on the opportunity they offer the expert to exercise more effective control over institutional sectors.[14]

We tend to look at 'research', for example, as providing empirically-grounded, reliable knowledge from which decisions can be made. But, as we scrutinize it, that knowledge comes into question, along with the whole purpose of educational science. Thus, in a review of research in teacher education, we found the knowledge in that area providing only a fragmented, disjointed, ahistorical and often trivial conception of professional life.[15] The way in which research is practised was found to misconstrue the nature of inquiry. But more important, the research functioned not to illustrate but to legitimate and to mystify. The conduct of research was uncritical and thus made the existing categories, actions and patterns of behaviour within teacher education and schooling seem normal and reasonable ways to proceed.

The approach to reform found in IGE can be considered from this perspective of the expert-as-legitimator. The reform did not create new institutional forms, but its language and procedures legitimated existing power and status arrangements. From this perspective, the reform programme can be considered as containing rituals, ceremonies and language styles which can create for both public and professionals a feeling that things are getting better. The dramaturgy reinforces a belief in institutional processes and professional competence; it makes social organizations seem progressive. This ability to generate new symbols of affiliation is important to institutional stability and credibility. The IGE reform, however, did not create any mechanism for self-criticism or scrutiny, except at the level of procedures related to improving efficiency. In contrast, when reform was held to improve school efficiency by definition, existing power relations tended to be preserved.

But to see how professional ideologies influence pedagogical practice, we must consider the occupation's categories, assumptions and definitions as in flux, responding to particular strains of institutional life. Different and conflicting conceptions of occupational mandate work themselves into pedagogical relations to give definition to schooling. Esland, for example, has identified the implicit epistemologies of two dominant educational psychologies.[16] One, drawn from the behaviourist tradition, assumes that knowledge exists outside the minds of individuals. A second tradition, closely related to developmental psychology, considers knowledge to arise out of participation in a community and the problem-solving process. Each epistemologic tradition has connections to organizational theory and to larger debates about schooling and professional mandates as well. Each conception has implications about the way children learn and develop, about the nature of knowledge and social control in the school, and about the way interaction and communication in the school should be ordered.

The fact that different competing occupational ideologies do exist in the world of schooling is illustrated in Wolcott's study of an attempt to develop an accountability programme.[17] Wolcott, an anthropologist, provides a detailed and often humorous account of how an irrational, unsystematic, and vague programme was developed in a school district to make teaching both rational and precise. The programme produced conflict within the school district, anger among some teachers who felt they were being abused, and embarrassment to members of the project.

In his analyses of the motives lying behind this project, Wolcott argued that there are two moieties, or divergent ideological subsystems, in schooling: teachers, who are concerned with teaching acts, and with understanding teaching and learning; and technocrats, who value information, rational planning, and progress.

> The technocrats struggle to define what they want to accomplish and then attempt to set a course that will accomplish their objective. Teachers, on the other hand, seem unable to explicate precisely what they want; their objectives are global and diffuse. Technocratic precision only helps teachers to recognize what they don't want when someone attempts to impose it on them.[18]

These educational moieties, Wolcott argues, have relations which can be described as conceptually antithetical, rivalrous, reciprocal and complementary. The importance of the moieties, for Wolcott, is that they facilitate adaptability and cohesiveness in the school system. They enable educators to respond to different clients of public education and be accountable to different publics.

But different and conflicting conceptions of occupational mandate do work themselves into pedagogical relations to give definitions to schooling. In constructive, technical and illusory schooling, the schools contain different forms of occupational practice and legitimacy which filter in classroom practice. The debate we saw within our constructive school is illustrative. The teachers in the school maintained a particular definition of professional autonomy. They considered their role to be that of choosing materials and constructing a curriculum in relation to the general pedagogical belief that children are active and responsible in the process of knowing. This relative and personalized view of knowledge, however, was in conflict with the ideology of the school district. District policy sought to introduce greater consistency and standardization among schools. The disagreement between district and school was also articulated within the school by a few teachers who believed that specified, determinate curriculum *made* teachers carry out and evaluate tasks in a more precise manner. The school superintendent referred to the policy of consistency by mentioning the professional obligation to use observable criteria to prove to the general public that its money was being spent wisely. The specific policies of consistency (terminal objectives, single textbook series, district approval of field trips) had little to do with improving quality; they did serve, however, to restrict options available to teachers and children in the school.

Occupational pressures from educational agencies outside the school and school district also constrain the practices that occur in classrooms. Efforts to establish accountability mechanisms to publicly demonstrate the school's efficiency in meeting certain goals of public education provide one example. As an accountability measure, schools in one State in the IGE study were required to administer criterion-referenced tests. These tests have a specific purpose: to test the range of skills and information a child has acquired at certain grade levels. Results were published in the county newspaper – as one might print the results of a horse-race. The principal of a technical school in this State related that his school did well on the tests and that, as a result, he was one of only two principals retained when a new superintendent came to the district. Observation of day-to-day instruction in the school revealed that technical learning had characteristics similar to the form and content of the multiple-choice items on the State's criterion-referenced tests. This pedagogical structure became more obvious approximately a month prior to the tests. The children's days were taken up with timed practice on tests similar to those provided by the State.

Thus it is important to consider the implications of the occupational work styles and patterns of communication that guide teachers as they reason and act in their school settings. What specialized bodies of images, allegories and rituals explain and interpret the role of teachers and the conduct of teaching? How are professional languages used to justify practices with *different* student populations? How do external professional organizations (teacher unions, teacher associations, State-education agencies, school districts) influence school practices? When State or local school district policy incorporates the language and technologies of an innovation, how do these technologies influence classroom practices and the priorities by which instruction is established? What strains and tensions result as external policies are translated into school instruction?

Social/cultural contexts and school forms

Understanding the institutional characteristics of schooling and educational change requires that educators consider more than the nature of school language and forms or the occupational community. Any school is subject to social demands which reflect both local concerns and larger social and cultural issues. The interplay of school and society, however, is an obvious and non-controversial aspect of life in our contemporary world. The school curriculum reflects what influential groups of people can establish as social priorities. Citizenship education, back-to-the-basics, and discipline-centred curriculum movements, no matter how noble their purposes, are political endeavours of groups trying to achieve their emphasis on particular social knowledges.[19]

The awareness of the relation of pedagogical practices and social forms is not, of course, a recent discovery. Durkheim's history of the French secondary school, for example, argues that changes in school content and methods during the Renaissance reflected profound social changes in European society.[20] In part, the development of a bourgeois class precipitated the demand for an educational system that could provide a curriculum which would legitimate the style and manner of the bourgeoisie in society. During the counter-Reformation, classical content was reformulated to emphasize the virtues, vices and great passions that exemplified the precepts of Christianity. Individualization of instruction was to be a means by which the Jesuit school could provide greater personal surveillance, manipulation and competition to encourage personal motivation.

Of course, such external socio-cultural demands are not presented in the form of carefully articulated arguments or forcefully documented concerns. Cultural expectations provide background assumptions for schooling and are absorbed into the discourse and practices of the school in a variety of ways. Teachers' perceptions of the lifestyle of the community, patterns of schoolwork, and selection of curriculum content mediate, through the everyday life of schooling, conditions and dispositions related to larger social and cultural patterns.

In the IGE study, the teachers' perceptions of the community's lifestyles, occupations and values influenced the definition of the mandates of schooling associated with the technical, constructive and illusory schools. In one of the technical schools, the superintendent of the district characterized the parents of the schoolchildren as 'the salt of the earth, hard-playing people where snowmobiling takes precedence anytime over symphony. The importance of this lifestyle is that when students do not have enough affluence to appreciate the arts, the school programme must limit itself to survival skills.' This perception of the community was translated into pedagogical language and the theories of psychology. This school's emphasis on efficiency in teaching utilitarian skills made school events appear independent of social and cultural considerations.

In this filtering of values between community and classroom, the relation of schooling and social and cultural arrangement is problematic. As I have suggested, pedagogical practices value and distribute only certain aspects of the total culture. For example, scientific and technological knowledge is culturally important. For some, its inclusion in schooling is necessary to maintain the productive base in society.[21] For others, such knowledge has the potential for unmasking the pretensions, propaganda, deceptions and self-deceptions by which people cloak their actions with each other.[22] In either instance, the inclusion of scientific and technological knowledge into school emphasizes certain styles of thinking and work as sacred in society.

By emphasizing a particular style of knowledge, schooling may legitimate social inequities. It has been argued, for example, that scientific and technological knowledge is the property of a distinct class, the middle class. Making that knowledge seem neutral and employing it as though all children have equal access to it gives the impression that schooling is itself a neutral process. In fact, such an emphasis favours those children whose social backgrounds provide them with the linguistic and social competencies of middle-class culture. The school, in this instance, reproduces the cleavages and divisions of larger society. It also legitimates certain social and political interests which dominate public institutions by establishing certain styles of thinking, tastes, attitudes and behaviours as naturally superior.[23]

When we examine school materials we find that they express a conservative bias toward social and political institutions. The discipline-centred curriculum movement in the social studies, as we see it in American schools, communicates little of the real curiosity, adventure and discipline of social science.[24] The materials instead crystallize the values of the scientist as expert and urge children to replace their own commonsense ideas with the more esoteric and formal language of the scientist. Anyon's analysis of current US secondary-school history textbooks' treatment of industrialization between 1866 and 1914 argues that these texts are more clearly ideological.[25] They rationalize the continuation of economic expansion and legitimate government intervention to bring about economic change, make élites (industrialists and managers) central figures in industrial development, and portray labour unions solely as a mechanism for protecting the rights of workers in a democracy. An impression of consensual, orderly change is provided, implying that we should regard the poor as responsible for their own poverty, and that we should accept uncritically myths about social, political, cultural and economic life.

Classroom observations of US schools also suggest that schools are organized differently for children of different social, economic and racial backgrounds. Teachers of children from low-income families minimize cognitive interactions with children while emphasizing rote learning. When these children ask questions that are marginal or tangential to points under discussion, their answers are rebuked or ignored. Schools of middle-class children, on the other hand, stress cognitive growth and student satisfaction: in the dialogue of the classroom, children's questions are taken seriously; classroom practices provide greater opportunities for students to work on committees and more tasks leading students to classroom discussion. The different treatment in school, DeLone argues, performs a function of occupational screening and selection, and awards status on the basis of inheritance, while obscuring the different expectations by means of the popular belief that those who succeed have been meritorious in the competitive, neutral system.[26]

The discourse and work of the three institutional conditions we saw in the IGE study can be viewed as responsive to different social and cultural backgrounds. In two of the three technical schools, for example, there was an emphasis on teaching the functional skills, responsibility and discipline that teachers believed would enable the children to succeed in the blue-collar or low-status service occupations of their parents. The intellectual and social point of view in the constructive school responded to the professional social and cultural orientation of a community in which interpersonal control, facility with language, and responsiveness to the subtle nuances of interpersonal situations are important. The illusory schools, located in poor communities, reflected the pedagogical ideology of pathology and therapy.

This differentiation of patterns of schooling, however, was hidden by the myth of a single, common school. The patterns of conduct in each of the schools in the IGE study had an appearance similar to any school in the United States. The children studied the same subject matter, took tests to measure achievement, and worked with materials and physical environments (desks, blackboards, lunchrooms, and so on) that might be found in any school. This apparent standardization and homogeneity helps to maintain the myths of continuity, formal equity, and opportunity that are important in the maintenance of the authority of the social order of schooling.

The homogeneity of schooling, however, is deceiving. Differentiating rituals marked these schools as offering different potential for students to compete in a meritocracy. These rituals were most significant in the illusory schools, where they took the form of compensatory educational programmes, expectations of different learning and teaching styles, and achievement results that corresponded to the low income and social characteristics of the community.

The significance of the illusory school as a social form becomes most apparent in the contradiction between the differentiation and standardizing rituals of schooling. The illusory schooling portrayed the particular categories, ways of working and communicating found in the formal subject-matter of schooling as being naturally superior to those found in the community, but did not provide teaching experiences that would make this style of learning accessible to students. Instead, the pathology of the children's home and community was stressed, along with therapy, obedience to the school's authority, and conformity to rules of conduct foreign to the children's lives.

The imagery of illusory schooling, then, had three distinct qualities. First, it established the sacredness of the categories and knowledge forms found in the formal curriculum of schooling. These were the knowledges that individuals should aspire to attain, as they defined how competence in society was to be judged. Second, the rituals of the illusory schooling established institutional competence in conveying the substance of that knowledge. Third, that institutional competence was juxtaposed with the incompetence of the person who came to the school. Student failure became personal, the result of inadequacies of personality or community. The social processes of schooling, while maintaining the myth of a common, standardized school, may legitimate the belief that those in the illusory school's community fail because they do not participate in schooled society.

Some discussions of the relationship between schooling and occupational structures in the larger society make the argument that the forms of schooling correspond directly to larger social conditions. Thus, schooling is viewed as reproducing the psychological and work requirements of social modes of production in a paper by Anyon.[27] She explored the styles of work in contrasting social-class communities and found work in the school reflecting children's potential relationships to the ownership of symbolic and physical capital, to authority and to control. These relationships are specific to those which the children experience in their own social circumstances and cultural location. *Working-class schools,* for example, provide work that is appropriate preparation for mechanical, routine wage labour. *Middle-class schools* provide work relationships experiences that are appropriate for a future bureaucratic relation to capital: 'one is rewarded . . . for knowing the answers to the questions one is asked, for knowing when or how to find the answers, and for knowing which form, regulation, technique, or procedure is correct'.[28] *Affluent professional* and *executive élite schools,* in contrast, communicate a potential relationship that involves acquiring the skills and strategies of linguistic, artistic and scientific forms of discourse which are necessary for interpersonal and intrapersonal control. The *affluent professional school* maintains a personalized and relative view of work and knowledge of schooling which affirms the potential for individuals to conceptualize and intervene in cultural life. The *executive élite school* extends the relationship to symbolic capital by giving students 'the opportunity to learn and to utilize the intellectually and socially prestigious grammar, mathematical, and other vocabularies and rules by which elements are arranged'.[29] Anyon concluded that these different cognitive and behavioural skills help to reproduce the relations of capital, authority, and control that exist in society.

Although this analysis points to some possible relationships between pedagogy and larger social conditions, its formulation is too static and reductionistic to adequately represent the dynamics involved.[30] We cannot assume that schooling is a mirror which reflects something else that is occurring in society. Thus we argue here that the competing ideologies of the occupational community in schooling create inconsistencies, contradictions and strains which need to be understood when considering pedagogical practices. Further, the school provides credentials that contribute to the formation of specialized cultural communities in which groups vie for occupational positions and rewards in larger society.

A functional analysis, in which schools' forms seem to be only the result of adaptation to external forces, ignores the self-generating capacity of schooling and acknowledges only its imitative powers. We can see some of the complexity of schooling and cultural/social conditions in the six schools in the IGE evaluation study. The discourse and practices of those schools exist within the decisions and beliefs of other layers of the social system. There was a clear relationship, for example, between constructive schooling and the occupations of its parents: the emphasis on interpersonal control, facility with language, and personalized knowledge corresponded to the intellectual and social point of view found in its community. The community was composed primarily of professionals whose position in society depended upon the creation and control of systems of communication. One of the illusory schools and its black, poor urban setting also showed such a clear relationship. This illusory school responded to a social predicament in which teachers saw the community as pathological and believed that the purpose of schooling was to establish the moral superiority and values of middle-class society. But while social class is important, its importance does not preclude the necessity of establishing relations to other dimensions of social/cultural life. Two of the three technical schools, for example, were similar both in pedagogy and community to Anyon's working-class schools. The third technical school, however, existed in an affluent business community; its style of work and knowledge seemed related more to an integration of certain dominant social and cultural beliefs with religious ones than to social-class position. In addition, different kinds of schooling can exist in similar communities. One illusory school and one technical school in the IGE study both existed in communities of blue-collar or low-status service occupations, similar in income level and occupational position.

Geographic location seems as important in illuminating the social predicament of the schools as community socioeconomic status. The technical school just mentioned was located in a rural, southern community; the illusory school was in a northern mid-sized industrial city. The rural school existed within a social context in which extended family relations went back for generations, and the school represented a valued communal feeling, and played a part in extended and intricate networks of communication. In this technical school, teachers had a sense of optimism that children could be taught technical skills and knowledge. The northern illusory school, in contrast, reflected no sense of communal obligations: the teachers viewed the neighbourhood's culture as pathological and its occupants as lazy and unsettled. In pointing to these instances, I am not arguing causality but complexity. School-community relations cannot be explained by social class alone.

Often, the language and assumptions of educational reform can obscure and mystify the different social and political conditions underlying school practices. The IGE programme is a case in point. The problem of reform is believed to be related to individual differences, technologies being developed to increase 'learning efficiency'. Individual variation and technological reform were part of a psychological abstraction in which human traits, aptitudes and attitudes were treated in isolation from school setting, cultural circumstances, and social location. The consequence of making school change a 'psychological' problem was a failure to consider, except in a limited sense, the impact of social structure on individual development. In each of the schools studied, individualization or human variability was a social category that celebrated three distinct styles of work or cognition. The irony of the IGE reform was that, by focussing almost exclusively upon the individual apart from social context, the reform effort resulted in different but unequal treatments. Indeed the programme may have given new credibility to the social differentiations already contained in the schools.

While not considered explicitly in the IGE study, relations between school and social forms have to be modified further to consider ways in which individuals and groups withhold their cooperation from history. Aronwitz's study of Lordstown workers identifies ways in which workers not only accommodate the pressures of the assembly line but also engage in acts of resistance and rebellion to the monotony, boredom and authority of the line.[31] Other studies of work cultures document forms of resistance, conflict and struggle in the day-to-day life of workers.[32] Forms of resistance are also found in a study of a working-class high school in England.[33] Some of the students of this school rejected the social values, ideologies and practices being offered by the school, regarding them as flawed myths and beliefs. The students spent their days working the system in order to gain control over their time in the school. The rejection and resistance, however, were not total. These students maintained sexist, racist and anti-intellectual assumptions that served to legitimate existing social and economic divisions in society.

In the IGE schools, too, some teachers and children were detached or resisted the institutional conditions. One teacher threw into the waste-basket a test she had just given the students; a group of children in one of the technical schools developed informal arrangements to permit them to talk and play while they were supposed to be working independently; interview sessions often revealed that teachers gave consideration to school arrangements other than those available. These incidents, however, were not dominant in the school situations. Most people seemed to accept the working relations and purposes of schooling as given, and developed elaborate rationales to justify them. The lack of conflict was most obvious in the technical schools where the strictly rationalized procedures and organizations made deviance readily apparent to other teachers and principals. In these schools, the question may not be 'What forms of resistance occurred?' but 'Why did so many teachers, students and parents accept existing patterns of conduct as reasonable?'

These and other studies suggest various relations between social and cultural forms and schooling. From this perspective, learning becomes only one of the functions of schooling. Schools can serve as a mediating agency between the individual's consciousness and society. They provide a body of practices and expectations, systems of meanings and values that give practical organization to our perceptions of self and the world. It is not clear how school relates to the larger social world, which pressures and strains it brings to bear upon pedagogical practices, or how it influences social structure. Nor are the ways social structures are made fragile by the tensions and contradictions within a school understood. The necessity for researchers to consider these factors is, however, clear.

Conclusions

I have argued that the problem of understanding schooling and its reform lies in the ways different social contexts interrelate to produce the institutional arrangements of schooling. Posing the problem in this way demands a reciprocal view of causality; the social definitions of schoolwork and knowledge, occupational ideologies and cultural and social values are related to each other and are at once dependent and independent variables. All the elements interact, mutually changing and sustaining one another. The linkage between the internal dynamics of schooling and external conditions requires researchers to consider the larger context of thinking and acting that makes the conditions of schooling plausible and credible. It also provides a more adequate way of understanding how school practices create responses to the social world, sustain relations in that world, and enable individuals to withhold their cooperation. The problem of schooling and its change lies in how the three contexts discussed here interweave, cohere or conflict in the day-to-day life of schooling.

Our discussion challenges certain assumptions about reform and research. First, it challenges the belief that reform is a well coordinated and well orchestrated effort to improve the efficiency of instruction. The assumption underlying much of the R & D movement, for example, sees change as related to a search for a universally-efficient method to improve schools. Sometimes this has taken the form of a centre-to-periphery model, with experts designing, developing and providing for the implementation of some programme. At the opposite end of the spectrum is a decentralized technical assistance model which enables local districts to develop greater efficiency. Both the centre-to-periphery and decentralized approaches make inherently social, political and ethical problems of schooling into seemingly neutral administrative changes. Our argument about three contexts views the liturgy and technology of the efficient approach as a ceremonial mask that uncritically solidifies existing school values and practices.

Second, research cannot take for granted the goals and purposes of the practices of schooling. Research cannot empirically detail logical elements of a school organization or identify discrete behaviours within a teaching act, as is common in teacher effects studies, without also considering questions about context.[†] The

---

[†] The problem of understanding how various contexts help to sustain and create meaning in schooling is conceptual as well as empirical. Better

problem of educational research lies in understanding dynamic social and political interactions and their coherence, strains and contradictions.

School reform and research raises problems central to the social predicament of schooling. We place great faith in schooling as an institution that can respond to our social and political ideals. But these hopes and wishes are shaped and fashioned in concrete social processes which contain different and sometimes conflicting interests. The life of schooling is not a life within a single social configuration, but one which contains different styles of work, conceptions of knowledge and ideologies of occupation and of community. These various configurations of schooling are not neutral; they contain underlying values about authority and control. The discussion of the three contexts of schooling we say in our study of IGE is intended as a heuristic device for considering these dynamic and complex interrelations and their assumptions, implications and consequences. Because of the different and possibly antagonistic consequences of schooling, we cannot take these contexts for granted.

Acknowledgements

I would like to thank David Hamilton, Michael Apple, Ian Westbury, Pinchas Tamir and Cathy Cornbleth for their thoughtful comments on early drafts of this essay.

References and notes

1   POPKEWITZ, T., TABACHNICK, B., and WELHAGE, G. (1980). *School Reform and Institutional Life: A Case Study of Individually-Guided Education.* Wisconsin Research and

---

conceptual perspectives are needed for considering schooling's nature and character. The argument offered here rejects positivistic notions which seek to tie what is known only to observable and quantifiable factors, and which limit the science of schooling to only that which can yield technical efficiency. Both explanatory and interpretative explorations are needed.[34] In the contexts of conceptual interest and the illumination of the complexities of schooling as a social endeavour, the issue is *not* simply one of qualitative versus quantitative techniques.[35]

Development Center for Individualized Schooling, University of Wisconsin, Madison.

2. This argument is developed in POPKEWITZ, T. (1979). 'The problem of reform and institutional life,' *Educational Researcher*, 8, 3 (March) pp. 3-8.

3. CICOUREL, A. *et al.* (1974). *Language Use and School Performance*. New York: Academic Press.

4. A premise of compensatory education and early childhood programmes is similar: children need to be taught the particular language forms, practices, and styles of thinking associated with schooling. Once these are learned, it is assumed children will be able to succeed in school tasks.

5. MacKAY, R. (1973). 'Conceptions of children and models of socialization.' In: DREITZEL, H. (Ed) *Childhood and Socialization*. New York: Macmillan, pp. 22–43.

6. KING, N. (1976). *The Socialization of Kindergarten Children*. Unpublished doctoral dissertation, University of Wisconsin, Madison.

7. KEDDIE, N. (1971). 'Classroom knowledge.' In: YOUNG, M.F.D. (Ed) *Knowledge and Control: New Directions for the Sociology of Education*. London: Collier-Macmillan, pp. 133-60.

8. A discussion of the three conditions of schooling can be found in POPKEWITZ *et al., op. cit.* (see Note 1.)

9. GOULDNER, A. (1979). *The Future of the Intellectual and the Rise of the New Class*. New York: Seabury Press.

10. KONRAD, G. and SZELENYI, I. (1979). *The Intellectuals on the Road to Class Power: A Sociological Study of the Role of the Intelligentsia in Socialism*. New York: Harcourt, Brace and Jovanovich.

11. POPKEWITZ, T. (1978). 'Educational research: values and visions of social order,' *Theory and Research in Social Education*, 6, 4 (December), pp. 20-49; POPKEWITZ, T. (1980). 'Paradigm in educational science: different meanings and purpose of theory,' *Journal of Education*, 162, 1 (Winter) pp. 28-46.

12. GRAMSCI, A. (1971). *Selections from the Prison Notebooks*. (Edited and translated Q. Hoare and G. Smiths.) New York: International Publishers.

13. EDELMAN, M. (1977). *Political Language: Words that Succeed and Policies That Fail*. New York: Academic Press.

14. MARGLIN, S. (1974-5). 'What do bosses do? The origins and functions of hierarchy in capitalist production,' *Review of Radical Political Economics*, No. 6 (Summer) pp. 60-112; 7, 1 (Spring) pp. 20-37.

15. POPKEWITZ, T., TABACHNICK, B. and ZEICHNER, K. (1979). 'Dulling the senses: research in teacher education,' *Journal of Teacher Education*, 30, 5 (September-October) pp. 52-60. See also LASCH, C. (1977). 'The siege of the family,' *New York Review of Books*, 24, 9 (24 November) pp. 14-18.

16. ESLAND, G. 'Teaching and learning in the organization of knowledge.' In: YOUNG, M.F.D. (Ed), *op. cit.* (see Note 7).
17. WOLCOTT, A. (1977). *Teacher vs. Technocrats.* Eugene, Oregon: Center for Educational Policy and Management.
18. *Ibid.,* p. 161.
19. Comparative education has long documented this relationship: See for example, LUNDGREN, U.P. and PETTERSSON, S. (Eds) (1979). *Codes, Context and Curriculum Processes.* Stockholm: CWK Gleerup; KAZAMIAS, A. 'The politics of educational reform in Greece: Law 390/1976,' *Comparative Education Review,* 22, 1 (February). Discussions of pedagogy in the United States, however, often ignore such relationships by paying primary attention to 'efficiency' in teaching.
20. DURKHEIM, E. (1977). *The Evolution of Educational Thought: Lectures on the Formation and Development of Secondary Education in France.* Translated by P. Collins. London: Routledge and Kegan Paul.
21. APPLE, M. (nd) *Some Aspects of the Relationship between Economic and Cultural Reproduction.* University of Wisconsin-Madison. in mimeo.
22. CLEMENTS, H., FIEDLER, W. and TABACHNICK, B. (1966). *Social Study: Inquiry in Elementary Classrooms.* Indianapolis, Indiana: Bobbs-Merrill Company.
23. BOURDIEU, P. and PASSERON, J. (1977). *Reproduction in Education, Society and Culture.* Beverly Hills: Sage.
24. POPKEWITZ, T. (1977). 'The latent values of the discipline-centred curriculum,' *Theory and Research in Social Education,* 5, 1 (April) pp. 41-60.
25. ANYON, J. (1979). 'Ideology and United States history textbooks,' *Harvard Educational Review,* 49, 3 (August) pp. 361-86.
26. DeLONE, R. (1979). *Small Futures: Children, Inequality and the Limits of Liberal Reform.* New York: Harcourt, Brace and Jovanovich.
27. ANYON, J. (1980). 'Social class and the hidden curriculum: correspondence theories and labor process,' *Journal of Education,* 162, 1 (Winter) pp. 47-66.
28. *Ibid.,* p. 88.
29. *Ibid.,* p. 89.
30. This issue is considered in: HAMILTON, D. (1978). *Correspondence Theories and the Promiscuous School: Problems of the Analysis of Educational Change.* University of Glasgow, in mimeo; GIROUX, H. 'Beyond the correspondence theory: notes on the dynamics of educational reproduction and transformation,' *Interchange,* in press; WEXLER, P. *Structure, Text, and Subject: A Critical Sociology of School Knowledge.* University of Rochester, nd. in mimeo, and KALLÒS, D. and LUNDGREN, U.P. (1979). *Curriculum as a Pedagogical Problem.* Stockholm: CWK Gleerup.
31. ARONWITZ, S. (1974). *False Promises: The Shaping of American*

Working Class Consciousness. New York: McGraw-Hill.

32.   For a summary of studies of work-cultures and their implications for school research, see APPLE, M. (1980). 'The other side of the hidden curriculum: correspondence theories and labor process,' *Journal of Education,* 162, 1 (Winter) pp. 47-66.

33.   WILLIS, P. (1977). *Learning to Labour: How Working Class Kids Get Working Class Jobs.* Teakfield: Saxon House.

34.   BELLACK, A.A. (1978). *Competing Ideologies in Research on Teaching.* University Reports on Education, No. 1. Uppsala University, Department of Educational Research.

35.   POPKEWITZ, T. and TABACHNICK, B. (Eds) (1981). *The Study of Schooling: Field Methodology in Educational Research.* New York: Praeger.

Teaching about Thinking and Thinking about Teaching

Magdalene Lampert

A 10-year-old boy asked his fourth-grade teacher: 'Does Dataman have eyes?' He was wondering about his hand-held computer game that looks like a robot. 'If not, how does he know if my answers are right?'

There are several different ways a classroom teacher might interpret and respond to these questions, depending on how she understands children's thinking and her role in their learning. If she sees herself as the source of students' knowledge and the judge of their 'wrong answers', her response might be a short lecture about how 'computers know the answers because they are programmed by people'. The boy's question would be taken as evidence that he is not very intelligent, and his teacher would relate to him in the future on the basis of this judgement. From another perspective, the teacher might think of the boy's question as a distraction from the task she has assigned to the class. She might see herself as responsible for planning appropriate lessons and activities for all of her students, throughout the day, to meet particular goals. She would thus respond by refocussing the boy's attention and behaviour on the lessons the class is supposed to be learning. In both of these views, the teacher is the source of knowledge and the organizer of its acquisition.

Another way to interpret the boy's question about Dataman's 'eyes', however, is to see it as his attempt to understand a new experience. He could be using an idea that makes sense to him as a way to figure out how computers process information. From this perspective, the teacher's response might be to explore the implications of *his* way of thinking about the mechanical toy, perhaps asking him, 'How do you think Dataman can tell what your answers are?' It would be crucial for the teacher to understand what the boy already knows about how 'dataman' works, so that she could direct his learning process in a way that would make connections with this knowledge. Even though his idea about Dataman's 'eyes' is at odds with the conventional way we explain how computers process information, it is intuitively meaningful to him, and therefore suggests an appropriate place for the teacher to begin her lessons.

The third – personal and active – view of the learning process redefines the teacher's work to include on-the-spot clinical research into the way a learner thinks about something. During the past four years, this concept of teacher-as-researcher has been the subject of a study at the Division for Study and Research in Education at Massachusetts Institute of Technology. The study was built around a series of weekly seminars attended by both researchers and public elementary school teachers. The seminars had several aims, and both their form and their content have raised some interesting questions about the relationship between scholarly inquiry and classroom practice.

The first goal of the project was to train the teacher-participants to recognize what its designer, Jeanne Bamberger, called 'intuitive knowledge'. In her view, each individual builds a store of this commonsense sort of information from personal experimentation on the physical environment. Such knowledge is not usually made explicit, but is often useful and powerful. It contrasts, therefore, with the 'formal knowledge' one is taught in school: a commonly accepted set of well-articulated 'descriptions' of experience, which may have little connection with the knowledge individuals regularly apply in their everyday lives.[1] The project staff devised activities which would help the teachers to distinguish between their own intuitive ways of making sense of various phenomena and the formal knowledge they had been taught in school.

Given this background, the teachers and researchers together were to pursue the second goal, and major purpose of the project: to explore how this appreciation of intuitive knowledge could be useful in educational practice. The hope was that this work would result in practical strategies to help individual children connect their intuitive ways of understanding experience with the conventional formulas everyone needs to know to succeed in school and society. Developing and implementing these strategies was to be the work of 'teacher-researchers':

> Center[ing] on the image of teacher as teacher-researcher as opposed to the prevalent image of teacher as link in a knowledge-delivery-system . . . extends the teacher's self-image and her intellectual engagement by providing a richer intellectual definition of her task.[2]

By this redefinition of the teacher's work, the project sought to bring teaching practice closer to the work of researchers trying to understand how children learn.

The staff of the project included two cognitive psychologists: Bamberger, who has done considerable research relating intuitive knowledge of music to learning formal music theory, and Eleanor Duckworth, who has endeavoured to make Piaget's theories and research accessible to teachers. Bamberger and Duckworth constructed musical, mathematical and physical tasks for the teachers which were meant to make them more conscious of the usefulness of their own intuitive knowledge. They demonstrated clinical research methods with children, and they led discussions with teachers of the use of these methods in the classroom.

The teacher-participants volunteered in response to an advertisement for the project which was circulated in their school district. It briefly described the idea of a 'teacher-researcher' and explained the proposed format of the project. The seven teachers who became involved represented a wide variation in grades taught, kinds of schools and classrooms in which they worked, age and years of experience, ethnic and educational background, and personal life styles. All of them participated actively in the project during the 1978-1979 and 1979-1980 school years. The teachers continued their daily work in classrooms while they met once a week with the staff of the project, and members of the staff observed periodically in each teacher's classroom to develop a shared context for discussion.

As an experienced school teacher and teacher-educator, my role in the project was to help the teachers articulate their perspective on classroom practice. I also documented the activities and discussions that occurred in the weekly seminars. It is the perspective of practice, therefore, which I bring to this case study of the project, informed by a careful analysis of what the teachers said about teaching in their conversations with one another during the seminars. From my perspective, as participant-observer, the identification of the teachers as both practitioners *and* researchers and the multiple aims of the seminar put them in a somewhat ambiguous and often frustrating position. I will address this problem in my analysis of the project. In training the teachers to do clinical investigations of children's thinking, the project looked like many other attempts at staff development or in-service training, with the teachers being 'students' of academic researchers who had ideas about how practitioners could do their job better. The notion that the teachers thus trained would then become collaborators in addressing a research problem defined by psychologists complicated their role considerably. The teachers who participated in this project were also paid and treated as 'consultants', and they were encouraged to articulate their own ideas about the problems of teaching. These varied definitions of the relationship between the teachers and the researchers often left everyone confused about who was 'in charge' of the weekly meetings. Yet the structure did allow the teachers to question the researchers' definitions of pedagogical problems and their assumptions about how to 'fix' the practice of teaching.

Whatever else it accomplished, the project raised fundamental questions inherent in the relationship between academic research and classroom practice. It is these questions that I wish to examine in this paper. In the first part of the paper I describe how the project operated; in the second I consider the conflicts that teachers faced as a consequence of participation. The teachers' conflicts arose out of their attempts to translate theory into practice. Ideas about children's thinking which had been useful to researchers in a loosely defined form led to impossible practical dilemmas as these practitioners tried to make sense of them in terms of concrete classroom procedures. However, when the same teachers diverged from the researchers' agenda and told informal stories about their work, the conflicts that they had conceived seemed to be managed within their sense of themselves as teachers. The teachers' stories reveal ways in which the practitioner uses her 'self' to manage the potential contradictions in her work, thus challenging the traditional notion that conflicts are resolved through research and then research 'implemented' by practitioners.

Teaching teachers about thinking.

The work of the teacher-researcher, as conceived by Bamberger, is 'helping the child to coordinate his own intuitive knowledge (what and how he knows already) with the more formal knowledge contained in the privileged descriptions taught in school and shared by the community of users'.[3] The belief that such coordination is necessary is built on the assumption that the *intuitive* knowledge of the individual child can be understood separately from the *formal* knowledge of school and society. Therefore, in order to build connections between these theoretically disparate elements, the teachers first needed to learn to be able to distinguish between them. They needed to acquire both the psychologists' way of thinking about knowledge, and the clinical research skills that would enable them to put aside conventional assumptions about what is worth knowing so as to examine a child's way of making sense of something.

Bamberger framed the following questions to guide the teacher-researcher's inquiry:

How are the child's descriptions different from those formal descriptions accepted as norms in the school setting; what is the nature of the mismatch; and finally, how can [the teacher] help him to integrate his own useful, even powerful, ways of knowing with the expectations of school and community?[4]

The view of knowledge underlying the project's design places a high value on the child's intuitive understanding. Intuitive knowledge is considered to be powerful and useful to the individual person. In contrast, formal knowledge is thought of as separate from the persons who are learners. It is considered 'privileged', and thereby presumably alien to the child. At the same time, it is the kind of knowledge, 'taught in school' and 'shared by the community of users'. Thus the design of the project echoed a familiar theoretical dichotomy between the individual and society.

As the teachers were trained to become teacher-researchers,

they were expected to use this dichotomous perspective to understand classroom practice. As they did this, the *distinction* between intuitive and formal knowledge was translated into a set of practical *dilemmas*. The job of making connections between these two kinds of knowledge, i.e. between the child, and school and society, thus became much more difficult than the project's designer had anticipated. While the teachers agreed that doing research on their students' ways of understanding something seemed essential, they perceived a conflict between that sort of attention to individual differences and implementing the school curriculum. The teachers' new appreciation of the psychology of individual learning seemed to be at odds with their understanding of the responsibilities of their job, yet a clear choice between these two alternatives was also out of the question if they were to take both the project and their jobs in schools seriously.

This dilemma did not surface immediately. At the beginning of the project, the teachers were involved primarily in examining their own thinking processes in areas unrelated to the subject matter they were teaching. They participated in a variety of activities designed to help them recognize the usefulness of their own, informal, strategies for solving problems. Bamberger chose to have the teachers do musical tasks in the early weeks of the project precisely because it was a subject in which they would not have had much formal training. She assumed that, although music was a domain in which nearly everyone has experience, it was not as encumbered with learned formal descriptions and societal expectations as the more central school subjects like mathematics and reading.

One of the first tasks the teachers were given, for example, was to compose a tune that would 'sound good', using a set of five individual metal bells. The bells would make sounds of different pitches when struck with a wooden mallet. Bamberger encouraged each teacher to articulate the various qualities which she thought made *her* tune sound good. The teachers thus practised doing clinical investigations of individual understanding by reflecting on their own ways of making sense of music. They also analysed videotapes of the researchers interacting with children who did similar tasks.

After doing these activities for several weeks, the teachers were asked to bring the group instances from their own classrooms in which a child talked about something in a way that seemed 'puzzling'. The research staff helped the teachers to speculate on the structure of the intuitive knowledge that the child was bringing to the situation. Suzanne, a fourth-grade teacher, told about Lenny, who had asked her, 'Does Dataman [a small computer] have eyes?' She reported her first reaction to his question as follows:

> My immediate thought was that he thought it was a living thing, had eyes, was connected with a living thing. At first, my aide and I were both so flattened by the idea that a fourth grader would think that Dataman could have eyes or could hear or speak that we just left it and said, 'No. It doesn't.' He said he thought it could see because it – 'he' – told you whether your answer was right and if 'he' wasn't able to see, 'he wouldn't be able to do that'.[5]

Suzanne explained that she and her aide were 'flattened' because they just couldn't believe that this 10-year-old boy did not know that machines could not have eyes, and she expressed her distress at the thought that Lenny might actually think computers are alive. She assumed, at first, that he did not *know* something he should know, and that explaining to him how computers work was *her* job. It was in such discussions of their own students that teacher views about the importance of formal knowledge in classrooms began to surface.

In presenting this problem to the group, Suzanne called Lenny's question 'silly' and wondered about the boy's 'intelligence'. She said that he 'was not very smart in math, either', she worried about whether he would learn all that she was supposed to teach him during that year, and said she had told him that Dataman recognized his answers because it is 'programmed'. However, she admitted that she did not really know exactly how the machine works. But what she did know, and what she said she really wanted Lenny to know, was 'that there was definitely not a person or a brain in there working'. Suzanne favoured transmitting formal knowledge rather than examining how she or the child might make sense of the machine's workings.

The staff asked the teachers: 'what might Lenny have been thinking that prompted him to ask his question in the first place?'

Although whether Lenny was right or wrong in his thinking, or whether he needed to be taught something about how computers work, were issues of some interest to the teachers, the group was directed to try and imagine how someone might think that a computer might have 'eyes'. The teachers began to wonder whether the boy may have been asking a question that was somewhat more complicated than the literal ones: 'Does it have eyes?' or 'Is it alive?' and they found themselves questioning just how Dataman could, in fact, tell you whether your answer was right or wrong if it didn't somehow 'see' your answer. One member of the group compared Lenny's reasoning process with the way she, and other adults, might think about computers:

> *We* talk about a computer as a 'brain' with a 'memory' and we also talk about memory being a human being's memory. The eyes are the pathway, the input to the brain. This is getting very theoretical about what this child was up to, if any of these things. But how *could* this thing know whether the answer was right or wrong?

This teacher was using her own way of thinking about computers to assess the legitimacy of the student's way of thinking. These considerations of how Dataman 'knows' led to the idea that it was not necessarily 'stupid' or 'silly' to refer to the computer as having 'eyes'.

What Suzanne had first presented as a 'silly question', which had distracted her and her student from what he was *supposed* to be learning, thus came to be understood as a question of considerable significance: 'He got a machine and he wondered about the essential differences between machine and man; but it's just that he wasn't sure . . . .' At the end of this session of analysing the child's question, Suzanne had quite a different view of Lenny's 'intelligence':

> I had not thought of this child as being very intelligent, but you're right, in that he *should* be thought of in that way since he did ask that kind of question. It's a higher level of thinking, if he's thinking about trying to make the distinction between robot and computer and man and whatever.

By working on this and similar 'puzzles', we hoped that teachers would gain a new perspective for looking at their interaction with students – the possibility of responding to a student's question, not with an answer, but with more questions constructed to help the teacher better understand the *student's* way of thinking.

An example presented by Helen, another fourth-grade teacher in the group, illustrates the development of the teacher's experiments with sustained inquiry into their students' ways of understanding what they learn. It represents the other side of the work of the project: an application of that research in classroom practice.

Mario had come into school one day asking his teacher, Helen, for an explanation of something he had been told by his father. Helen told the group:

> Mario, in his usual (somewhat belligerent and challenging) way said: 'My father said we didn't have whatever that thing was yesterday'. Then I said, 'The *eclipse*. What did your father tell you about it?' Mario answered (with doubled assurance) 'He said we didn't have it because it was snowing'.

Helen recognized Mario's confusion, and at first, she believed it would be relatively simple to clear up. She thought that he had misunderstood his father. What he needed to know was that the eclipse was happening behind the clouds even though he didn't see it because it was snowing. But the lesson turned out to be not so simple: 'I told Mario we had it; even though it was snowing, you look behind the clouds. He walked back to his seat and about half an hour later, he said to me, "My father doesn't lie to me, we didn't have it".'

Initially, Helen perceived a difference between the boy's understanding of the eclipse and her own. But rather than simply telling him *her* understanding, she also tried to explore *his* construction of what happened to the eclipse. She explained her initial attempts to get the matter cleared up:

> That next day was also a very cloudy day, and so I asked, 'Where do you think the sun is today? and he just shrugged his shoulders. I took a book and put it in front of the shade cord and asked him if he could see the cord. He said 'no', and I

explained to him that is how it is with the sun when it is behind the clouds. And he said, 'But my father –'. I concluded that he still couldn't understand that it [the eclipse] happened behind the clouds. So anyway, I didn't know what to do.

When Helen presented this problem for discussion, the staff encouraged the group of teachers to try to figure out what *Mario* might have been thinking.

At the next seminar session the following week, Helen said that what she thought was 'how I could phrase my question [about the sun] to him so he would say, "It's in the sky", which is what I want to know if he understands'. Her approach to Mario became a combination of figuring out how *he* was thinking about the problem and finding out whether he knew what *she* considered to be some essential basic information about how the solar system works.

She reported her subsequent interaction with him as follows:

So when it was a cloudy day on Friday, I said to him, 'What happened to the sun today? and he looked at me like I was from Mars, and said, 'It's in the sky'. He must have seen the look of relief on my face because he said 'What's the matter?'

Having ascertained that he understood that the sun was there, behind the clouds, on a cloudy day, Helen then came back to the question of the eclipse:

Then I said to him 'you know that eclipse we had? Did we have it here?' He said 'Well, no. Well, I guess. Well, I'm not sure'. I said, 'I guess what I'm asking you is did it happen in the sky over us?' He said, 'Yah'.

Still testing her understanding of Mario's understanding, Helen said she had asked him some more questions and found that he was aware that the eclipse did happen behind the clouds, even though we couldn't see it. By 'not having it', he had meant 'not seeing it'. She presented her conclusions to the group: 'I have been on such a wrong track with him. The "where" meant: he wanted to point to "there, there it is". But I was thinking he didn't know it was there at all. So I was happy to find out he did.' Helen's probes demonstrated to her that Mario thought she had initially been asking him to point to the exact point in the sky where the sun was behind the clouds. He did not think he could do that when he made his first comments, and so she had tentatively concluded that he didn't know that the sun was there behind the clouds. Yet after the second interaction, she thought that *she* was the one who had not understood what he was thinking.

Helen had decided that Mario did not need a lecture about where the sun is on a cloudy day. In fact, such a lecture may have only served to confuse his sense of the relationship between the sun, the clouds, and the Earth. Through discussion of Mario with the group Helen had developed a different sense of the *purpose* of teachers asking students questions. She had not simply judged Mario's answers to be right or wrong, but had considered them as indicating how *he* perceived the position of the sun on a cloudy day.

Based on my analysis of examples like these and teachers' reflections on their own intuitive ways of making sense of various phenomena, it became clear that the teacher-participants had changed their thinking in at least three significant ways: they had expanded their sense of what it means to know something so as to include what the knower figures out for himself or herself, thus complicating the meaning of a 'right' answer and their sense of what makes a student 'intelligent'; they had become more confident in their own ability to figure things out, ranging from problems in music and physics and mathematics to problems of how and what to teach in schools; they had begun to think that clinical-style research investigations, with individual children in classrooms, *might* be a part of their classroom work.

The teachers seemed equipped to examine and appreciate students' intuitive ways of making sense and to see, by reference to their own experience, how such individual ways of making sense were different from the formal descriptions accepted as norms in the school setting. However, having learned that *researchers'* distinctions between intuitive and formal knowledge, these teachers had a difficult time with the idea that the two different ways of knowing could be *integrated* in the classrooms where they worked. As they thought concretely about how their teaching was organized and their own position as knowledgeable authorities, they raised several problems which had not been among the researchers' concerns:

> If students construct their own understanding of something, like how machines work, or relationships in the solar system – what is the connection between what they understand and what a teacher knows to be 'the right answers?'
>
> And these right answers, which are printed in the textbooks we use, and measured on the tests we give – where did they come from? And aren't they important? And what does it mean for teachers and students to know something if they don't really understand it?

What Bamberger had called 'formal knowledge', the teachers called 'right answers'. This distinction suggests some of the reasons why what had been an interesting difference for the researchers became a *practical* problem for the teachers. The formal knowledge that is 'taught in schools' is, in fact, taught by *teachers*. It is the source of their power and authority in the social institutions where teaching and learning occur and where norms are established. These norms include what is to be defined as useful knowledge in the classroom. It is not surprising, then, that formal knowledge would have a different *functional* meaning for teachers than it has for researchers.

In school, formal knowledge is not one among many ways of knowing; it is the 'right' way. When the teachers worked as teacher-researchers, however, they were expected to be detached from this formal standard. They were supposed to accept intuitive knowledge as useful and powerful, and to refrain from judging the child in terms of what they or other authorities thought he should know. At this stage of the project the teachers began to sense some of the contradictions involved in adopting the project's view of their role *vis-à-vis* knowledge. Here, the case of Lee is instructive.

Lee, a sixth-grade teacher, wondered whether accepting the reality of differences in individual understanding meant that she would have to give up assigning the *same* textbook work to her whole class. If her students came to an assignment with different ideas about what they were supposed to do, she concluded that she would not be able just to look at their answers as a way of judging what they did or did not understand. Her dilemma was a choice between acknowledging individual differences and measuring students' knowledge by textbook standards. She knew she had to do both, but in the context of the project, she was worried: 'I have the terrible feeling that if this process [the research] goes too far, I'm *never* going to be able to assign page 98 again.'

Here, Lee uses 'assigning page 98' to represent an essential aspect of the way teaching and learning are organized in schools. In a given classroom, one teacher is responsible for instructing a large group of children, all of whom have roughly the same level of knowledge of the subjects taught in school. Textbooks are a standard measure of the class's and the teacher's assignment and their *progress*.

In giving an assignment in a textbook to a whole class, Lee assumes that these 20 or 30 different students are supposed to be able to do something – long division, let's say – and she has a clear responsibility to ensure that her students can do long division correctly. It is not surprising, therefore, that being asked to give up the functions served by the knowledge needed to complete 'page 98' correctly might give this teacher a 'terrible feeling'.

This use of knowledge is different from exploring a child's knowledge about 'Dataman' or 'the eclipse'. In these cases it was not too difficult for the teachers to imagine themselves as *researcher*, exploring and appreciating *one* student's particular way of thinking and indeed, their sense of a student's 'intelligence' was enriched by such exploration. There were no curricular guidelines on these particular subjects to provide a sense of school norms or expectations. No long division was there to be mastered by all of the students.

In the seminar, Bamberger responded to Lee's worry about giving up the standards reflected in the textbooks with the comment: 'It would be interesting to see how all these different mixes of things would interlace with page 98', i.e. what different children, with different prior knowledge and different abilities, would do with the same assignment. As a researcher, for whom the 'mismatches' between individual understanding and the school curriculum are *valuable* data, she has no responsibility for what children have or have not learned. However, the teachers had a different view of the situation. Jessica, for example, responded to the nature of the *researcher's* interest in children's thinking with the assumption that Lee probably *'already knows . . .* how many different things can be done on page 98!' – implying, by her tone of voice, that for a teacher to have such information would be, not interesting, but troublesome. If it is the teacher's job to get students to learn what is in the textbook, different answers indicate that her job has *not* yet been accomplished. There may be little feeling of accomplishment for a teacher in recognizing that a *variety* of answers may result from each student's unique interpretation of an assignment. But more importantly, Lee thought that she must decide *either* to continue to assign 'page 98' and disregard individual interpretations *or* to give up making uniform assignments based on the textbook which she considered to be a necessary tool of her trade. Her sense of the demands of the theory she was learning seemed to make the first inappropriate and the nature of her practice as a sixth-grade teacher, to make the second impossible. She felt immobilized by the contrary ways in which her responsibilities seemed to be defined. Lee saw herself faced with a choice between understanding individuals and succeeding as a teacher in terms defined by the institutions within which she was working. As one of the other teachers put it, her 'thoughts' about theories of individual learning seemed to be contrary to the 'facts' of practice in a public school classroom. Such ambiguous interpretations of what they were supposed to be doing left the teachers frustrated, and sometimes even angry about their participation in this project. We turn now to an analysis of these contrary tendencies which flowed from assumptions of the project.

Thinking about teaching

The way these teachers analysed their work into contradictory responsibilities is not unqiue. Although their thinking could be attributed to the dichotomous way in which the project defined the work of the teacher-researcher, the conflicts they felt parallel those identified by several scholars who have attempted to understand the work teachers do. Philip Jackson, for example, describes the institutional standards of classroom life as 'threatening to the student's sense of uniqueness and personal worth'; he sees the teacher's role, therefore, as 'fundamentally ambiguous': '[The teacher] is working for the school and against it at the same time. He has a dual allegiance – to the preservation of both the institution and the individual who inhabit it"[6]. In these terms, if a teacher distinguishes among the individual learners in her classroom, according to the differences in how they understand something, her allegiance to school standards like textbooks and tests is called into question. Gertrude McPherson, who did an intensive study of teaching in a small-town school, found similar contradictions in the job. She analysed the differences in expectations placed on teachers in their various professional relationships: by students, other teachers, administrators, parents, the larger community. These relationships define the teacher's 'role set'. McPherson concluded:

> It should be clear from this study that much of the teacher's internal conflict is built into the role set; that the conflicting expectations of different interested parties are not easily changed or made congruent either through organizational changes or improved communiction.[7]

One endemic conflict in the teacher's 'role set' is between the needs of students and the standards of the institution. McPherson found that what the teacher has come to believe is appropriate practice in relations with *individual* learners is contrary to what is expected by others outside the classroom, who have the power to decide whether she is doing a good job. Teachers cannot easily resolve their dilemmas by allying themselves with one set of expectations or another. The nature of the relationships among the people who can influence what they do – parents and children, for example, or the principal and the other teachers in the school – makes that solution impossible.

When Dan Lortie asked teachers how they manage the conflicting expectations that result from the way schools are organized, he found them to be 'ambivalent' and conflicted about how their job should be defined. He summed up their sentiments as follows:

> There is a certain ambivalence, then, in the teacher's sentiments. He yearns for more independence . . . but he accepts the hegemony of the school system on which he is economically and functionally dependent. He cannot ensure

that the imperatives of teaching, as he defines them, will be honoured, but he chafes when they are not . . . In any event, the feelings I have discerned among Five Towns teachers are internally contradictory and reflect dilemmas in the role.[8]

Lortie interpreted teachers' general feelings about their work as expressing a contradiction between their own ideas about how to relate to students as individuals, and the constraints and rewards of the organization in which their teaching occurred.

The teachers who participated in the MIT project seem to have arrived at the same conflicted conclusions. Bamberger had hoped that the teachers could find pedagogical strategies for making *connections* between individual understanding and institutional expectations. But as the teachers examined the purposes of their work in terms of the distinctions between individual and formal knowledge, and as they continued their work in classrooms, these connections seemed to them something of a *practical* impossibility. The more they accepted the theorists' view of learning and teaching, the more they were frustrated – alternately wanting to understand individual children better, and feeling that such understanding might actually *get in the way* of the job they have to do in the classroom. These teachers' sense of contradiction between a researcher's concerns and their own practical concerns in the classroom (such as class size, behaviour problems and external interference) parallels that described by John Elliott in his analysis of a programme in Great Britain designed to train teachers to plan activities to match an individual child's developmental level. In Elliott's view, teachers could not assume a researcher's perspective on their students because it did not take account of the complexity of their responsibilities; they saw the programme's expectations as 'isolating certain events for special attention to the neglect of others'.[9] Even though the teachers may have concurred that the researcher's concerns for individual children were important, they could not give them the absolute attention that seemed to be expected.

The tension between individual and social standards seems to be at the very heart of teachers' work. Students have had different experiences and have different ways of making sense of those experiences, and therefore bring a wide range of interpretive frameworks to the lessons they are learning in school. It is also the case that there are certain things taught in school that are useful for *everyone* to know, and that a student's success in learning them may affect his or her whole life. From the perspective of an individual's system of ideas, however, this standard knowledge is only one among many ways of understanding and describing experience. From the project's point of view, an individual's way of understanding his or her own experience was considered to be a more useful and powerful way of knowing, and, in the long run, a more powerful base on which to erect teaching strategies.[10]

As these teachers sought to move from being teacher-researchers, it is not surprising that they felt some contradictions in their work. While learning to recognize children's ways of constructing their own knowledge from experience had informed their teaching and the way they thought about children, the dichotomous ways of thinking about practice which they derived from the project's psychological theory did not appear useful. Trying to figure out whether it would be better to pursue a child's intuitive knowledge *or* to teach the formal curriculum seems to have been counter-productive. While arguing for the superiority of one purpose or another might have been an appropriate *academic* activity, it did not seem to the teachers particularly connected to the problems they worked on every day in their classrooms. These problems surfaced when teachers told 'stories' to each other at informal moments during our meetings about what they actually *did* in their classrooms.

The contrast between the contradictions the teachers expressed in their speculative *seminar* discussions and thus the ideas about teaching that can be found in 'stories' they tell about their practice is significant. It raises two questions that seem useful in examining the relationship between theory and practice. First, what is it about this *project* that led these teachers to feel that they needed to make impossible choices between children and curriculum, between inquiry into individual understanding and upholding school standards, between their own intellectual interests and their classroom responsibilities? And, secondly, what is it about *teaching* that made these choices seem essentially unrelated to their practice? The teachers' 'stories' about themselves at work suggest some answers to these questions and point to a possible framework for furthering our understanding of what teachers do.[11]

In one such story, a kindergarten-first grade teacher told the group about how she had used the occasion of a new child joining the class in the middle of the year as the subject of a lesson in counting, addition and subtraction. One girl in her class, Penny, counted the new boy twice, adding him both to the number of children who were 'present' *and* to the number of children who were absent. When Jessica finished her story, the other teachers in the group eagerly took up the puzzle, exploring what the girl might have been thinking. This was the problem from the perspective of a group of teacher-researchers. But as she spoke about her classroom, Jessica considered several other issues. First of all, she said she wanted everyone to be clear about the fact that there was a total of 24 children in the class, i.e. that 22 here, and two absent, added up to 24 altogether. She could not give equal legitimacy to Penny's conclusion that there were 25 without confusing the other children. The girl's understanding of the situation was not something she wanted anyone else to share. She needed to teach all of the children, including Penny, that each member of the group should only be counted once.

A teacher has a special position as the person in the class who knows formal mathematics. Her students look to *her* as the authority on addition. She personally represents the order of arithmetic in contrast to their own shaky sense of how it works. Particularly because Jessica was interacting with Penny in front of all the other children in the class, she thought it was important for her, as teacher, to stand behind the formal knowledge represented by the correct sum and the correct procedure for arriving at the total number in the group.

Of course, there are many different ways of understanding this mathematics problem, and that might be what Jessica ought to have tried to understand about Penny's thinking. But examining how Penny constructed the problem was not possible; in addition to the mathematics lesson, Jessica said she also needed to give her attention to managing the transition of a large group of young children from one sort of activity to another. Penny's irritation, which may have caused some problems among the other children in the group, needed to be dissipated. These aspects of classroom teaching made it difficult for Jessica to engage in or even think much about an exploration of Penny's intuitive understanding of addition. From the distance of the seminar, however, Jessica reflected on what a good researcher might have done in the same circumstances, in contrast to her own, teacherly, response. She said to Duckworth, one of the researchers in the group:

> I wanted *you* there, because I knew you would ask her the right question. I kept saying, 'this is perfect, Jessica get it out'. But I couldn't think of a question to ask. Of course, *I* was worried about a few other items . . . I couldn't defuse her anger because I couldn't understand what she was talking about. And I didn't have the time – I tried – I gave it three sentences.

A researcher could have gone off on Penny's tangent with the confidence that someone else was responsible for managing the whole class's behaviour and teaching this girl (and the rest of the class) how to add.

Although Jessica felt that she had not acted as a researcher would have in these circumstances, it was obvious that her participation in the project influenced her response to the child's way of thinking about arithmetic. She said she was aware of the child's intuitive understanding and how it differed from the formal knowledge first graders are supposed to learn about addition. She assumed that there was some 'sense' to Penny's way of thinking and she tried to get her to articulate it. Even though there was clearly a tension between individual thinking and conventional social standards in this instance of practice, Jessica did not need to make a choice between them in the way she spoke about her work. Like Helen, who wanted Mario to know about the eclipse, she was able to manage both the child's understanding and the formal knowledge she wanted to convey.

In contrast to their stories, the teachers' discussions of the dichotomy between intuitive and formal knowledge communicated the belief that if they were going to value their own or any other individual's way of thinking about something, then they would have to disassociate themselves from the formal standards that are used to measure learning and teaching in schools. What was a distinction of interest to theorists (intuitive versus formal knowledge) had become a set of contradictory categories for defining their task: *teacher-researchers versus school and society*. If the teachers had fully identified with the researchers in the project, they might have settled on that self-definition. However, the structure of the project also encouraged them to see themselves as school practitioners. The researchers valued the teacher's perspective on their classroom practice, and recognized them as authorities in matters of classroom life; the teachers were told that they knew things about work in schools that the researchers did not know. Thus the teachers' authority as collaborators in the project was based on their work in schools. In order to perform this function they defended the importance of the formal knowledge that is taught to children in schools. From this perspective, they reasoned that aligning themselves with schools meant they could not also be researchers, and so they divided things up differently. The dichotomy became: *researchers versus teachers and schools and society*. They had been asked to collaborate on the project's research *because* they were public school teachers. Yet their association with all of the aspects of that role made it difficult for them to pursue the kind of inquiry which the researchers had hoped for.

Given these two quite opposite ways of thinking about themselves, it is not surprising that the teachers were frustrated by trying to play the role of both teacher and 'teacher-researcher'. The way they understood the project's assumptions led them to a choice: should they align themselves with children by focussing on the individual's intuitive knowledge? Or should they align themselves with the school as teachers of society's formal knowledge? They faced a dilemma; it seemed to them that they could not do both.[12]

What is most striking about the thinking of the MIT project teachers is that although they *analysed* their work into a set of forced choices, they did not seem to have to make such choices in their *practice*. Their 'stories' about themselves imply a variety of alternative strategies for coping with conflicts that enabled them to work *without* choosing. This is the significant point we should consider. The teachers' management, in practice, of concerns that they talked about as contradictory in their analysis of practice raises some very interesting questions about the relationship between *thinking* about teaching and doing it. They did not have an analytic language for reflecting on their practice to counter the contradictory themes that developed in their thinking about intuitive and formal knowledge. But what they did have was a way of working and a concrete way of talking about their work, and there is much to be learned from listening to their 'stories' about particular interactions with students.

How did they manage the tensions and contradictions inherent in their work? And why did their ability to manage them surface in their stories when it was absent from their more abstract analysis? In the stories the teachers told about specific instances of practice, they were talking about *themselves*. All of the various expectations that are a part of learning in schools seemed to be filtered through the person of the teacher in the act of teaching. She used her 'self' as a tool to manage the contradictions of her trade. Jessica portrayed herself as *more* than simply a conduit through which formal knowledge passes to students. When she talked about herself as a teacher of mathematics, it seemed important to her that children learn what *she* is teaching them. In talking with a child to find out what he or she thinks about something, her *personal* attitude towards the child and towards the skills being assessed made a significant difference in how she understands what the child 'knows'. Yet what Jessica's students learn from her is also part of the shared knowledge that is important to their success in school and society. The way this knowledge is structured by teachers themselves in relation to their students makes it difficult to say whether it is 'intuitive' or 'formal'.

The way the teacher uses her self in her practice suggests that the dichotomy between these two kinds of knowledge is a false one. In the person of the teacher, knowledge is conveyed to students in a way which is both socially useful and meaningful to the teacher herself. In the course of instruction the teacher attempts to make knowledge meaningful to students through her formal authority and the relationship she has established with them as individual persons. On the part of the student, there is a certain degree of trust that if something 'makes sense' to the teacher, it will eventually 'make sense' to the learner; both are part of a society in which the knowledge taught and learned in school has some usefulness. The 'mismatches' between intuitive and formal knowledge, posited by Bamberger, may thus be managed by the teacher without deliberate research into their incongruence.

The tensions in a teacher's work are the same kinds of tensions everyone feels as an individual growing up in society, writ large because of the teacher's official role in the growing-up process. We all feel enduring contradictions, for example, between what it seems other people, in various positions of power, want us to do and what *we* think we should do. But teachers have a special responsibility for managing these kinds of tensions in themselves and in their students. Given what these teachers have said, it seems appropriate, therefore, to consider the notion that teaching involves *inventing personal strategies for working with universal contradictions that cannot be finally resolved.* Coping with these conflicts in one's self seems related to how they are managed in practice, and we need to persist in trying to find out how teachers do cope, in practice, with these enduring and unresolvable tensions.

Theories of self like those of George Herbert Mead, which I have drawn on here in thinking about the teacher's self, may be useful in examining this aspect of the teacher's work.[13] In Mead's view, a person is both a spontaneous actor on the environment and an interpreter of the ways in which actions are received by others. The 'self' develops in the course of managing the tensions between one's own actions and the expectations of others. The perspective from which a person acts is thus different from a 'theory' of action, developed at some distance from the problems to be managed. At the same time, a person is understood to direct his or her own actions rather than involuntarily reaction to social expectations. A teacher's 'story' about *herself* at work might be understood, therefore, as something different from either a reflected-upon theory about why she did what she did or a list of impulsive behaviours.

Analysing such stories may lead to a reflective language for talking about practice that is more congruent with what teachers do in classrooms. This language could be used by both researchers and teachers for teaching about thinking as well as thinking about teaching. Finding such a language is of critical importance for curriculum change.[14] With such a language teachers may be able to contrast the *personal* aspect of their work with the more abstract contradictory themes that emerged when they were asked by theorists to speculate about becoming teacher-researchers.

Clearly the project influenced the teachers' sense of the internal contradictions in their work, and the researchers on the project did not offer any way out. The problem stems from more universal characteristics of relationships between theories about teaching and practice. Our experience in the project points to a gap in the way researchers understand practitioner thinking: the gap emerges because teachers' particular 'stories' about what they do in classrooms have been given little attention in research and writing about practice. Teachers who participate in university seminars are often criticized for the 'stories' they offer about themselves and their students. Their contributions are considered irrelevant to focussed discussions of educational theory and research. Judged by academic standards, the 'stories' seem like evidence for inadequate problem-solving ability; what teachers say they do seem uninformed by all the careful theoretical analysis of teaching and learning that goes on outside the classroom.[15] Even though the designers of the MIT project did not take this perspective, the emergent differences between 'thinking like a teacher' and 'thinking like a researcher' had similar implications.

The way teaching has been thought about and written about by academics certainly has had an influence on how teachers themselves think about it. The conventional relationship between theory and practice has assumed that practitioners should be *consumers* of theory which is created by someone else. When researchers have tried to separate how teachers themselves think about their work from academic descriptions of practice, they have concluded that the language practitioners use is too concrete, too context-bound, and too inconsistent to inform good teaching.[16] Teachers who want to improve their practice, therefore, are expected to use the language of *researchers* both to define problems and to understand their solutions.

Researchers conceive of their own job as actively searching for *solutions* that can be applied to the problems of practice. A recent review by Richard Shavelson and Paula Stern of a wide range of research that has been done on teacher decision-making is illustrative; the authors admit, however, that the fundamental formulation of the research problem that has been examined in this work 'ignores multiple, potentially conflicting goals which teachers have to balance daily'.[17] Yet a teacher who tells 'stories' about *managing* problems rather than *solving* them is considered intellectually passive, if not helpless. Coping with conflict, rather than getting rid of its source, goes against our society's deep-seated hopes for progress. Enduringly unsolved problems remain something of an embarrassment, and thus while research is valued, it is a struggle to see a teacher's everyday acts of teaching, in spite of the essential contradictions in her work, as productive and creative. When compared with the problem-solving researchers, she appears to be naïve or indifferent.

Much educational research has been built on the model of the sciences, in which the validity and reliability of a solution are defined by the qualities that a number of events have in common. We have, therefore, been drawn away from the 'anecdotal' ways teachers talk about themselves at work (and what that can tell us about what is problematic in that work) towards solutions for problems that are defined to be useful for improving 'teaching' in general. The specific ways in which a teacher manages her classroom are not as interesting, from this perspective, as are general principles derived from research that can be developed into a universal theory of practice.[18]

Our thinking about how the teacher affects what she does in the classroom by using her 'self' to manage conflict has also been limited by the psychological concept of 'personality'. Instead of thinking of each teacher as an intentional agent in the moment-by-moment management of contradictory ways of thinking as Mead suggests we do, we have placed teachers in theoretically derived trait categories like 'warm and friendly' or 'authoritarian', based on a statistical average of classroom behaviours. This led to attempts to 'solve' educational problems by identifying which sort of teacher produces the most learning and figuring how to get those kinds of teachers in classrooms. Such solutions could not take account of the *dynamic* nature of the teacher's identity. As Mead points out, who a person is and what she does is expressed in and shaped by the environment in which she works, and yet she may appropriately *decide* that it is useful to be warm and friendly in one instance and authoritarian in another. The teacher, while affected by the environment, is not driven by it.

No matter what kind of teacher is placed in a classroom, the essential contradictions in teaching persist. Jessica, for example, cannot choose between accepting the fact that students come to school with different ideas about the structure of counting *or* teaching them to add and subtract according to conventional mathematical rules. Lee does not have a choice beween expecting students to correctly answer the questions on 'page 98' of the textbooks which the school district assigns to her or trying to make sense of the individual variations in students' answers on a class assignment. Theoretical arguments might lead to apparent resolutions of these dilemmas, but such arguments seem remote from what teachers do in their classrooms. Although a resolution may be accomplished in each particular incident of teaching, the underlying tensions do not go away. It is this difference – between the specific momentary, creative acts of management on the part of teachers, and the more general picture of their work as contradictory – that makes the MIT teachers' stories about their own practices so important.

Our project might have gone much farther if we had taken account of the richness of these teachers' language for talking about their work. Instead, we provided them with a researcher's language in the cause of teaching them about thinking. We did not concurrently examine *their* ways of thinking about teaching. If we could better understand the special qualities of the thinking revealed in the way teachers talk about their own work, researchers might be able to participate in a different sort of conversation with teachers about improving practice. Taking teachers' stories as evidence for their thinking about why they do what they do means developing both new ideas about what 'thinking' is and a different attitude towards teachers. If teachers are to be considered as 'intentional' practitioners whose own thoughts and feelings serve as the rationale for their actions, what researchers have to offer in the improvement of practice needs to be reexamined.[19]

The MIT teachers' stories suggest a conceptualization of the practitioner's teaching self – an actor in a situation who brings her personal history, knowledge and concerns into a relationship with her working environment. Her own ideas about what should be happening in that environment (informed by educational research and theory or not) must be adjusted, by her, to the concrete reality which she faces in each situation. Because the teacher must thus use her 'self' in the Meadian sense, in her teaching, and because the materials on which she works are the 'selves' of her students, the relationship between thinking and doing, between research and practice, is created by her in moment-by-moment classroom interaction. She does not put aside the formal aspect of her own or a student's knowledge while she examines the intuitive, nor can she simply impose the formal without making some kind of sense of it for her self and for her class. It is the essence of the teacher's job to be a person who can manage both conventional social expectations and individual understanding, even though the two may often be in conflict.

Acknowledgement

The research reported in this paper was partially supported by a grant from the National Institute of Education (Grant No. G78-0219) awarded to the Division for Study and Research in Education at Massachusetts Institute of Technology, Cambridge, Mass.

References and notes

1.   For a more complete description of the distinction between intuitive and formal knowledge, see BAMBERGER, J. (1978a). An experiment in teacher development. A proposal submitted to the National Institute of Education, Basic Skills Group, June; and BAMBERGER, J. (1978). 'Intuitive and formal musical knowing: parables of cognitive dissonance.' In: *The Arts, Cognition, and Basic Skills, Second Annual Yearbook on Research in the Arts and Aesthetics Education.* CEMREL, Inc.
2.   BAMBERGER, J. *op. cit.* (1978a), p. 1 (see Note 1).
3.   *Ibid.,* p. 3.
4.   *Ibid.,* p. 9.
5.   The quotations in this essay are all taken from transcriptions of tapes that were made during the teachers' weekly discussions. First names are used to identify the teachers in an attempt to convey the personal quality of their exchanges with one another and the staff. The quotations have been edited only in so far as was necessary to make them readable.
6.   JACKSON, P. (1978). *Life in Classrooms.* New York: Holt, Rinehart and Winston, p. 154.
7.   McPHERSON, G. (1972). *Small Town Teacher.* Cambridge: Harvard University Press, p. 212.
8.   LORTIE, D. (1975). *Schoolteacher: A Sociological Study.* Chicago: University of Chicago Press, p. 186.
9.   ELLIOTT, J. (1977). Some key concepts underlying teachers' evaluation of innovation. Paper presented at the British Educational Research Association Conference, London, p. 8.
10. DUCKWORTH, E. (1979). Learning with breadth and depth. The Catherine Molony Memorial Lecture, City College School of Education Workshop Center for Open Education, June.
11. These 'stories' are treated in greater detail in LAMPERT, M.

Teaching about thinking and thinking about teaching. Mimeo.

12. Olson also applies the term 'dilemma' to the situation in which teachers find themselves as implementers of curriculum innovation. See OLSON, J. (1981). 'Teacher influence in the classroom: a context for understanding curriculum translation,' *Instructional Science,* 10, pp. 259-75.

13. MEAD, G.H. (1956). *On Social Psychology.* Chicago: University of Chicago Press. See also BLUMER, H. (1971). 'Sociological implications of the thought of George Herbert Mead.' In: COSIN, B.R. *et al.* (eds.) *School and Society: A Sociological Reader.* London: Routledge & Kegan Paul; and BERLAK, H. and BERLAK, A. (1975). 'Towards a political and social psychological theory of schooling: an analysis of English informal primary schools,' *Interchange,* 6, pp. 11-22, for applications of Mead's theory to teaching.

14. See also OLSON, J. (1980). 'Teacher constructs and curriculum change,' *Journal of Curriculum Studies,* 12, pp. 1-11.

15. JACKSON, P. (1971). 'The way teachers think.' In: LESSER, G.S. (ed.) *Psychology and Educational Practice.* Glenview, Illinois: Scott, Foresman, and Co., pp. 28-9.

16. A similar critique of this perspective on teachers thinking can be found in HAMMERSLY, M. (1979). 'Towards a model of teacher activity.' In: EGGLESTON, JOHN (ed.) *Teacher Decision Making in the Classroom.* London: Routledge & Kegan Paul; and FLODEN, R. and FEIMAN, S. (1980). 'Should teachers be taught to be rational?' Paper presented at the Annual Meeting of the American Educational Research Association, Boston, April.

17. SHAVELSON, R. and STERN, P. (1981). 'Research on teachers' pedagogical thoughts, judgements, decisions and behavior,' *Review of Educational Research,* 51, p. 471.

18. For a similar criticism of generalized approaches to curriculum problems see REID, W.A. (1978). *Thinking about the Curriculum.* London: Routledge and Kegan Paul.

19. The implications of this view for improving practice have been examined by FENSTERMACHER, G.D. (1978). 'A philosophical consideration of recent research on teacher effectiveness,' *Review of Research in Education,* 6.